THOMAS AQUINAS AND THE NEO-THOMIST TRADITION

BERNIE VAN DER WALT

THOMAS AQUINAS AND THE NEO-THOMIST TRADITION

A Christian-Philosophical Assessment

PAIDEIA PRESS

PAIDEIA
PRESS

Thomas Aquinas and the Neo-Thomist Tradition: A Christian-Philosophical Assessment

Paideia Press (P.O. Box 1000, Jordan Station, Ontario, Canada L0R 1S0). Copyright © 2021 by Paideia Press and Bernie van der Walt. All rights reserved. Except for brief quotations in critical publications or reviews, no part of this book may be reproduced in any manner without prior written permission from Paideia Press at the address above.

Cover Design by: Steven R. Martins
Typesetting by: Paul Aurich
Edited by: Paul Aurich and Michael Wagner

ISBN 978-0-88815-318-0

Printed in the United States of America

Re-published under Paideia Press with permission by the author, Bernie van der Walt

Contents

PREFACE	1
INTRODUCTION	5
LASTING WORLDWIDE INFLUENCE	5
INFLUENCE ON THE REFORMED THEOLOGICAL TRADITION	6
INFLUENCE ON REFORMATIONAL PHILOSOPHY	7
RETURNING TO THE ORIGINAL AQUINAS	8
METHODOLOGY	8
CONTENTS	8
SEVEN CENTURIES OF NEO-THOMISM	9
ACKNOWLEDGEMENTS	10
CHAPTER 1 THE RELIGIOUS DIRECTION OF THE PHILOSOPHY OF THOMAS AQUINAS	11
INTRODUCTION	12
1. ITS PLACE WITHIN THE BROAD OUTLINE OF THE RESEARCH PROJECT	12
1.1 TOPICALITY	13
1.1.1 IMPORTANT FOR UNDERSTANDING ROMAN CATHOLIC THINKING	14
1.1.2 IMPORTANT TO PROTESTANT SCHOLASTICISM OR ORTHODOXY	14
1.1.3 INFLUENCE ON THE FOUNDERS OF THE REFORMATIONAL PHILOSOPHY OF THE TWENTIETH CENTURY	15
1.1.4 INFLUENCE ON CONTEMPORARY THEOLOGICAL THINKING	15
1.2 NUMEROUS INTERPRETATIONS OF AQUINAS	16
1.3 BIBLIOGRAPHICAL LIMITATION	17
1.4 THE LAYOUT	18
2. AQUINAS' PHILOSOPHICAL EVOLUTION	18
2.1 FIRST ACQUAINTANCE WITH ARISTOTELIANISM	18
2.2 GROWING INFLUENCE BY THE MAN FROM STAGEIRA	19
2.3 IN DEFENCE OF ARISTOTLE'S PHILOSOPHY	19
2.4 REJECTION AFTER HIS DEATH	20
3. THE PLACE AND PURPOSE OF THE SCG	21
3.1 THE PLACE OF THE SCG IN AQUINAS' PHILOSOPHICAL EVOLUTION	21
3.2 REASON FOR AND INTENTION WITH THE SCG	22
4. THE NORMATIVE DIRECTION IN THE PHILOSOPHY OF THE SCG	23
4.1 THE BROAD PERSPECTIVE	24
4.2 SYNTHESIS IN THE SCG	25

4.3 THE METHOD OF SYNTHESIS IN THE SCG	26
4.3.1 BIBLICISM	26
4.3.2 PARADOX	26
4.3.3 TWO REALM DOCTRINE	27
4.4 NATURE AND GRACE IN THE SCG	27
4.4.1 GRACE AND FAITH	28
4.4.2 TWO SEPARATE DOMAINS	28
5. AN APPRAISAL	29
5.1 IT IS NOT BIBLICALLY FOUNDED	29
5.2 IT CONFLICTS WITH GOD'S SOVEREIGNTY OVER THE WHOLE OF LIFE	29
5.3 IT IMPLIES A CONFUSION OF STRUCTURE AND DIRECTION	30
5.4 IT ENTAILS AN INHERENT DUALISM	30
5.5 IT DOES NOT PREVENT MUTUAL INFLUENCE	31
5.6 IT HAS ENORMOUS IMPLICATIONS	31
5.7 CONTEMPORARY THEOLOGICAL THINKING IS STILL INFECTED BY IT	32
5.8 IT ALSO IS PRESENT IN ECCLESIASTICAL LIFE	32
6. CONCLUSION AND LOOKING AHEAD	33
CHAPTER 2 THE IDEA OF LAW AS A KEY TO THE PHILOSOPHY OF THE CATHOLIC "DOCTOR COMMUNIS"	**35**
1. INTRODUCTION	36
1.2 STILL A CHRISTIAN SCHOLAR	37
1.3 A POSSIBLE KEY TO HIS ONTOLOGY	37
1.4 SOURCES	38
1.5 LAY-OUT	38
2. A COSMOLOGICAL AND DUALIST ONTOLOGY	39
2.1 ONE REALITY DIVIDED INTO TWO	39
2.2 THE LAW DISAPPEARS IN GOD AND COSMOS BUT REMAINS DETERMINATIVE	39
3. GOD AS LAW	40
3.1 GOD IS PURE ACT	41
3.2 GOD IS PURE FORM	41
3.3 GOD IS HIS BEING	41
3.4 GOD'S BEING IS INTELLECT AND WILL	42
3.5 GOD IS THE HIGHEST GOOD AND ABSOLUTE TRUTH	42
4. THE COSMOS MADE INTO LAW	43
4.1 "EXEMPLAR"	43

4.1.1 God Encompasses Everything	44
4.1.2 God is Omniscient	44
4.1.3 A Deterministic Idea of God and the Reaction to It	45
4.2 "Similitudo"	46
4.2.1 "Similitudo" and "Forma"	46
4.2.2 The human being looks like God	46
4.2.3 God Does Not Look Like His Creatures	47
4.3 "Ratio"	47
4.3.1 The Same as Likeness	47
4.3.2 The Same as Exemplar	47
4.3.3 A Mirror Image of the Trinity	48
4.4 "Verbum"	48
4.5 "Lex naturalis" and "Lex Divina"	49
5. A Hierarchy of Reality	49
5.1 A Pyramid of Being	49
5.2 A Pyramid of Law	50
5.3. Conclusion	51
6. The New Interpretation	51
6.1 The Author's Own Interpretation	51
6.1.1 The Cyclic Motive	51
6.1.2 Two Underlying Reasons	52
6.1.3 A Natural Desire for the Supernatural	52
6.2 An Alternative Ontology	53
CHAPTER 3 AN ANALYSIS OF THE ONTOLOGY OF THE "SUMMA CONTRA GENTILES" (1261-1264)	**55**
1. Introduction: Reference, Focus, Sources and Lay-Out	56
1.1 Reference	56
1.2 Focus	57
1.3 Sources	57
1.4 Lay-out	57
2. A Hierarchical Ontological Philosophy	58
2.1 Risks Attached	58
2.2 God's Being to be Fathomed	58

2.3 Relativism of Being	59
3. Purely Cosmological Philosophy	59
3.1 Two Viewpoints	59
3.2 The Role of the Idea of Law	60
3.3 The Light of the Scriptures for Philosophy	61
3.4 A Philosophy of Creation?	61
3.5 A Static View of Creation	62
3.6 The Positive Side	62
4. An Ontological Dualism	63
4.1 Two Different Theories	63
4.2 Influence of His Idea of Law	64
4.3 Comment	64
5. Partial Universalism	65
5.1 Different Theories	65
5.2 The Doctrine of Form and Matter	66
5.3 Once Again His Idea of Law as The Key	66
5.4 Comment	67
6. Analogy of Being	67
6.1 The Heart of Aquinas' Philosophy?	67
6.2 Likeness in Difference	68
6.3 His Idea of Law as Background Again	69
6.4 Epistemological Implications	69
6.5 Application	69
7. Participation	70
7.1 The Link with "Exemplar" and "Similitudo"	70
7.2 The Difference Between the Doctrine of Similitudo/Exemplars and Participation	71
7.3 A Platonising Trait	72
7.4 A Full Circle	72
8. The Implications of Aquinas' Idea of Law	73
8.1 Serious Reservations	73
8.2 Already Queried By His Contemporaries	73
8.3 Even Protestant Philosophy Influenced	74
9. Summary	74
9.1 Direction and Idea of Law	74
9.2 View of Reality	75
CHAPTER 4 THE THOMIST ANTHROPOLOGY AND EPISTEMOLOGY	77
1. Introduction	78
1.1 Link	78

1.2 LIMITATION	78
1.3 SOURCES	79
1.4 LAY-OUT	79
2. THE ORIGIN OF HUMAN BEINGS	80
2.1 THREE PARTS OF THE SOUL	80
2.2 HOW THE SOUL DOES NOT ORIGINATE	81
2.3 EACH SOUL IS CREATED BY GOD HIMSELF	82
2.4 ARGUMENTS EMPLOYED AGAINST THE CREATION OF AQUINAS	82
3. THE RELATIONSHIP BETWEEN INTELLECTIVE SOUL AND BODY	84
3.1 FORM AND MATTER	84
3.2 SIGNIFICANT IMPLICATIONS	85
4. THE INTELLECTIVE SOUL: AN INDEPENDENT, IMMORTAL AND SUPRATEMPORAL SUBSTANCE	85
4.1 THE INTELLECTIVE SOUL AS A SUBSTANCE	86
4.2 THE INTELLECTIVE SOUL IS IMMORTAL	86
4.3 COMMENT	87
4.4 A SUPRA-TEMPORAL SOUL	88
4.5 SUBSISTENCE THEORY	88
5. THE ABILITIES OF THE INTELLECTIVE SOUL	89
5.1 INTELLECT AND CONDUCT	89
5.2 INTELLECT AND FAITH	90
6. KNOWLEDGE OF THE UNIVERSAL FORM OF LAW	90
6.1 DIFFERENCE BETWEEN TWO KINDS OF KNOWLEDGE	91
6.2 KNOWLEDGE OF THE LAWS	91
7. "EMPIRICISM"	92
7.1 SENSORY PERCEPTION	92
7.2 NATURAL SENSORY KNOWLEDGE OF GOD	92
7.3 THE BEGINNING OF THE PROCESS OF KNOWING	93
8. "PHANTASMA"	93
8.1 A SUBSEQUENT STEP NEEDED	93
8.2 NOT YET SUFFICIENT	93
9. "INTELLECTUS AGENS" AND "POSSIBILIS"	94
9.1 THE ROLE OF THE ACTIVE INTELLECT	94
9.2 ILLUMINATION	95
9.3 ABSTRACTION	95
10. "INTELLECTUS POSSIBILIS"	96
10.1 KNOWLEDGE OF THE ESSENCE	96
10.2 INTENTIONALLY ORIENTED	96
10.3 KNOWLEDGE NOT YET APRIORISED	97

11. AGREEMENT	97
11.1 A Likeness of Reality	97
11.2 Correspondence	98
11.3 Determinative Role of the Doctrine of Exemplars	98
12. Knowledge by Faith	99
13. The Value of the Preceding Research	99

CHAPTER 5 DIVINE PROVIDENCE IN THE PHILOSOPHY OF THE "DOCTOR ANGELICUS" — 101

1. Introduction: Topicality, Links, Lay-out and References	102
1.1 Topicality	102
1.2 Links	103
1.3 Lay-out	103
1.4 References	104
2. Idea of God	105
2.1 Proofs of God's Existence	105
2.2 The Various Substantiations	105
2.3 Comments	106
3. Providence as a Fact in General	107
3.1 Everything Directed at an End	108
3.2. Everything Pursues the Good	108
3.3 Everything Pursues God	108
3.4 Creaturely Perfection Means Deification	109
3.5 God Himself the Mover	109
3.6 Intellectual Creatures Pursue God Through their Understanding of God	110
3.7 Biblicist Eisegesis and Exegesis	110
3.8 Comments	111
4. How God Wields His Providence	112
4.1 God Sets An Order For Things	112
4.2 God is Omnipresent	112
4.3 Comments	113
4.4 Primary and Secondary Causes	114
4.5 God Rules By Means of Intellectual Creatures	115
4.6 The Higher Ones Rule The Lower Ones	115
4.7 Why Specifically by Intellectual Creatures?	116
4.8 God's Rational Plan	116
4.9 God Subjected to His Own Plan	117
4.10 Conclusion	117

5. THE PROVIDENCE OF GOD IN RELATION TO	117
THE HUMAN BEING	117
5.1 THE ISSUE	118
5.2 AQUINAS' SOLUTION TO THE PROBLEM	118
6. DIVINE PROVIDENCE AND HUMAN FREEDOM	119
6.1 FREEDOM OF WILL	120
6.2 FREEDOM AS THE FREEDOM OF CHOICE	120
6.3 FREEDOM OF WILL AND CONTINGENCY	121
6.4 COMMENTS	122
6.5 HUMAN FREEDOM AND DIVINE SOVEREIGNTY	123
6.6 COMMENTS	124
6.7 DETERMINISM	125
7. PROVIDENCE AND PRAYER	125
7.1 AQUINAS' PROBLEM	126
7.2 AQUINAS' SOLUTION	126
7.3 COMMENTS	127
8. PROVIDENCE AND EVIL	127
8.1 EVIL IS SOMETHING ACCIDENTAL	128
8.2 EVIL IS A LACK OF THE GOOD	128
8.3 EVIL IS CONNECTED TO THE GOOD IN A NEGATIVE WAY	129
8.4 COMMENTS	129
8.5 THE CAUSE OF EVIL LIES WITH BOTH THE SECONDARY AND THE PRIMARY CAUSE (GOD)	130
8.6 COMMENTS	132
9. PREDESTINATION, ELECTION AND REPROBATION	132
9.1 PREDESTINATION AS AN ETERNAL, DIVINE DECREE	133
9.2 FURTHER EXPLANATION	133
9.3 COMMENTS	133
9.4 THE HISTORICAL LINE CONTINUED	134
10. CONCLUSION	135
10.1 THE HAZARD OF SYNTHESIS PHILOSOPHY	135
10.2 THE HAZARD OF DETERMINISM	*135*
10.3 THE LAW-IDEA AS THE ROOT CAUSE – SOME HISTORICAL GLIMPSES	135 *135*
10.4 A FELICITOUS REVERSAL	136
10.5 LOOKING AHEAD	137

CHAPTER 6 CHRISTIANISING HELLENISM IMPLIES THE HELLENISATION OF THE CHRISTIAN FAITH   139
1. INTRODUCTION: MOTIVATION AND LAY-OUT   140

1.1 Motivation	140
1.1.1 Von Harnack on Hellenization	141
1.1.2 Vollenhoven and Dooyeweerd on Synthesis	141
1.1.3 Klapwijk's View of Synthesis Philosophy	142
Klapwijk's Point of View	142
Comment on Klapwijk's View	143
1.1.4 Helleman's Sympathy with Synthesis Philosophy	144
1.1.5 The Debate By About The Nineties	145
Classical Philosophy	146
The More Broadly Based Debate	146
1.1.6 The Struggle of Sweetman and Others	146
1.1.7 The Viewpoint of Some Contemporary Theologians	147
1.1.8 A Preliminary View	148
1.2 Lay-out	149
2. Synthesis Philosophy	149
2.1 What Synthesis Means	150
2.2 Based on The Idea of Neutral Scholarship	151
2.3 It Differs From Syncretism	151
2.4 Two Kinds of Synthesis	151
2.5 Different Motives	152
2.6 Synthesis is not merely a Matter of Terminology, and Methods are Not Neutral	152
2.7 Different Methods of Synthesis	153
2.7.1 Method of exegesis and eisegesis	153
Four Kinds of Hermeneutics	153
Allegorical exegesis	154
Biblicism	154
Threefold Revelation	155
2.7.2 The Paradoxical Method	155
2.7.3 The Method of Nature and Grace	156
Implications	156
2.8 Hazards of Synthesis Philosophy	157
An Example	157
No Slave of Aristotle's and yet...	157
Unresolvable Tension	158
Anachronistic Thinking	158
Taken over by Aristotle	158
2.9 A Different View of the History of Western Thought	159
2.10 A Permanent Temptation	159
2.11 Thetic-Critical Philosophy	160

3. SCHOLASTIC PHILOSOPHY	161
3.1 STEMMING FROM TWO NEEDS	161
3.2 BOUND BY TRADITIONAL SOURCE	162
3.3 THE ROLE OF LOGIC	162
3.4 SPECIFIC METHODS	163
3.5 A WIDER DEFINITION	163
3.6 CONCLUSION	164
3.6.1 NATURE AND GRACE	164
3.6.2 THE GREAT INFLUENCE OF ARISTOTLE	165
4. AQUINAS' SYNTHETIC ACCOMMODATION OF	166
ARISTOTLE'S PHILOSOPHY	166
4.1 A BROAD OUTLINE	166
4.2 THE REASON FOR ARISTOTLE'S POPULARITY	166
4.3 NO EASY TASK	167
4.4 REACTIONS TO ARISTOTLE'S PHILOSOPHY	167
4.5 THE OUTCOME OF THE WHOLE COURSE OF EVENTS	168
4.6 ARISTOTLE, ARISTOTELIANISM AND ARISTOTLE	169
INTERPRETATION	169
5. CONCLUSION	169

CHAPTER 7 SEVEN CENTURIES OF NEO-THOMIST THINKING AFTER AQUINAS — 171

1. INTRODUCTION: HOW THIS CHAPTER LINKS UP WITH PREVIOUS CHAPTERS, THE MOTIVATION FOR IT, ITS LIMITATIONS AND LAY-OUT	172
1.1 CONNECTION	172
1.2 MOTIVATION	173
1.2.1 FELLOW-CHRISTIANS	173
1.2.2 INFLUENCE ON ORTHODOX REFORMED THEOLOGY	173
1.2.3 INTERRELATIONS	174
1.2.4 CONFRONTED BY THE SAME PROBLEMS	174
1.2.5 RECENT ATTEMPTS AT A SYNTHESIS	175
1.3 CONSTRAINTS	175
1.4 LAY-OUT	176
2. HOW A TRADITION IS HANDLED	176
2.1 WHAT A TRADITION IS	176
2.2 ELEMENTS OF A TRADITION	177
2.3 HOW A TRADITION SHOULD BE HANDLED	177
3. A BRIEF OUTLINE OF THE NEO-THOMIST TRADITION	178
3.1 THE PHILOSOPHY OF AQUINAS CANONIZED	179
3.2 INFLUENCE ON OTHER ORDERS	179
3.3 DECREES BY VARIOUS POPES	179

3.4 NATURE AND GRACE	180
3.5 THE DUTCH-BELGIAN CONTRIBUTION	181
4. NEO-THOMIST INTERPRETATIONS OF DEVELOPMENTS DURING SEVEN CENTURIES	181
4.1 HALDANE	182
4.2 DELFGAAUW	182
5. TWO DIFFICULT QUESTIONS	183
5.1 WHICH AQUINAS?	183
5.2 ILLUSTRATING THE ISSUE	184
5.3 WHOSE THOMISM?	185
5.4 THE IMPORTANCE OF A DEVELOPMENT IN THE PHILOSOPHY OF AQUINAS	185
6. TWO HISTORIOGRAPHICAL METHODS	186
6.1 A TYPOLOGICAL CLASSIFICATION	186
6.2 A CHRONOLOGICAL ACCOUNT	187
7. CONCLUSION: THE NECESSITY FOR A MORE DISTINCTLY PHILOSOPHICAL HISTORIOGRAPHY	188
CHAPTER 8 A PROBLEM-HISTORICAL ANALYSIS OF NEO-THOMIST SCHOLARSHIP	**189**
1. INTRODUCTION	190
1.1 LINK	190
1.2 LAY-OUT	190
2. CONSIDERING THE CONSISTENTLY	191
PROBLEM-HISTORICAL METHOD AS A POSSIBILITY	191
2.1 THE CHARACTER OF TYPES	192
2.2 THE NATURE OF SCHOOLS OR TRENDS	192
2.3 THE INFLUENCE OF SCHOOLS ON TYPES	193
3. THE TYPE OF PHILOSOPHY FUNDAMENTAL TO THOMISM	193
	193
3.1 EARLIER REPRESENTATIVES	194
3.2 MORE RECENT REPRESENTATIVES	194
3.3 A BRIEF DESCRIPTION OF THE TYPE OF PHILOSOPHY OF NEO-THOMISM	195
3.3.1 PURELY COSMOLOGICAL PHILOSOPHY	195
3.3.2 DUALISM	196
3.3.3 NATURE AND GRACE	196
3.3.4 VERTICAL PARTIAL UNIVERSALISM	197
3.3.5 SUBSISTENCE THEORY	198
4. SHIFTS IN NEO-THOMIST VIEWS OF THE NATURE-GRACE THEME	198

4.1 EARLIER VIEWS	199
4.2 NEWER TENDENCIES	199
4.3 TWO DIFFERENT VIEWS	200
4.4 UNSOLVED ISSUES	201
4.5 A CONFIMATION	201
5. THE PHILOSOPHIES "BEHIND" THE CHANGED VIEW OF THE RELATIONSHIP BETWEEN NATURE AND GRACE	202
5.1 NEW IRRATIONAL SCHOOLS	202
5.2 K. RAHNER AS AN EXAMPLE OF A NEW PHILOSOPHICAL CURRENT	202 202
5.3 M. BLONDEL AS AN EXAMPLE OF ANOTHER TYPE OF PHILOSOPHY	203
5.4 AN APOLOGETIC MOTIVE	204
5.5 INCONSISTENCY	204
5.6 FAILED APOLOGETICS	205
5.7 CHAMPIONS OF A CHRISTIAN PHILOSOPHY?	205
5.8 AN EXCEPTIONAL VIEWPOINT?	206
5.9 DOOMED TO FAILURE	206
6. A REFORMATIONAL RESPONSE	207
6.1 A FALSE PROBLEM	207
6.2 THE CORRECT BIBLICAL CONTRAST	208
6.3 MODIFICATIONS OFFER NO SOLUTION	208
6.4 EXAMPLES OF UNFINISHED REFORMATION	208
6.5 THE ALTERNATIVE?	209
BIBLIOGRAPHY OF CHAPTERS 1 - 8	**213**
CHAPTER 1	**213**
1.1 ORIGINAL TEXTS	**213**
1.2 TRANSLATIONS	**213**
2. PROCEEDINGS OF THE INTERNATIONAL CONFERENCE IN COMMEMMORATION OF THE SEVENTH CENTURY OF AQUINAS' DEATH (17-24 APRIL 1974 AT ROME AND NAPELS). ED. BY THE SECERETARIAT, A. FERNANDEZ & A. SALIZZONI.	**214**
3. SECONDARY SOURCES	**215**
CHAPTER 2	**220**
CHAPTER 3	**221**
CHAPTER 4	**224**
CHAPTER 5	**226**
CHAPTER 6	**229**
CHAPTER 7	**234**
CHAPTER 8	**238**

PREFACE

It is hardly necessary to argue that Thomas Aquinas is one of the giants of Western philosophy. The philosophy of the *Doctor Angelicus* is a fundamental *locus* to the understanding of Christian thought, both past and present. His philosophy is also essential to grasping past and present non-Christian philosophy. People might regard Aquinas' system of thought as the centre of Western philosophy. On the one hand, Aquinas' thinking draws from the Greek past, as it is "appropriated" and re-interpreted to fit into the framework of Christian dogma. On the other hand, his thought process branches out in and influences many modern and late-modern movements. One needs to think, for example, of phenomenology (a philosophy of lived-out experiences) and its interest in essence and being.

At the same time, Aquinas is a complex author. His works are difficult to read because they are monumental (in-depth and in size). Furthermore, his works are ancient works, which belong to another time and culture, being a challenge for the modern reader to access. Thomist philosophy is difficult to read because, after many centuries of interpretations and comments, there seem to be several perspectives on Aquinas, each confirming or condoning the views of past or recent movements within the Roman Catholic tradition.

Not reading his works nor commenting on them is not an appropriate response to Aquinas. Each interested reader and philosopher, whatever their position may be, needs to know what Aquinas said and what impact this may have on one's tradition. Reformational philosophy has paid a lot of attention to Thomist philosophy, primarily through Dooyeweerd's works. If one could say that Dooyeweerd focused on key figures of Western philosophy, then Aquinas is undoubtedly in the company of those essential authors. Among those who studied and wrote on Aquinas and Medieval philosophy from a Reformational perspective in more recent times, we also find SU Zuidema, MC Smit and BJ van der Walt.

In this book, Professor Van der Walt enriches this tradition of reformational reflection on Medieval philosophy. His contribution, in my opinion, is new in at least two senses: first, it focuses with particular emphasis on neo-Thomism and second, it utilizes Vollenhoven's method for the study of the history of philosophy.

Concerning the first point, extending the discussion to neo-Thomism, has the advantage of highlighting the consequences and sometimes the hidden tensions of Aquinas' philosophy. Van der Walt conceives neo-Thomism as beginning very early, in the 13th century, not just in the revival of this movement during the 19th century. We can, therefore, say that he takes into account various interpretations of Aquinas since his death. The questions and observations developed in this regard are undoubtedly important. First of all, for reformational philosophy, a movement regarding itself as *neo*-Calvinist. Secondly, this book, utilizing a reliable method for studying the history of philosophy, has the proper credentials to offer a genuinely reformational position on Thomist philosophy. Van der Walt doesn't simply provide a slightly modified version of previous assessments but attempts to break new ground from its original work. Van der Walt's contribution is thus valuable not only to reformational circles but the whole philosophical community.

This text has several other plus points, which I will also mention. Van der Walt does not focus on peripheral issues. Instead, he deals directly with ontological, epistemological and anthropological issues. His insightful analysis grants a thorough systematic character to the text.

On the other hand, he does not neglect the historical side of things either as they are well-informed and quite pleasant. This balance between the systematic and the historical perspectives allows us to experience this text as an integrated whole. It is not simply an accumulation of a-historical and abstract lucubration; it is also not a pile of historical reports on interpreters who disagreed, popes who canonized, commentators and betrayers. Finally, the author tries to bring to light the very soul of Thomist philosophy: the worldviews, pre-scientific or "religious" level, which is essential to an understanding of the "heart" of Aquinas' philosophy (and any other philosophy for that matter).

This book will therefore benefit at least historians, theologians and philosophers. We live in a time of compromise, where many, even in Reformed circles, confusedly recommend a return to "orthodoxy" with an attitude willing to make historical and philosophical concessions. They often regard the "borrowing" of past or present philosophical ideas as the only possible strategy. This book returns the Christian scholar a sense of dignity and hope.

Prof. Renato Coletto
School of Philosophy
Potchefstroom Campus of the Northwest University

INTRODUCTION

LIKE EVERY GIANT IN the history of Christian philosophy and theology Thomas Aquinas (1224/5-1274) still deserves our attention. The greatness of this man is already evident from the fact that he was not only declared a saint but moreover became the universal *doctor Angelicus,* whose teachings guided the Roman Catholic Church and its theology. Consequently, his heritage continues in many centuries following his death.

Lasting worldwide influence

His thinking has had remarkable endurance over the past 750 years, as illustrated by the following examples.

Firstly, throughout the ages, his ideas have been accepted, interpreted, and in countless ways, reworked by many of his Neo-Thomist followers – not only by his closest Dominican brothers but also by Jesuits and Franciscans. Thomas Aquinas also significantly influenced the Neo-Thomists—chapters 7 and 8 of this book especially trace his massive impact on their thinking.

Secondly, Aquinas' heritage was not limited to only like-minded Catholic philosophers and theologians, having a wide-ranging influence even in Protestant circles. Soon after the sixteenth-century Reformation, both Reformed and Lutheran theologians, because of a lack of their own, genuine Reformational philosophy, also accepted Thomistic synthetic philosophy as a basis for their theological works. This trend is called Reformed Orthodoxy or Scholasticism.

Influence on the Reformed Theological Tradition

I published several scholarly journal articles to prove this influence over the last few years (cf. Chapter 1). Unfortunately, I wrote most of them in my mother tongue, Afrikaans. But in the interest of those wanting to consult them, they are mentioned here – with the prospect that eventually they will also be available in English.

An introductory article appraises Reformed Orthodoxy in general and appeared in *Tydskrif vir Christelike Wetenskap,* 47 (1):97-116, 2011.

The following three articles were devoted to the Synod and Canons of Dordt (1618-1619). The first one discussed the Reformed-Scholastic view of the relation between God and man in the works of F. Gomarus (1563-1641) and J. Arminius (1560-1609), two prominent figures at the Synod (Published in *Tydskrif vir Geesteswetenskappe,* 51(3):269-287, 2011). The second one (in *Tydskrif vir Christelike Wetenskap,* 48(1 & 2):91-110, 2012) focussed on the Aristotelian-Scholastic philosophical influences on this crucial meeting and its "confession" accepted by the Reformed churches.

Then followed an essay on the Aristotelian-philosophical influences at Dordt (in *Tydskrif vir Geesteswetenskappe,* 52(3): 174-195, 2012), followed in the same year by a more comprehensive treatment of the same issue (in *Tydskrif vir Christelike Wetenskap,* 48(1 & 2):91-110, 2012). Only one article was written in English, viz. "Flagging philosophical minefields at the Synod of Dordt (1618-1619); Reformed Scholasticism reconsidered" (Published in *Koers,* 76(3): 505-538).

Next, *The Synopsis Purioris Theologiae* published two of my contributions, a journal written at the request of the Synod of Dordt and first published in 1625. In the first (in *Tydskrif vir Christelike Wetenskap,* 47(2): 1-34, 2011), I argued that the title of this Reformed Dogmatic textbook was inappropriate: without a pure biblically oriented philosophical basis, it could not be a *purioris theologiae* (a purified theology). The second article (in *Tydskrif vir Christelike Wetenskap*, 47 (3 & 4):4986, 2011) indicated similar philosophical impurities reflected in the theological anthropology and epistemology of the *Synopsis*.

A subsequent *third* indication of the impact of Aquinas and Neo-Thomism on Reformed theologians is discernible in Herman Bavinck (1854-1921) and Abraham Kuyper (1837-1920). One only has to read Bavinck's *Reformed Dogmatics* and Kuyper's *Encyclopedia of Holy Theology* carefully to see the extent to which they still relied on Aquinas.

Influence on Reformational Philosophy

Fourthly, and quite surprisingly, traces of Aquinas' philosophy are even detected in the thinking of reformational philosophers, who would otherwise distance themselves from his influence. Herman Dooyeweerd (1894-1977) in the Netherlands and Hendrik G. Stoker (1899-1993) in South Africa. (cf. my book of 2014 *At the cradle of a Christian philosophy in Calvin, Vollenhoven, Stoker and Dooyeweerd*.) both come to mind.

A last, *fifth* example of Aquinas' lasting significance is the contemporary movement known as the Radical Orthodoxy of John Milbank and his followers (cf. e.g. J.A.K. Smith: *Introducing Radical Orthodoxy* (2004). Milbank, with his followers, intends to develop a post-secular theology by returning to a newly interpreted version of Aquinas and other Medieval thinkers, like Duns Scotus. Milbank even makes an effort to reconcile Radical Orthodoxy and the European Reformational philosophical tradition (cf. J.K.A. Smith & J.H. Olthuis (Eds.) *Radical Orthodoxy and the Reformed Tradition*). The present monograph takes a more critical stance on the whole Thomistic heritage.

Aquinas (unlike many Evangelical and Reformed theologians) realized that he required a philosophical basis to develop his Christian theology. But I do not regard the enduring influence of Aquinas and Neo-Thomism as beneficial for contemporary Christianity in general and Reformational philosophy in particular.

Returning to The Original Aquinas

The present writer decided to read the original Aquinas (in Latin) again. The focus fell on his *Summa Contra Gentiles*, regarded as his main philosophical work, tracking the deepest, philosophical basis of his theology.

The first result of my research was written up long ago (1968) for my master's degree in philosophy: *Die wysgerige konsepsie van Thomas van Aquino in sy "Summa Contra Gentiles"* (The philosophical conception of Thomas Aquinas in his "Summa Contra Gentiles").

In 1974, I was privileged to attend and deliver a paper at the International Congress (in Rome and Naples) as I commemorated Aquinas' death seven centuries ago.

In 1975 (for part of my doctoral dissertation in philosophy), I again paid attention to his view on natural theology.

Recently (2012-2014), I wrote a series of eight articles (translated for this volume) on Thomas and Neo-Thomism, published in the South African *Tydskrif vir Christelike Wetenskap/Journal for Christian Scholarship*, vol. 48-50 (See *Acknowledgments*).

Methodology

The method employed in this book to evaluate Aquinas' philosophy is the consistent problem-historic method. The reader will find an elementary explanation in various previous publications and my monograph of 2014: *Constancy and change: historical types and trends in the passion of the Western mind*.

Contents

The first five chapters of this book provide a systematic overview of Aquinas' philosophy.

Chapter one uncovers the primary religious direction of Aquinas' thinking, while the *second chapter* describes his peculiar idea of law, considered a key to comprehending his entire philosophy.

The *third chapter* is an exposition of Aquinas' ontology or view of reality (God and cosmos). *Chapter four*, subsequently, indicates how these ontological starting-points are determinative for his anthropology and epistemology.

Chapter five discusses the implications of the preceding four chapters and illustrates how, in his doctrine of providence, Aquinas viewed the relation between God and human beings in, for instance, his ideas about human freedom, prayers and the issue of evil.

In *Chapter six*, I retrace my steps and return to the question of whether justice has been done (in the first chapter) by characterizing Aquinas' thinking as an unacceptable scholastic synthesis or an accommodation between pagan Greek and biblical ideas.

Seven Centuries of Neo-Thomism

Chapters seven and *eight* move beyond the *Doctor Angelicus*. *Chapter seven* provides a bird's eye view of how Neo-Thomist thinkers themselves tried to understand their own long and complex history. Their key question has been: what exactly does it mean to be a Neo-Thomist? To what degree should a follower of Aquinas connect his/her thinking to the "original" Aquinas, and to what extent may she/he deviate from him? Because of the many divergent interpretations of Aquinas, one can state the problem differently, asserting the question: Which Aquinas and whose Thomism?

Neo-Thomists employed two methods, portraying their development. The *first* is an ontological categorization (according to types of philosophy). And the *second* is a chronological-historiographic methodology (according to different trends in the philosophies of Neo-Thomists).

The author, however, regards these approaches as unsatisfactory. He proposes a consistent problem-historical method to better grasp the protracted and involved history of Neo-Thomism. In addition, *chapter eight*, the concluding chapter, provides a critical evaluation of the shifting perspectives – without any real solution – in the philosophy and theology of Aquinas and his followers on their fundamental doctrine of nature and super-nature (grace).

For the convenience of the readers, each chapter starts with a brief abstract (printed in italics), providing an overview of its contents. Considering that the eight chapters originated from eight separate articles, a certain amount of repetition and overlap is inevitable but can be of value for readers who may only be interested in a specific chapter.

Acknowledgements

I want to express my sincere gratitude to the following persons. Without their assistance and contributions, this publication would not have been realized:

Dr. Marietjie Nelson, for translating the often difficult philosophical material.

Prof. Renato Coletto of the School of Philosophy, Potchefstroom Campus of the Northwest University, who introduced this volume with a preface.

I want to thank the editorial board of the *Journal for Christian Scholarship* for granting permission to republish the articles in English.

Finally, I want to thank my wife, Hannetjie, for typing the original articles, editing and typesetting this new English text.

May this humble contribution encourage renewed interest and further reflection on a Christian giant of the past whose influence is still reverberating today.

Potchefstroom Bennie Van der Walt
June 2017

CHAPTER 1
THE RELIGIOUS DIRECTION OF THE PHILOSOPHY OF THOMAS AQUINAS

THIS INVESTIGATION ABOUT THE *famous Catholic thinker Thomas Aquinas and his philosophy is part of a more comprehensive research program. The project intends to trace the influence of Aquinas on subsequent thinkers historically during the following centuries, focussing on Reformed Orthodoxy or Scholasticism from 1550 to 1700 and afterward. Previous articles already investigated the main philosophical lines from Aquinas (via Suarez and Zabarella) to Beza, the Synod and Canons of Dordt (1618-1619) up to the* Synopsis Purioris Theologiae *(1625). The founders of Reformational philosophy (viz.) continue the line of scholastic thinking, Stoker, Dooyeweerd and Vollenhoven. Today again, we witness a new revival in Reformed circles of this kind of orthodox-scholastic theology and philosophy. Understanding the philosophy of Aquinas can therefore be of great help in an appraisal of subsequent developments – not only in Catholic but also Reformed thinking up to the present day.*

This one and the five proceeding chapters focus on the Summa Contra Gentiles, *Aquinas' main philosophical work offering a new interpretation. Observers should view Aquinas' law idea as the central motive behind his whole philosophical-theological system. But before one discusses his ontology of law, it is necessary to explain the religious direction of his thinking – the main topic of this introductory chapter.*

Introduction

SOME INTRODUCTORY REMARKS ARE essential to: (1.) Explaining the place of this and the following four articles in the author's research programme. (2.) Bringing to the attention its topicality. (3.) Pointing out the various interpretations of Aquinas' thinking. (4.) Motivating the essential bibliographical limitations regarding secondary sources. (5.) Explaining the planned layout of this part of the research project.

1. Its Place Within the Broad Outline of the Research Project

The scope of this program is an effort to *characterize* and *evaluate* Reformed scholastic philosophy (also called Reformed Orthodoxy) (cf. Van der Walt 2011a), but also to determine the course of its historical lines (evolution). In this respect, intellectuals debate a specific kind of theology, but the primary focus falls on the philosophical foundation of theology. Unfortunately, within this program, all results could not be published in the correct chronological order. For this reason, readers should read the different articles in the proper order given here. Chronologically, readers should first read this article (and the following four articles) on Thomas Aquinas (1224-1274). Due to his synthesis thinking with Greek philosophy, readers can follow the historical line from him going back in history to Aristotle (384-433 B.C.).

After the reformation in the sixteenth century, the scholastic thinking of Aquinas became popular in Reformed Orthodox circles, employing several intermediate links like i.e. Suarez (1548-1617) and Zabarella (1532-1589). Van der Walt (2011a) offers a general typification and evaluation of this from a philosophical angle. This is followed by (cf. Van der Walt, 2011d) a historical outline, developing the issue of divine sovereignty and human responsibility by amongst others Augustine, Aquinas, Calvin, Beza and Ursinus. Subsequently, various contributions (cf. Van der Walt, 2011e, 2012a and 2012b) examined the Synod of Dordt (1618-1619) and the Canons of Dort. Under the authority of this famous Synod, four professors at the University of Leiden published a dogmatic handbook, the *Synopsis Purioris Theologiae,* in 1625. However, Van der Walt (2011b and 2011c) demonstrates that, despite the suggestion by the title that it contained sound Reformed theology, philosophically seen, it was not so pure since it exhibits distinctly Aristotelian scholastic features. The initial research we hope will be resumed by following the historical lines from the *Synopsis* further to the following mileposts in the history of the Reformed tradition.

During the seventeenth and eighteenth centuries, the *Nadere* Reformation of the "old writers" (like Smytegeld and A'Brakel") of the Netherlands was almost the only literature that profoundly influenced their thinking. The European Reveil (awakening) among writers like Da Costa, Bilderdijk and Groen van Prinsterer (in the Netherlands) was during the end of the eighteenth and the first half of the nineteenth century.

- Afterwards, we learn something from the fathers of a Reformational philosophy: Vollenhoven and Dooyeweerd (in the Netherlands) and Stoker (in South Africa). (On the philosophy of these three individuals, the author's research will already be published in 2012 in three contributions in *In die Skriflig*.)

- Finally, after examining all the philosophical tracks in the sandy roads of the past—this comprehensive research project will bring us to our South African history and, more specifically, to the Christian National ideal, which for a long time indicated the normative direction.

At the end of the whole project, we hope it will be clear how the threads run between the various mileposts of history; how ideas have feet that travel right through history; what Reformed identity meant in the past and should mean today.

1.1 Topicality
One can enumerate at least four reasons for the topicality of this part of

the research project on Aquinas.

1.1.1 Important for Understanding Roman Catholic Thinking

In 1323, Aquinas was declared a saint. During history, no less than 66 popes referred to his philosophy. His school of thought received a new injection for employing this through the papal encyclical *Aeterni Patris* (cf. Aeterni Patris, 1948) 1879. Pope Leo XIII declared that all Roman Catholic philosophers, theologians and educationalists had to follow the philosophy of the *Doctor Angelicus*. Although this encyclical is no longer carried out to the letter nowadays (cf. 3.1 below), the philosophy of Aquinas still has a vital role in Roman Catholic thinking.

1.1.2 Important to Protestant Scholasticism or Orthodoxy

In the work of Aquinas, the synthesis thinking of the Middle Ages, which attempted to reconcile the Bible and Greek philosophy reached a climax and became well-rounded. His synthesis would serve as an example for many centuries to come to Roman Catholic and Protestant thinkers – including Reformed ones. It happened, among the latter, already from the time of Beza (Calvin's successor in Genèva) and lasted until about 1700, but was revived once again in the nineteenth century by Bavinck (For seventeenth-century Protestant Scholasticism especially in Germany compare the comprehensive investigation by Wundt, 1939). E.A.Venter rightly remarks: "On the Western history of civilization, the philosophy of Thomas of Aquinas had a determining influence; even Protestantism did not evade its allure" (s.a. 63).

I want to specify the meaning of "allure:" the later appeal to Reformed philosophers – which is reviving today – has nothing to do with *ecclesiastical, confessional* differences (e.g. on the sacraments). In this regard, Reformed thinking followed its way.

Reformed theology gave into scholastic synthesis philosophy. The greatest future danger to real Reformational thinking (obviously apart from the growing secular influences) will be a synthetic-scholastic philosophy (cf. 1.2.4 below).

1.1.3 Influence on the Founders of the Reformational Philosophy of the Twentieth Century

In the third instance, the philosophy of Aquinas is essential not only to theology but also to Christian philosophy. Taljaard, as far back as 1976, indicated that the philosophical conceptions of two founders of Reformational philosophy, namely Dooyeweerd (1894-1977) and Stoker (1899-1993), can be linked to two phases in the evolution of Aquinas. (Dooyeweerd to Aquinas' initial monarchistic thinking and Stoker to his later subsistence theory.) According to Tol (2010), Vollenhoven, who was under the influence of Scholasticism earlier on, later pursued a different road. Since approximately the middle of the previous century, Christian philosophers sought similarities between the Christian philosophy of Dooyeweerd and various Catholic scholars (cf., e.g. Marlet, 1954, 1961, Robbers, 1948, 1949 and Smit, 1965).

1.1.4 Influence on Contemporary Theological Thinking

Fourthly, theologians nowadays tend to foster the cause of a revived Medieval Scholasticism (including Aquinas) and the later Reformed Orthodox Scholasticism, utterly devoid of criticism. This tendency, among current theologians, indicates the direction of contemporary Reformed thinking (Such representation, in my opinion, entails keeping one's eyes on the past and walking back into the future).

In the Netherlands, by way of example, Van Asselt (1996), Van Asselt & Dekker (2001), and Te Velde (2006, 2007, 2010a, 2010b,) all defend Medieval and later Scholasticism.

In the USA, this tendency toward Scholasticism among theologians is also apparent. Take Müller (2003), who rehashes Reformed Orthodox theology (from ± 1550-1700) once more for today. At the same institution (Calvin College, Grand Rapids), we have the philosopher Smith (2004), who advocates for a new movement known as Radical Orthodoxy as he wants to reconcile it to the Reformational philosophical tradition. Millbank, the "father" of this movement, started this kind of "return to the good old times," and his thinking has already gained support in South Africa, as evident from the recent doctoral thesis of Kruger (2011).

This information is given here merely to show how relevant Aquinas' thinking was not only for the centuries directly after him but right up to the present day. My own much more critical view of this uncritical relapse into scholastic philosophy will be explained in more detail later (cf. the fourth article in this series).

1.2 *Numerous Interpretations of Aquinas*

On the philosophy of Aquinas, there is an almost disorderly variety of neo–Thomistic (and other) interpretations. In the 1950s, E.A. Venter (s.a. 135 et seq.) grouped different Thomistic philosophers into three groups. *The first group* regarded Aquinas' thinking as a *philosophia perennis* which should hold good for all times and places without change. *The second group* attempted to present modern thinking as having already been foreseen by Aquinas. *The third group* felt even more free to take new philosophical tendencies into account and merely wanted to connect these with the essence of Thomism.

Robbers (1961), for instance, tried to reconcile Aquinas' philosophy with existentialism. (On what the "essence" of Aquinas' philosophy is, there is no consensus either!) Smit (1950) is another valuable source for understanding something of this variety among Aquinas' followers as well as their diverse interpretations of the *Doctor Angelicus*. Most probably, the nature–grace issue (cf. 4.3.3 and 4.4) is today still the most outstanding feature of Thomistic thinking.

The five hefty volumes which appeared during and after the International Thomas Conference (1974) (cf. Thomaso d'Aquino, 1974, 1975, 1976a, 1976b and 1976c respectively under Part 2 of Bibliography) is a further example of the differences in interpretation.

For more particulars on this conference at the time of the seventh century, since Aquinas' death, see Van der Walt (1974b and 1974c and 1976) for his lecture on this occasion. The following are examples of questions raised in the various lectures during the Thomas conference. Did he think more Platonising or more Aristotelianising? Or the question: what was the "key" to understanding his philosophy/theology? Was it his teaching on God, on creation, participation, analogy, or what exactly?

In the light of all the above–mentioned, the author, therefore, decided to drink from the fountain itself, not relying on secondary sources but instead reading Aquinas' main philosophical work in original Latin. In the proceeding next article, this investigation will also offer its interpretation—namely that one can better understand Aquinas from the angle of his specific cosmogonic idea. Therefore, this interpretation will differ from the numerous Roman Catholic interpretations and even from Reformational interpretations like Aertsen (1982).

1.3 Bibliographical Limitation

A chaotic number of magazines, articles and books on Aquinas already exist, which could quickly fill a library. (Only the lectures at the above-mentioned Thomas conference already number 2696 pages!) Here we will, only by way of exception, refer to secondary sources. The focus, particularly on newer sources, was not yet available during the author's previous (still unpublished) research (cf. Van der Walt, 1968 and 1974a). I also include some of my more current insights.

The endeavour to study Aquinas' numerous works, which could, indeed, fill an entire shelf, is an ambitious lifetime task. We will, thus, only focus on *Summa Contra Gentiles* (in future abbreviated SCG), his thesis against the heathen, generally considered to be his main philosophical work (the *Summa Theologiae* is his theological *magnum opus*). It takes up four books dealing in this order: God, creation, providence and redemption.

I consulted two Latin texts, *S. Thomae Aquinatis*, 1935 and *Santo Thomas de Aquino*, 1967. Since I consider the English translation published by Doubleday a reliable one (cf. Thomas Aquinas, 1955, 1956a,b,c and 1957), this research followed and quoted it. This translation takes up *five parts* since the original Book 3, *God's providence*, was translated into *two parts*. Therefore, in the English quotes, the reference method to the four books and page numbers is the following: I,10; II,200; IIIa,100 or IIIb,120 and IV,90. For checking, an earlier German translation was also used (cf. Thomas Aquinas, 1942-1960) as well as English translations (cf. Thomas Aquinas, 1945 and 1950).

1.4 The Layout

I will focus on Aquinas' philosophy in five successive contributions. In this first article, by way of background, something is first said on (1) Aquinas' evolution, (2) the place of the SCG in Aquinas' thinking, as well as (3) his (probable) intention with it. Subsequently, (4) I focus on the religious-normative direction of his philosophy (This includes his synthesis thinking, the method he applies for reaching unity between Aristotle and the Scriptures, namely distinguishing between nature and grace), while (5) finally evaluates.

2. Aquinas' Philosophical Evolution

Through the following glimpses from Aquinas' life story, one can trace his philosophical evolution (For more on his life history, cf. Van der Walt, 1975). His initial development from a Platonising philosopher to an Aristotelianising philosopher (or better formulated: Aristotle's interpretation) is one of his most discerning traits (Note: however, Aquinas' Platonic influences do not exclude Aristotle's influence on his philosophy). Early on in his life, Aquinas became acquainted with the work of Aristotle, but this was through the Patoni influence of the Arabic philosopher Avicenna. In short, Aquinas' philosophical course ran as follows as the progress of this discussion will convey.

2.1 First Acquaintance with Aristotelianism

Aquinas, the brilliant young man (born 1224/5), began his studies at the State University of Naples at the young age of fourteen. This university setting was the ideal place to get acquainted with the Greek philosopher for Aquinas because it, for centuries, served as the meeting point of Arabic and Western culture, conserving Aristotle's writings. Since it was a secular institution, Rome's ban on studying and teaching the works of the man from Stageira did not apply to the University of Naples and one of Aquinas' masters, Petrus Hibernus, availed himself of this freedom. During this period, Aquinas joined the Dominican Order (founded at the beginning of the century by the Spaniard Dominicus). This order required intense study from its members, and Aquinas became one of their top students.

2.2 Growing Influence by The Man from Stageira

In 1245 (more or less at the age of twenty), Aquinas departed to Paris, the Mecca of the theological world of the time, particularly to continue his studies under Albertus Magnus (1193-1280). Aquinas, as already mentioned, first was substantially influenced by Avicenna and still thought in a Platonising way. Although the papal ban on Aristotle applied in Paris, he still studied there, and his influence on Aquinas would gradually increase. From 1260, he taught in various places in his land of birth, Italy. Among other sites also (1261-1265) at the court of Pope Urbanus IV, who continued the efforts of Pope Gregory IX to make known to the Christian world the philosophy of Aristotle in a way that would maximize the gain and minimize the damage. At the same court, William van Moerbeke also translated several works of the famous Greek into Latin. It was also here, between 1259 and 1264, that the more significant part of the SCG had its origin.

2.3 In Defence of Aristotle's Philosophy

From 1268 to 1272, Aquinas received a call to be a professor in Paris. He now had to defend his Aristotelianising philosophy (Platonising and later non- Platonising) against other philosophical schools. Secular professors, opposing the Dominicans, and conservative Franciscans, oriented towards Augustine, and the Neo-Platonists unanimously opposed Aristotle's philosophy. One representative of the latter group (Asalo of St.Victor), for instance, declared openly – and rightly so – "that the spirit of Christ cannot rule where the spirit of Aristotle prevails." But Aquinas also needed to defend his progressive Aristotelianising philosophy against other forms of

Aristotelianising philosophies and that of the Arabic philosopher Averroës and his followers like Siger van Brabant and Boëthius the Dacian. This group adhered to the teaching of the so-called double truth (or paradox). According to them, there could be no connection between the Scriptures (or theology) and (Aristotelianising) philosophy, yet they accepted both as the truth.

Over against all these schools, Aquinas set his "Christian Aristotelianism" in which, using his distinction between natural and supernatural grace, he could demonstrate how the Christian faith could assimilate Aristotelian philosophy without jeopardizing either the Christian or the Aristotelian convictions. He, therefore, was an intentional synthesis thinker. Vollenhoven writes:

> In the same way that Augustine had used Plato in the explanation and defence of church doctrine, Thomas did with the philosophy of Aristotle. To be sure, he met with vehement opposition from his contemporaries but finally Thomas did prevail, to such an extent that Aristotelian philosophy became the basis of all of medieval scholasticism (2005c: 414).

Pope Gregory summoned Aquinas to attend the Council of Lyon, calling him back to Italy. Aquinas, however, fell ill and died on July 7, 1274, at Fosso Nova, near Terracina (between Rome and Naples). He was merely 49 years old. He did, though, accomplish far more than other philosophers who lived much longer than him.

2.4 Rejection After His Death

The fact that all and sundry did not accept Aquinas' Christian synthesis thinking at the time already became clear from his sojourn in Paris, but even after his death, the debate continued. Only three years after his death, the church rejected some of his Aristotelian ideas. His former master, Albertus Magnus, had to hurry to Paris to defend his deceased disciple's ideas. After this, both a Dominican and a Franciscan Archbishop of Canterbury likewise opposed Aquinas' writings. When his ideas were canonized in 1323, the hatchet was buried fifty years after his death. Thus the

Christian synthesis thinking of Aquinas was even at that time not taken for granted. Why would it today (once more) be acceptable?

After this general outline, we now say something more about Aquinas' main philosophical work. However, Gaybba (1998: 41) adeptly summarizes the above as follows:

> By the time Aquinas appeared, all of Aristotle's philosophical works had been discovered and not only his works on logic. The entire corpus of Aristotelian writings posed a major challenge to Christian thought, since it not only provided a well-reasoned survey of the entire field of human knowledge, but did so in a way that stressed the human mind's inherent ability to discover truth in the world around it. The rationalist threat that this posed to Christianity cannot be imagined any longer. But it was an immense threat and it was Aquinas who took up the challenge by mastering Aristotle's thought and forcing it to serve Christianity. He recast the entire Christian faith in Aristotelian categories of thought, thus ending the centuries–old domination of Platonic categories. So successful was he, that Scholastic Theology and Aristotelian Philosophy came to be seen as inextricably intertwined, to the point where Luther had to protest against the idea that one could not be a good theologian without using Aristotelian Philosophy!

3. The Place and Purpose of The SCG

First, we now ask the reader's attention for the place of the SCG in Aquinas' philosophical evolution and secondly for its purpose.

3.1 The Place of the SCG in Aquinas' Philosophical Evolution

As demonstrated above, Aquinas' thinking progressed from an initially Platonisingng to an increasingly Aristotelising philosophy. (While "Platonic" or "Aristotelian" denotes an exact following of these two great Greek philosophers, the terms "Platonising/Aristotelising" or Plato/Aristotle interpretation mean that only elements of their philosophies are taken over and re-interpreted according to a new conception). According to Vollenhoven (2000: 237, 238 and 2005c: 415), in the work of Aquinas, two phases can be discerned, each having two sub-phases.

A Platonising (monarchistic) period had two phases. During the *first phase* (1255), Aquinas still thought *without* the theme of nature—grace on the lines of the Arabic philosopher Avicenna (980-1037). However, as a Dominican, Aquinas was accused of heresy by some priests (e.g. Gerhard from Abbeville and Willem of St. Amour c.s.), and he began solving the problem as he employed a distinction between a natural (philosophical) theology and a supernatural (Christian) theology. During *the second phase* (1255-1259), Aquinas philosophized *with* the nature—grace method of synthesis thinking.

From 1259-1274, Aquinas' conception changed to a more purely *Aristotelising* subsistence theory in two phases: (a) From 1260-1265, the influence of Aristotle via Aquinas' tutor, Albertus Magnus (1206-1250), grew. However, he was still thinking in a Platonising way, seeing his Aristotelising philosophy through Platonising glasses. (b) From 1265 until 1274, however, he followed a non-Platonising version of Aristotle's interpretation. His last important theological work, the *Summa Theologiae,* was written during this final phase. As will become apparent, the SCG (his main philosophical work written between 1258/9-1263/4) falls in phase 2(a).

3.2 Reason for and intention with the SCG

It is no longer sure what the exact reason was for Aquinas to write the SCG. Van der Walt (1968: 40-44) goes into this in great detail and mentions the following. Aquinas wrote the SCG at the request of a Dominican missionary among the Muslims in Spain, Raymundus from Pennaforte (*obiit* 1275).

Tallying with Aquinas' words in Book I, Chapter 2 (p. 62). The Old Testament could convince the Jews to faith, and the New Testament could not sway the heretics. However, the Muslims do not accept the authority of the Bible. "We must, therefore, have recourse to natural reason, to which all men are forced to give their assent," meaning that the Bible was declared useless in the case of missionary work among Islamists. Moreover, it implies that one can change somebody's faith through rational arguments – instead of one's faith determining one's thinking. This kind of apologetic, in my opinion, is, therefore, doomed from the very beginning!

Take note, too, of the double irony of history. In the first place (as shown above), the Medieval Christians were indebted to the Arabs for their knowledge of Aristotle. Secondly, in the SCG, the Islamic Aristotelising philosophy is attacked by Aquinas, who employed Christian Aristotelianism!

It could be that the SCG was simultaneously also directed against the Averroic Aristotelising philosophy at the University of Paris (cf. 2.3 above and Van Steenberghen, 1955: 75 et seq.).

In summary: People regarded Aristotle as *the* philosopher, and Aristotelising philosophy was all the vogue. The Muslims attempted to reconcile Aristotle with their Islamic faith, while the Christians were trying to connect the same kind of philosophy with their biblical faith – and persuade the Muslims that it would be a better synthesis!

However, one kind of synthesis cannot be better than another. Aquinas fell into a pitfall that would determine his philosophy's normative direction with his reconciliation between Aristotle and the Word of God.

In this way, he accepted two – conflicting – sources of authority which he had to obey. Therefore, he could not point to a clear normative direction (cf. E.A. Venter, s.a.: 69) but found himself on a veritable see-saw that he had to keep stable all the time. Some more about the disunity in his philosophy.

4. *The Normative Direction in the Philosophy of the SCG*

Every proper philosopher should ask and answer at least the following two fundamental questions: (1) What *are* the things that exist in reality? And (2) What *should* it be like? The first is more a *structural* question, and the second a *directional*. The answer to the first question is a specific *type* of philosophy and the answer to the second is a particular *school, spirit* or *direction* in philosophy. We will start with Aquinas' answer to the second normative question and afterwards (in subsequent contributions) deal with his response to the first.

4.1 The Broad Perspective

Vollenhoven (2005a: 29. Cf. also 2005b) distinguishes three main periods in the history of Western philosophy: (1) the *pre-synthesis period* from ancient Greek, Hellenistic and Roman philosophy to approximately 50 AD; (2) the *synthesis thinking* of the Church Fathers and the Middle Ages from about 50 to 1550 AD; (3) the *post-synthesis thinking* since 1550 to the present. The latter period further distinguished in the anti-synthetic left (since the Renaissance) and right (since the sixteenth century Reformation). The left (secular) direction rejects the Scriptural Revelation accommodated within synthesis thinking, while the right (Christian) thinking wants freedom from the pagan element.

Synthesis thinking is, therefore, Vollenhoven's point of departure, a classification of Western philosophical history. One could also call it his greatest adversary. Why? Not because he denies that the philosophers from this long period were also sincere Christians. But because he thought that their philosophy did not do justice to the Word of God by attempting to connect it with themes from heathen, Greek-Hellenistic-Roman thinking – which is a religious sense having no connection at all. In Aquinas' philosophy, this synthetic mentality reached a climax— according to Vollenhoven, therefore, there was instead a record low. Why?

Because thinking synthetically also determines the *primary normative direction* of one's thinking, the question is, "How *should* I think?" It can no longer be answered unambiguously. The pre-synthesis thinking, for instance, accepted only the human intellect as its norm. In synthesis thinking, the Christian faith (based on the Scriptures) is added to it, resulting in a divided loyalty between an autonomous reason and faith and a muddled normative direction for the philosophy.

4.2 Synthesis in the SCG

One need not even read through all four books of the SCG to prove that Aquinas was a synthesis thinker. He starts his first book with a quotation from Proverbs 8:7: "My mouth speaks what is true...", but from what follows, it becomes evident that it is not only the truth of the Scriptures. On the same level of authority as God's Word, we also find pagan Greek philosophy.

Aquinas quotes Aristotle in the very first sentence. While Aquinas did not name him, he introduced Aristotle to the reader as "the Philosopher." *Philosophus* is also written with a capital letter, for there was no other philosopher who had such authority over Aquinas' way of thinking.

This beginning also characterizes the rest of the SCG. There hardly is a chapter in which there is no quote from the works of the man from Stageira. And where there is no explicit reference to his philosophy, the traces of his philosophy transpire very clearly from the contents.

Venter is correct when he writes that Aquinas' philosophy results from a *deliberate* effort to reconcile the Bible and Aristotle. To this, he adds:

> Thomas did not make this effort due to a lack of taking life seriously. On the contrary, he intended rendering Christianity a service. However, a false philosophical view of the relationship between faith and reason prevented him from realizing the fatal dangers inherent in such attempts at synthesis (E.A. Venter, s.a.: 64.).

On the face of it, however, Aquinas is so successful at giving both the Scriptures and heathen philosophy a place in his philosophy and theology that he is suspected on two sides (cf. 2.3 above). On the one hand, those who wanted nothing to do with pagan philosophy, while on the other hand, some found it most alluring. The suspicion of Venter's opposition was not without reason, for as a synthesis thinker, Aquinas did not concur with either of the two parties. Not with those (conservative) Christians who had turned their backs on the ancient philosophies, neither with the (liberal) Christian thinkers who (as one contemporary sharply put it) turned themselves into heretics in their effort to turn Aristotle into a Christian.

4.3 The Method of Synthesis in the SCG
The question is how Aquinas, despite vehement opposition, could succeed in effecting this synthesis. Vollenhoven (2005a: 62,65 and 2005b: 66,69) distinguishes three different ways synthesis thinking took place in the past – and still does.

4.3.1 Biblicism
The first is the method of reading alien thoughts, which even conflict with the Scriptures into the Bible (eisegesis) and then, now with biblical sanction – read it from the Bible again (exegesis). The intention of the early Biblicist Christian philosophers was often not wrong, for, in this way, they could show their pagan contemporaries that the Bible also contains (good) philosophy. "We do not believe it because you preach it, but we know it from God's Word" (sic!). Vollenhoven conludes: therefore in, such cases, one attempted to derive one's entire philosophy from the Bible biblicistically.

However, one had introduced a specific philosophy into the Bible and imagined that Scripture now sanctioned it (Vollenhoven, 2005a: 62.)!

This kind of Biblicism is evident in Aquinas' exegesis in the SCG of numerous passages from the Scriptures and is still fashionable today, even among Reformed theologians.

4.3.2 Paradox
The second synthesis method on its face does not seem to be accommodation but eventually still results in it. Above (2.3), we said that Aquinas met with this method (among the Averroists) but rejected it— this was the method of paradox, which accepted a double truth, consisting of both the pagan philosophy as the revelation of Scripture – even though there was the awareness that these two are irreconcilable. On reading someone like Tertullian (usually regarded as the father of this approach), one soon discovers that he failed in keeping apart his understanding of the Bible and pagan philosophy– the latter undoubtedly defiling the former.

4.3.3 Two Realm Doctrine

We mentioned (cf. 3.1) Aquinas (in 1255) accepted nature and grace as a method—Vollenhoven (2005a;65) states that this originated during the Synod of Orange (529 AD). One could say that this approach was a middle-of-the-road solution between the all too easy *reconciliation* between the Bible and Greek philosophy by the Biblicists (on the one hand) and the *tension* between them as presented by the paradoxical philosophers (on the other hand). According to Aquinas, one had to adhere to both the *unity and the difference* between pagan philosophy and God's revelation.

According to the nature–grace scheme, the relationship between pagan philosophy and the Christian faith was not paradoxical. The former was a *forerunner* or *threshold* to the latter's *perfection*. An age-old heathen dualism between the profane and the sacred is thus accepted here and used as a solution.

In this way, Aquinas could attempt to reconcile two spheres of knowledge (nature and grace) and two forms of knowing (reason and faith). "Nature" here represents all of life in this world as seen in the light of heathen philosophy, that is, without God's Word, the ecclesiastical offices or the sacraments. "Grace," on the other hand, means the preaching of the Word, fulfilling the ecclesiastical offices and taking the holy sacraments.

If one expresses this in an image, one could say that this view supposes a kind of two-story reality (nature being the lower story and grace the first floor). Aquinas wanted to examine this conceived reality with double-focused glasses all the time.

4.4 Nature and Grace in the SCG

The doctrine of nature-grace emerges in the SCG, particularly in Aquinas' anthropology. In Book 3, he deals with the fact that a human being cannot reach its highest goal without grace. Amongst other things, he says: "The end to which man is directed by the help of divine grace is above human nature. Therefore, some supernatural form and perfection must be superadded to man whereby he may be ordered suitably to the aforesaid end" (IIIb, 232).

The doctrine of grace as a *donum supperadditum* (an added gift) emerges from this.

4.4.1 Grace and Faith
Coupled with grace goes faith:

> To... man, in order that he may attain his ultimate end, there is added a perfection higher than his own nature, namely, grace, as we have shown. Therefore, it is necessary that, above man's natural knowledge, there should also be added to him a knowledge which surpasses natural reason. And this is the knowledge of faith, which is of the things that are not seen by natural reason (IIIb, 236).

In Book 4, it becomes clear why grace and faith have to be *added* to the structure of a human being before he can reach his highest goal. Aquinas writes: "because that nature has been stripped of that help of grace which had been bestowed on it in the first parent to pass on to his descendants along with the nature". (IV, 221). Afterwards, he says, "that good of nature which grace added over and above nature could be removed by the sin of our first parent." Aquinas emphasizes that the first human being had the gift of grace *before* the fall and that after the fall, he was deprived of this gift. (Cf. IV, 223).

4.4.2 Two Separate Domains
From this, it is clear that in the work of Aquinas, we find approximately the same idea regarding a human being that we see in the statement of the Synod of Orange (529 AD). God has structurally divided the human being into a *domain* of nature and a *domain* of grace. Only grace is lost at the fall. Grace is added again to the human being by the deliverance of Christ so that he can reach his highest goal.

Kok (1998:105) maintains that the nature–grace theme emerged most distinctly in the theology and philosophy of Aquinas. Therefore, to this day, it remains typical of Thomistic thinking (with modifications, of course). The natural human being, according to this, did not fall radically into sin, for his rational nature remained unblemished, and this applies to all human beings. Naturally, though, a human being does not progress far enough but needs grace as a means to perfection. In contrast to the doctrine of paradox, Aquinas teaches that grace does not *conflict* with nor *rejects* nature but merely *perfects* it.

5. An Appraisal
Various points of critique can be levelled at the nature–grace scheme of Aquinas.

5.1 It is Not Biblically Founded
Before the fall, it is impossible to speak of grace in the same sense as the Scriptures. Grace is the favour shown to a human being by God. One can only speak after the fall because the relationship between God and human beings was still perfect before the fall. Therefore, grace does not stand opposite/above nature (as Aquinas says) but opposite the wrath of God. Grace is not the antipode of sin either, but grace towards sin means forgiveness. As on God's side, grace is the opposite of wrath; on the side of a human being, forgiven sin stands over and against sin, which remains against him (cf. Vollenhoven, 2011: 87).

Aertsen (1991:116) rightly describes the difference between the view that Rome and the Reformation have of nature and grace as follows: Grace, according to Aquinas, is a perfection, elevating a human being above its nature to a supernatural state.

Human nature is such that a person cannot complete the *conversion* to the origin. The infusion of divine grace is required. According to the Reformation, grace must first and foremost be related to sin, to aversion with God. Grace, properly understood, is the remission of sins by which God restores people into fellowship with God. To the Reformers, grace is not the *elevation* of human nature but its *restoration* and liberation.

5.2 It Conflicts with God's Sovereignty over the Whole of Life
Aquinas claims that reason is the highest authority in the domain of na-

ture, while the authority of God and the Bible are restricted to the spheres of faith, the church, and theology. His thinking, here, is an apparent departure from the biblical narrative, which asserts the sovereignty of God over the entirety of creation, Christ's kingship over the whole of life, and the proclamation that his kingdom is all-encompassing. Aquinas narrows God's kingdom down to ecclesiastical life. And the redemptive work of Christ is also restricted to our "spiritual" life and is not needed for natural, everyday life.

5.3 It Implies a Confusion of Structure and Direction

The fact that Aquinas views nature and grace as two spheres of domains indicates confusion between the (ontic) structure of a human being and the (religious) direction of good and evil. He attempted to *localize* the twofold focus in the life of a human being to two spheres, namely that of nature (the less good) and that of grace (the good). In this way, the religious antithesis between evil and good is sought in the wrong places. Politics, labour, science, *et cetera* belong to the natural sphere and are, therefore, "neutral" domains. In contrast, ecclesiastical life would be good, to the glory of God. Over against this, we have to state that good/evil are not that easily localized. The religious direction influences *all* structures of reality from the human heart.

5.4 It Entails An Inherent Dualism

Since it is impossible to unite two conflicting religious directions – that of a pagan Greek and God's Word – Aquinas could not prevent a deep-seated dualism or disunity in his philosophy. Underlying the apparent unity, one could never evade the tension (seen distinctly by paradoxical scholars). Synthetic philosophy is, thereby, not sustainable!

Therefore, E.A. Venter (s.a.: 73,74) says no proper synthesis is possible between non–Christian and Christian religious motives. Due to an inherent dialectic tension, the two poles (the Christian and the non–Christian) drift further and further apart and eventually once more (as in the beginning) antithetically stand opposite to one another. According to him, even Aquinas' greatest effort failed.

5.5 It Does not Prevent Mutual Influence
Neither could Aquinas in his philosophy succeed in upholding the purity and authority of God's revelation in opposition to pagan philosophy. The heathen philosophy (in the domain of nature) thoroughly influenced his so-called Christian, holy or supernatural theology (in the domain of grace). Instead of "Christianising" Aristotle, the message of the Bible was "Aristotelised."

5.6 It has Enormous Implications
The nature–grace approach in itself already bore the seed which would assist secularisation. In other words, to live part of one's life as if God and his commands were irrelevant. Until approximately the sixteenth century, the powerful Roman Catholic Church could, however, ward off the tension between nature and grace – even by using violence. But during the Renaissance, this age-old union was shattered. Nature was liberated from its enslavement to the supernatural, and the former so-called Christian West began secularizing.

E.A. Venter (s.a.: 73-75) describes the situation as follows: the *Christian* culture of unity to which Aquinas aspired was at most an *ecclesiastical* culture of unity which was upheld only by the authority of the pope. Outside the ecclesiastical domain, medieval "Christianity" never was more than a label that represented ecclesiastical sanction. As long as the church (the sacred) still held sway over the state (the secular), the semblance of Christian society was maintained, though it was a struggle that lasted for centuries. But when (from the end of the Middle Ages and afterwards), no one could recognize the overarching authority of the church, only the profane, secular domain remained – the semblance of Christianity just disappeared.

5.7 Contemporary Theological Thinking is Still Infected by It

Tragically, Aquinas could not foresee that his duel philosophy and double normative would eventually lead to irreligious secularism.

An even greater tragedy is that contemporary Christians – after seven centuries – still do not understand the significant risk of such a way of thinking about the world. They, therefore, look for the cause of secularization of life somewhere *outside* their faith and life in the church.

On closer analysis, numerous Christian bodies– the Protestants too – are still consciously or unconsciously prisoners of this age-old nature–grace dualism – it is accepted as evidence without criticism.

Do I mean that Protestants and Reformed theologians do not differ from the Roman Catholic followers of Aquinas? Yes and no.

Yes, because they still have not overcome the dualism of Aquinas. The fact that they usually emphasize only the Word, grace and faith often indicates that they underline the one pole of the fundamental dualism – without rejecting the pole of nature.

No, because of confessional, dogmatic and ecclesiastical differences between the Roman Catholic Church (e.g. their differences on the sacraments). But this does not exclude the existence of more profound typical lifeviewish-philosophical dualism among both these two groups.

5.8 It Also is Present in Ecclesiastical Life

However, the same dangerous virus is also present in the blood of millions of ministers, pastors and ordinary church members. They, consequently, lead a dual existence that is schizophrenic, simultaneously living out their lives both in the "spiritual" and "neutral" spheres. They regard Bible reading and going to church as obviously "Christian." Still, they also allow for their secular professions to be more or less "neutral," for which the redemption of Christ is not that relevant or even essential.

This attitude is reinforced nowadays by the false distinction between the so-called private and public life. In the former, religious convictions are still tolerated, but they are banned in public – there, the secularist religion must prevail.

Kok rightly remarks (1998: 109) that, unless Christianity gets rid of the poison of Aquinas' nature–grace view, "the Christian community will continue to become increasingly impotent and irrelevant." This statement proves true in present-day South Africa as well.'

6. Conclusion and Looking Ahead

Vollenhoven (2011: 75,76) warns that one should not fight a synthesis philosopher – and this would also apply to Aquinas – as if he thought in a purely heathen way, for then one's critique becomes unfair, one does an injustice to such a Christian. The Greek-Roman-Hellenistic philosophy was pagan, but not the Christian synthesis thinking of the Church Fathers and the Middle Ages. A Christian philosopher should therefore oppose the pagan philosophy much more severely than the synthesis philosophy.

Simultaneously, Vollenhoven says that synthesis philosophy is much more hazardous to a Christian since it cannot be recognized as distinctly as full-blooded heathen or secular thinking. We hope that this article has spelled out the risk of synthesis in the work of Aquinas: it had a decisive influence on the normative direction of his philosophy.

The primary *direction* of Aquinas' philosophy has become apparent. Due to his accommodation (synthesis thinking) of especially the religiously alien Greek philosophy (of Aristotle), he could no longer – though he did not realize this himself – point a clear, unambiguous biblical *direction* for life in its *entirety*. His answer to the crucial normative question: "How *should* one live?" cannot satisfy a human being who is faithful to the Bible.

The article that follows deals with a second fundamental (structural) philosophical question: "Of what does reality consist?" It also builds on this article. For it will become evident that Aquinas does not, due to his synthesis thinking, give the rightful place to the independence of God's scripturally grounded law, which provides direction for the entirety of our lives.

CHAPTER 2
THE IDEA OF LAW AS A KEY TO THE PHILOSOPHY OF THE CATHOLIC "DOCTOR COMMUNIS"

THE DOCTOR COMMUNIS, THOMAS AQUINAS' (1224/25–1274) philosophy has been interpreted and reinterpreted in many different ways by Catholics and Protestants. The present effort is aware of the danger of explaining a philosopher's or theologian's conception from one single or leading idea, reducing the rest of his/her thinking to such a central motive.

I am, however, of the opinion that one's idea about law and normativity does play an important contributing role in his/her whole system of thought. Therefore, this chapter (following the previous introductory one on the primary religious direction of Aquinas' philosophy) investigates Aquinas' view of law as a kind of steel structure that keeps together, determines and explains other aspects of his philosophy and theology in his Summa Contra Gentiles. *With this "key," the rest of his complicated thought may be "unlocked." In summary, his idea of law boils down to the following: The laws exist (1) before creation (as archetypes) in the* mind of God, *(2) they were created by God into the cosmos, and (3) the human mind can contain them after abstracting them from creation.*

The investigation develops as follows: (1) It first explains how the law exists (as essence – or pure form) in God since He is the essence of the law. He is, therefore, the absolute truth. (2) Secondly, it is indicated how the law and the cosmos (subjected to God's laws) are not clearly distinguished but confused in Aquinas' thinking. The law (viewed as a "thing") is "cosmologised," evident from Aquinas' use of concepts like exemplar, similitude, ratio and verbum. (3) Thirdly, his hierarchical view of the cosmos, derived from Aristotle, is also based on a pyramidal view of the law. (4) The conclusion explains the writer's philosophical point of departure.

In place of Aquinas' hierarchical ontology, implying only a relative difference between God, his law and his creation, and consequently, a primarily ontic relationship between God and creation, the writer proposes a radical ontic distinction between them, as a close religious relationship.

1. Introduction

BY WAY OF INTRODUCTION, we bring the following to the reader's attention: (1.) A painting, which reflects the direction of Aquinas' philosophy. (2.) The fact that – despite his synthesis philosophy – he intended to think as a Christian. (3.) A possible key to his worldview. (4.) A remark on the used sources. (5.) The further lay-out of this chapter.

In the previous introductory chapter, the focus was mainly on the primary religious-normative direction of Aquinas' philosophy. First, something more on this issue before coming to the second important question which every philosopher has to answer, namely how reality is structured. It will become clear that, while structure (how *it* is viewed) and direction (what *ought* to be) are closely related, they should at the same time be distinguished.

1.1 Aquinas' Synthesis

The contents of the previous chapter are visually emphasized in a painting by Francesco Traini dating from 1344 (cf. Van den Berg, 1958 opposite title page for a reproduction). The following scene depicts Aquinas sitting in the middle of a wide circle with rays of light, shooting in all directions from the four books in his hand. The top one of the four books is the *Summa Contra Gentiles* (SCG), and the other three are possibly his *Summa Theologiae* (i.e. both his main philosophical and theological works). Above him and on both sides are the individuals who inspired him to write these books. Directly above Aquinas (in the middle), Christ appears. To the left and right above him are Moses, Paul and the four evangelists with their gospels. To the right of Aquinas stands Aristotle, and to his left Plato, each with a book. Directly under his feet, the conquered Averroës appears, and to the left and right of this, two groups of theologians and philosophers are portrayed, praising Aquinas.

This painting (on the altar of the Dominican church in Pisa in Italy) vividly shows the duality of Aquinas' inspiration, being both the Bible and Greek philosophy, as he attempted to effect a synthesis between the two.

1.2 Still a Christian Scholar

Despite his synthesis thinking, we may not forget that Aquinas was a devout Christian and that his intentions were honest. For instance, at the beginning of the SCG, he writes the following:

> In the name of the divine mercy, I have the confidence to embark upon the work of a wise man, even though this may surpass my powers, and I have set myself the task of making known, as far as my limited powers allow, the truth that the Catholic faith professes, and of setting aside the errors that are opposed to it. To use the words of Hilary: 'I am aware that I owe this to God as the chief duty of my life, that my every word and sense may speak of Him' (I, 62).

1.3 A Possible Key to his Ontology

Apart from the fact that every philosopher should answer how a human being *should* live and think (the religious-normative direction), he/she should also have to answer what exists and what reality includes. Dealing with this constitutes a philosopher's ontology. This chapter will address how Aquinas answered this question in part and more extensively in the following chapter. Against the broad background of his complete conception, we highlight only his idea of law as a person's view of the law and how it determines the direction of his/her thinking. The author regards Aquinas' specific view of the law as a crucial element of his philosophy and a key to understanding his philosophical and theological system. Thus, I propose a perspective that differs from Aertson's analysis (1982 and 1991), which presents the idea of a cycle as the central motive in Aquinas' philosophy. I am aware of the risk attached to efforts to explain a scholar's philosophy in the light of a single, central, guiding idea – especially when the rest of his philosophy is reduced to it. Nevertheless, a philosopher's idea of law plays a significant role in his/her whole system. Therefore, it is used here as *a* "key" – not the only possible one – to "open up" the complicated philosophy of Aquinas.

1.4 Sources

As in the previous chapter, we here limit reference to secondary sources as much as possible since we want to listen primarily to Aquinas himself. For the original Latin text of the *Summa Contra Gentiles*, an edition of 1935 was used (cf. S. Thomae Aquinatis, 1935). The English translation of this work, quoted here, is the Doubleday edition (cf. Thomas Aquinas, 1955-1957). The citation reference is first made in Roman numbers to the specific book of the SCG and then in Arabic numerals to the page numbers of this translation (e.g. II, 120). Since book three was translated into two parts, they are referred to as IIIa and IIIb. In this contribution, the author builds on previous research (cf. Van der Walt, 1968 and 1974) – with corrections and new insights.

1.5 Lay-out

The investigation proceeds as follows: (1.) First Aquinas' (dualist) God-cosmos philosophy is dealt with; then (2.) his view of God as law is explained; (3.) how he turns the cosmos into law (in concepts like *exemplar, similitudo, ratio* and *verbum*); (4.) his hierarchical ontology derived from Aristotle, and (5.) an explanation of the author's own point of departure. The author simultaneously proposes a radical ontic distinction between God, his creation and his law for creation with a close religious relationship. Here, the author's purpose is an alternative to the dualist and hierarchical ontology, which only permits a relative distinction between God and his creation as something ontic.

2. *A Cosmological and Dualist Ontology*
According to Aquinas, theology is the study of God and philosophy is the study of creation. So his thinking is purely cosmological (cf. Vollenhoven, 2005a: 415) and confines Scriptural Revelation to the cosmos' creation, fall and redemption. What then about God? Aquinas regards God, in his natural theology, as Creator, and in his supernatural theology, the Redeemer of creation.

2.1 One Reality Divided Into Two
Aquinas recognized only one existence or reality. However, as a Christian, he could not be a monist (it easily leads to pantheism) but assumes an ontic dualism (cf. Vollenhoven, 2005a: 415). The Greek philosophy of Aristotle made a distinction between a transcendent part (the deity) and a non-transcendent part (the cosmos) of one reality. As stated in Christian terminology, however, Aquinas designates the two components as God and creation. But if God and creation are taken together in one concept of existence, then one cannot maintain a distinction between them. As will become evident later, this has far-reaching consequences for the rest of Aquinas' philosophy and theology.

2.2 The Law Disappears in God and Cosmos but Remains Determinative
If Aquinas recognizes only one reality (with two "levels"), what did he do

with biblical revelation, namely that God subjected all creation to his laws?

Aquinas knows that God subjected His creation to His ordinations (a third reality according to the Scriptures). Still, in his philosophy in the SCG, justice is not done to the independent character of God's laws. Therefore, one has to analyze his idea of God and his view of the cosmos to trace his hidden concept of law which (remarkably enough) determines his concept of God and cosmos. What follows his understanding of God and the cosmos is not treated in detail, but mainly determines how Aquinas regarded God's law.

3. God as Law

Below follow some glimpses of Aquinas' idea of God from which it transpires that he does not make a clear distinction between God (the transcendent) and His law – Aquinas made God into a kind of law. What is more: God becomes a law unto Himself. Aquinas subjugated God to His law.

First, Aquinas' natural idea of God (cf. SCG, Book I, Ch. 13) is fraught with the thoughts on how Aristotle described his deity as the first (non caused) cause, the first (immovable) mover of all non-transcendent things (cf. Den Ottolander, 1965). One is simply amazed at the fact that Aquinas could think that two such diverging and conflicting ideas on god/God – a pagan and a biblical one – could be reconcilable. Although we will not deal with it here, Aquinas' Christian idea of God (which he deals with in his supernatural or holy theology, cf. Persson, 1957) is not devoid of Aristotelian influences either. Aquinas, in the SCG, reads scriptural passages from an Aristotelian perspective in keeping with his natural or philosophical theology (Also, in the case of the *sacra doctrina* (in the *Summa Theologiae*).

Note further that Aquinas' attempts to analyze or fathom God scientifically (as the highest part of a hierarchy of being). Such a theo-ontology is not only in principle impossible but reveals a severe degree of intellectual arrogance, for the true God is unfathomable to insignificant human beings. Furthermore, it leads to speculation, clearly emerging from the following.

3.1 God is Pure Act

In God, according to Aquinas, there is nothing potential: "God has no admixture of potency but is pure act" (I, 101). For this view, he calls upon the authority of Aristotle, who spoke of his deity as the *actus purus*. That God is pure act, however, does not mean that He is changeable.

He is "absolutely immutable" (I, 106). Note the link with Aristotle's monarch as the "immovable mover" of everything.

3.2 God is Pure Form

Since in Aristotle's philosophy the potential is linked with matter and the actual with form, the next step is also understandable: Chapter 17 of Book I, Aquinas argues that there is no matter in God, for "Whatever matter is, it is in potency" (I, 101). Between God and the *materia prima* there is a radical difference: "God and prime matter is distinguished: one is pure act, the other pure potency and they agree in nothing" (I, 103).

If God is pure act, there cannot be any composition or compound in Him either (Chapter 18), nor can He be a body (Chapter 20) or even have the form of a body – for He is only pure form (Chapter 27). "Form" to Aquinas is none other than law.

Suppose it is kept in mind that the law has the character of being enforced, of laying down boundaries. Aquinas' following statement reveals, that in his opinion, the form has the character of law: " in things composed of matter and form, the form has the character of a term".

Later: "matter, as that which is determined, and form as that which determines" (II, 324). Or: "It is the function of a form to limit" (IIIa 275). Elsewhere: "the form of a body is not the being itself, but a principle of being" (I, 133. Also compare I, 129).

3.3 God is His Being

So if God is pure form, He also is pure law. Aquinas expresses it even more explicitly by saying: "God is his essence, quiddity or nature" (I, 116). The concept "being" (translated *essentia*, *quidditas* and *natura*) was associated with the law throughout history up to Aquinas (It is the same as the concept *ousia* in Aristotle). In creatures, there is a difference between their existence (*esse*) and essence (*essentia*) but not in God (cf. Chapter 22). Therefore, God is being or law. We could thus speak of Aquinas' God as a "law God." In saying this, we have already stated the heart of Aquinas' idea of God. But there is more.

3.4 God's Being is Intellect and Will

God's being is the same as his intellect. For instance, Aquinas says: "divine understanding is His essence" (I, 173). Also, compare Chapter 46: "the divine intellectual operation is God's essence" (I, 175); "the divine essence, which is the intelligible species by which the divine intellect understands, is absolutely identical with God and is also absolutely identical with His intellect" (I, 176) and, "His knowledge is His essence" (I, 197).

Elsewhere, Aquinas says: "the understanding of God is His substance" (I, 204): "the divine intellect and will are of an equal simplicity, for both are the divine substance" (I, 250). *Substantia* is the Latin translation of the Greek *ousia,* so that in these two statements, Aquinas says the same as in the preceding. God's being, therefore, is also His will. (Compare chapter 73 *et seq.*) "God's will... is His very essence" (I, 243). So the will of God also is connected with His being (law).

Note that Aquinas ascribes human features (of will and intellect) to God. However, it becomes evident that God's intellect or reason is more important than His will. Aquinas holds an intellectualistic idea of God over against a voluntaristic one.

3.5 God is the Highest Good and Absolute Truth

In Book I, Chapter 38, Aquinas states that God is good, that He is goodness itself: "He is good essentially" (I, 153. Note the "essentially"). He is the highest good, or the universal good (I, Chapter 41). The universal good indicates that the good here is the law. Aquinas identifies the universal and the law. In Chapters 60-62, Aquinas argues the same regarding the truth and concludes: "The divine truth, therefore, is the first, highest and most perfect truth" (I, 208).

The fact that Aquinas accepts the three ideas (of the true, the good and the beautiful) in God (*ante rem*) indicates the Platonising trait in his philosophy in the SCG. To Plato, the three ideas were the laws for visible reality. But Aquinas differs from Plato (his conception is not Platonic but Platonising) since he sees the ideas not the way Plato does as things existing separately (Plato's realism). In the very last phase of his philosophical development, Plato derived the duality of foreground and background from still more primary principles. This more primary principle in the Neo-Platonic philosophy of Plotinus became located in the deity (*Hen*). In the synthesis philosophy of Augustine, the deity became the God of the Scriptures.

Meanwhile, the theme of apriority had originated (during the Hellenistic philosophy), also adopted by followers of Plato. The result was that the ideas were now also prioritized *in mente Dei,* in the knowing spirit of God. Aquinas' philosophy is similar to the Neo-Platonism of Augustine in that he places the ideas in the intellect of God. However, he goes further: the laws are not only *in* God, God *Himself* is the law. And He also creates His laws *into* the cosmos.

4. *The Cosmos Made into Law*

Aquinas' idea of God in turn also provides the key to understanding his idea of the cosmos. The laws for creation are not only in God, but the law of God is also created into cosmic things, becoming evident in the concepts *exemplar, similitudo, ratio* and *verbum in the* SCG.

4.1 "Exemplar"

To Aquinas, God's being or law is the exemplar of all things: "His essence, being one and simple, is the exemplar of all manifold and composite things" (I, 200, 201). "His essence is the exemplar of all things" (I, 249). Elsewhere: "The form through which God produces the creatures is an intelligible form in Him" (II, 141). That is why he can say God has "the proper form of a plant ... God has the proper form of animal and so forth" (I, 191).

4.1.1 God Encompasses Everything

Therefore, God's being encompasses (the laws or forms of) all things: "God embraces in Himself all creatures ... in a simple mode" (II, 142). In His intellect (which is the same as His being), God has "the perfections of all things" (I, 172). Therefore, he can also say: "God's intellect is the principle of the production of creatures" (II, 140). And Aquinas says:

> Since the proper exemplar of one thing is distinguished from the proper exemplar of another thing, and distinction is the source of plurality, we must observe in the divine intellect a certain distinction and plurality of understood exemplars, accordingly that which is in the divine intellect is the proper exemplar of diverse things (I, 191).

However, this does not mean a plurality or composition in the divine simplicity (*simplicitas*) (cf. I, 250). Therefore, one has to represent it so that God, apart from His own (peculiar) law, also has laws for every particular thing in Himself.

Aquinas calls these laws exemplars. The exemplars thus are not identical to the law-god but are implied in the god-law. As a result of the exemplars being law, there is a similarity to the god-law. Because they are not the same as the law-god, there is a difference.

4.1.2 God is Omniscient

Since God contains the exemplars of the things, He can also be omniscient, for by knowing his being, He also knows created things: "By knowing Himself, God knows whatever proceeds from Him" (I, 182); "the divine intellect knows all things by knowing its essence" (I, 199). Also, compare p. 225): "God knows other things by His essence as through a certain exemplary means" (I, 228). Further: "the divine essence is the principal object known by God and in this object ... all others are known" (I, 234).

Therefore, God can know things that do not yet exist beforehand since their forms are present in Him from eternity. Aquinas explains this with an image:

> The artisan knows things through his art, even those things that

have not yet been fashioned, since the forms of his art flow from his knowledge to the external matter for the constitution of the artifacts. Hence, nothing forbids that there be in the knowledge of an artisan forms that have not yet come out of it. Thus, nothing forbids God to have knowledge of the things that are not (I, 217).

This train of thought has significant implications. Amongst other things, it means that God determines everything in creation beforehand. Since He is confused with His laws, He is not *above* the law but is *subject* to His law. He, therefore, also has to act according to this law in His providence (cf. IIIa, Ch. 64) and election (cf. IIIb, Ch. 163).

These speculative ideas have endured from Aquinas' time to the present day in the form of so-called eternal, divine decrees on predestination (e.g. the Synod of Dordt (1618-1619) and even up to today with some Reformed theologians).

4.1.3 A Deterministic Idea of God and the Reaction to It

Furthermore, according to the law or *exemplar*, existing from all eternity in God, everything reaches its destiny, created into everything. J.J. Venter, therefore, writes that Aquinas:

> By means of his exemplarism came to the conclusion that God knows everything in their exemplars in Himself and by this therefore determines the contingent future events. Not only can this theory hardly accommodate the biblical notion of the personal relationship between God and human beings; it also entails complete determinism (1988: 182).

Both God and the created things, in summary, are therefore bound to the eternal archetypes/exemplars/laws in God's mind. No wonder that Aquinas' contemporaries and the succeeding generations rebelled violently against such determinism, which abolishes human responsibility. Ockham, for instance, later says that it is unacceptable to think that God who made everything – including the laws – may be made subject to His own laws. However, in reaction to the determinism of Aquinas, he lapses into an arbitrary (voluntarist) concept of God.

Reformational philosophy stresses that the law is not *in* God (Aquinas). But neither does the law exist *apart* from God (Ockham). Although God is "above" his law (Ockham was correct in this respect), He is still faithful to it and maintains it (One must reject Ockham's ideas in this respect). Therefore, there is a clear distinction between God and His laws, which applies to His creation. A second core concept in Aquinas' idea of law is *Similitudo*.

4.2 "Similitudo"

Aquinas uses *exemplar* and *similitudo* to denote the same phenomenon. For instance, he says:

> Whatever being a thing has God knows through his essence. For his essence can be represented by many things that are not, nor will be, nor even were. His essence is likewise the likeness (*similitude*) of the power of every cause, through which effects pre-exist in their causes. And the being that each thing has in itself comes from the divine essence as from its exemplary source (I, 220).

4.2.1 "Similitudo" and "Forma"

The *similitudo* is identical to the Aristotelian forms: "things are likened through their diverse forms to the one simple reality that God is" (I, 149). Elsewhere: "all things are like God ... so far as they have forms " (II, 130).

Intellectual creatures are, for this reason, nearest to God: "an intellectual creature chiefly becomes like God by the fact that it is intellectual, for it has this sort of likeness over and above what other creatures have, and this likeness includes all others" (IIIa, 99). Once again, there is a clear indication of Aquinas' inheritance of Greek intellectualism and the subsequent influence on Reformed Scholasticism.

4.2.2 The human being looks like God

If Genesis 1:26 reveals that God made human beings in his image (*imago*) and likeness (*similitudo*), it also points, according to Aquinas, to the divine form in the human being (cf. I, 138). Therefore, he says: "God can be seen in His substance in this life, but only as in a mirror ... this mirror, which is the human mind, reflects the likeness of God" (IIIa, 161). So concerning his intellect, a human being exhibits the image of God, which implies intellectualist anthropology.

Aquinas can also say for this reason: "Likeness is a certain kind of relation" (II, 42). Consequently, a likeness between God and His creatures exists in the relationship between the forms in God and creatures.

4.2.3 God Does Not Look Like His Creatures
Since creatures owe likeness to God (because of the form that God creates into them), they show the likeness of God, but not the other way round. God namely bears a likeness to the creature: "a form of a lower grade cannot by acting extend its likeness to a higher grade; rather, the higher form by acting can extend its likeness to a lower grade" (I, 216). This brings us to the third important concept in Aquinas' idea of law.

4.3 "Ratio"

4.3.1 The Same as Likeness
The word *ratio* (= reason), mostly translated into English as "model." Sometimes it also is translated as "likeness." So, for instance, in the following: "the divine essence ... is the proper model (*propria ratio*) and likeness (*similitudo*) of diverse things" (I, 189; so also I, 190). Elsewhere: "all things in a certain manner pre-exist in Him through their proper models (*proprias rationes*)" (I, 246).

4.3.2 The Same as Exemplar
From this, it emerges clearly that by *ratio*, Aquinas most probably means the same as by *exemplar* or *similitudo*. Book 3, Chapter 47, where he calls these *rationes* eternal because they exist in God, is particularly revealing. Therefore, he can write: "law is a rational plan of divine providence" (IIIb, 124). No wonder that the idea of God's providence plays such an important part in Aquinas' thinking – the third book of the SCG (dealing with this) is the most voluminous of all four books.

4.3.3 A Mirror Image of the Trinity

However, Aquinas takes it further. Things look like the god-law in general and like the three persons in the divine being. When he deals with the Trinity in Book 4, he says that the image of God in a human being is the image of the triune God (cf. IV, 146). Further, he is consistent in teaching: "One also finds in other things a likeness of the divine Trinity ..." (IV, 146). However, since God is not represented as clearly in the other (lower) things as in the human intellect, Aquinas does not call them an image (*imago*) of God but only tracks (*vestigia*) of God: "Accordingly, because of the remote and obscure representation in irrational things, one speaks of the 'vestige' of the Trinity in them, not of the 'image.' So we read in Job (11: 7): 'Thou wilt comprehend the steps of God'" (IV, 146). Note that Aquinas cannot help but read the Word of God from the perspective of his particular philosophy and here clearly reads his philosophy into the Bible (eisegesis) in order – with biblical sanction – to read it out of God's Word again (exegesis).

A last key concept which links up with the preceding three and which further explains Aquinas' law-idea is *verbum*.

4.4 "Verbum"

In Chapter 13 of Book 4, Aquinas deals with the Son being God's Word (*Verbum*). He then makes the statement that there also are "words of the Word:" "Thus, then, not only is the conception of the divine intellect called a Word, which is the Son but even the unfolding of the divinely conceived in exterior works is named the word of the Word" (IV, 96). "Necessary, then, the things made by God have pre-existed in the Word of God from eternity, immaterially, without any composition" (IV, 96). Therefore, the essentiality of created things exists particularly in one person of the Trinity (Christ).

In the following quotation, Aquinas connects the word *Verbum* with *exemplar en image:* "The Word of God must be referred to the other things understood by God as *exemplar*, and must be referred to God Himself whose Word He is as *image*. Hence, one reads of the Word of God in Colossians (1:15) that He is 'the image of the invisible God' (IV, 86). So as Word, Christ contains the essence of all things!

4.5 "Lex naturalis" and "Lex Divina"
Aquinas also calls the natural law (*lex naturalis*), the laws that God creates in things. Meanwhile, he calls the commandment of love the divine law (*lex divina*). The study by Kuhlmann (1912), in this respect, still contains valuable information, which proves his synthesis between preceding Greek philosophies and the Scriptures according to the method of nature and the supernatural.

5. A Hierarchy of Reality
As stated above, some things exhibit the image of God more than others because the divine law is found more distinctly in them. In Aquinas' view, the perfection of a creature depends on the extent to which it shows the image and traces of God.

5.1 A Pyramid of Being
Consequently, Aquinas' doctrine of reality shows the image of a pyramid.

To Aquinas, like Aristotle, being is hierarchical, ascending from the lower to the higher, according to the degrees of perfection.

At the base of the pyramid, there is *materia prima*, and at the top, God, who is pure form and highest being. Lovejoy (1973) calls it "the great chain of being." According to Aquinas, God is "super law" likened to a yardstick, which determines the value of the lower things in their different degrees. Aquinas writes: "the gradation of nobility and lowliness among all things is measured according to their nearness to and distance from God, Who is the peak of nobility" (I, 232). The other way round: "the nearer a body is to prime matter, the less noble it is, being more in potentiality and less in complete act" (II, 310).

The higher, the more divine the creatures are, says Aquinas, for instance, about the separate substances (angels): "Now the higher the rank of a separate substance, the more is its nature like the divine; and thus it is less limited, in as much as it approaches nearer to the perfection and goodness of the universal being, enjoying, therefore, a universal participation in goodness and being" (II, 333).

However, the lower creatures are from God, the lesser they are in being: "The more a thing is from that which is a being by virtue of itself, namely, God, the nearer it is to non–being; so that the closer a thing is to God, the further is it removed from non–being" (II, 86). Aquinas' doctrine about being is like a stepladder with different rungs or like a chain that holds itself together: "the higher nature in its lowest part touches the lower nature in its highest part" (II, 313).

The matter in the higher thing becomes the form for the lower. Or the other way round: the form for the lower is the matter for the higher thing. So actually, everything has a law-like nature. The only true subject for Aquinas is the *materia prima* (because it cannot become the form for something lower). This first matter is, however, something metaphysical, an abstraction. It does not exist, for "matter exists only in potency, while form is that by which something is, since it is act" (II, 129).

5.2 A Pyramid of Law

Aquinas' whole hierarchy of being, therefore, is none other than a hierarchy of law! Not only is God regarded as law, but also the angels (as separate intellectual substances) and the human being (in whom the intellect is compounded with matter). Plato's laws (ideas and numbers themselves) existed in the intelligible world. But Aquinas' laws lie in the world that the senses can observe (The evident influence of Aristotle).

Plato's realism viewed laws as real things (the law has been cosmologised). In Aquinas, we find the opposite: things were turned into laws (the cosmos has been made into law). Summed up: (1.) according to Aquinas, the law for creatures exists *ante rem* (*before* the things) in God. (2.) God creates these archetypes *in rebus* (*into* the cosmic things). (3.) The law also exists through rational abstraction *post rem* (*after the* cosmic things) in the intellect of human beings. It is clear that when such a central position is assigned to the idea of the law, it will be determinative for the whole of Aquinas' philosophy and theology.

5.3. Conclusion
The above concludes that Aquinas' ontology or doctrine of reality is a type of nomology (a view of the law). His philosophy tends towards nomism or an absolutization of the idea of law. As a result of this idea, Aquinas' nomism even determines the being of God. Aquinas, consequently, turns God into a law-god. The same happens with the cosmos: he turns it into law things.

6. The New Interpretation
First, something in defence of my particular interpretation as opposed to another exegesis of Aquinas' philosophy. *Second*, the author explains his ontology from the perspective of Aquinas' law-ontology, assessed on the foregoing pages.

6.1 The Author's Own Interpretation
My interpretation of Aquinas' philosophy differs from another scholar, Aertsen (1982, 1986, 1990 and 1991), who regards a cyclic motive as the central theme and key to Aquinas' philosophy. According to this view, everything flows from God and also returns to Him. Such a motive appears to be solidly biblical in the light of Romans 11:36: "For from him and through him and to him are all things."

6.1.1 The Cyclic Motive
Aquinas himself indeed mentions this motive. For instance, he says:
> The effect is most perfect when it returns to its source; thus the circle is the most perfect of all figures, and circular motion the most perfect of all motions, because in their case a return is made to the starting point. It is therefore necessary that the creatures return to their principle in order that the universe of creatures may attain its ultimate perfection (SCG II, 46).

Aertsen (1990: 86) claims that this cyclic motive also determines the structure of Aquinas' *Summa Theologiae*. Its first part deals with how all things come from God, while the second part describes the movement of reasonable creatures back to Him. According to Aertsen, this is the consequence of the influence of the Neo-Platonic doctrine of participation (cf. Chapter 3).

Meijer (1944: 55) indicated eariler that the SCG is the most important source of this doctrine of the "cycle of the things" (from God unto God) in the work of Aquinas. In the first three books of the SCG, it is worked out in such detail that one could see keynote in it, or the great synthesis of what the *Doctor Communis* (as a philosopher) teaches on the relationship between Creator and creation.

6.1.2 Two Underlying Reasons

I would like to differ with the interpretations of Meijer and Aertson. In my opinion, this cyclic motive is not the main key to the philosophy of Aquinas, but is the *result* of his underlying view of the law which is much more basic. Everything is 'from God' since He creates the *exemplar, similitude, ratio*, or *verbum* from Himself into cosmic things. However, everything is also 'unto God,' since these same exemplars, similitudes or rational germs which come from God, point back to Him.

Futher, I also connect this doctrine of a cycle of a cycle (cf. Van der Walt, 1974: 264-268) with Aquinas' doctrine of nature-grace (or the supernatural). Grace not only *perfects* nature (gratia non tollit sed perfecit naturam) but the *natural* itself pursues this perfection.

6.1.3 A Natural Desire for the Supernatural

Aquinas teaches a natural longing for God in a human being *(homo insitus est desiderium naturale)*. However, should one ask *why* it is that the natural longs for or pursues the supernatural, one once more has to consider Aquinas' law-idea: the law which God created into the things (*exemplar, similitudo* etc.) points back to their exemplars in God's intellect.

One may ask about this doctrine of *desiderium naturale* of Aquinas many questions. For instance (cf. Van der Walt, 1974: 265): How can there in nature be an ontic pursuit of the supernatural, since such a pursuit would then no longer be purely natural? Formulated differently: nature has to know that it is imperfect to long for perfection. However, such a kind of knowledge supposes at least something of a supernatural nature.

The other way round, the same applies: If nature is to be *perfected* and not *abolished* (as Aquinas emphasizes continuously), then even in the supernatural, there must be something natural.

In modern times this issue sparked off no less than some sixty different interpretations among Neo-Thomists. It is not possible to go into this issue in further detail at this stage. Bastable (1947) is still one of the best sources to be consulted. He deals with Aquinas' view on p. 31 et seq., and on p. 83, he gives a schematic outline of the different later interpretations. Meijer (1940), too, thoroughly investigated the so-called natural longing for the supernatural in the work of Aquinas. He not only deals with Aquinas' view (p. 53-75) but also with those of various commentaries during the heyday of Scholasticism, which attempted to elucidate this paradox in the philosophy of Aquinas. In addition, he also discusses the "solution" by the twentieth-century Thomist scholar Blondel.

6.2 An Alternative Ontology

The above critique is the perspective of an alternate philosophical ontology.

Vollenhoven (2005b: 14-15) puts the following three basic questions to the Scriptures: (1.) Who is the Creator? (2.) What is it that He created? (3.) What is the limiting boundary as well as the bridge between them? According to Vollenhoven, the answer given by the Bible entails the following distinction between three realities:

1. The *first question* is unambiguously answered by the Holy Scriptures. The Bible never sees "God" as a regulative idea [i.e. law – BJvdW] or a theoretical concept [as in the work of Aquinas – BJvdW]. But He is always as the living God ... in short, the Sovereign in the absolute sense of the word (p. 14).
2. The answer to the *second question* concerns creation's complete

dependence on the Creator, wholly subjected to His sovereign law, Word revelation and guidance (p. 14).

3. The answer to the *third question* answers that one should understand "limit" so that one can say that everything that stands on that side of this line is God. Everything that lies on this side is created ... Now, this demarcation is the law of God, which God permanently posited for creation. The only being who sovereignly gives laws to the cosmos and maintains them is God. On the other hand, all that which is created is subjected to laws. Accordingly, it is impossible to mention anything divine that stands under the law or anything created that stands above the law (p. 14–15).

These concise words contain a fundamental critique of Aquinas' philosophy. At the same time, this is a remarkable critique since Vollenhoven himself initially also thought on semi-Thomistic lines. (For details, cf. Tol, 2010.)

According to Vollenhoven, such a view of the *ontological distinction* between God, law and creation does not exclude their *religious connection* (cf. Vollenhoven, 2005b: 77-79 on the nature of religion).

In the work of Aquinas, one finds neither this clear *distinction* nor the correct *relationship*. He views the relationship between God and His creation as something *ontic* instead of *religious*. As will become evident from the next chapter, Aquinas' incorrect ontological point of departure has implications for all other facets of his philosophy in the SCG.

CHAPTER 3
AN ANALYSIS OF THE ONTOLOGY OF THE "SUMMA CONTRA GENTILES" (1261-1264)

FROM A REFORMATIONAL PERSPECTIVE, *this chapter provides a critical appraisal of the view of reality (ontology) of the* Summa Contra Gentiles, *the main philosophical work of the famous medieval thinker Thomas Aquinas (1224/5-1274). For centuries afterwards, his ideas had a decisive influence, not only on Catholic philosophy and theology but also on Reformed Orthodoxy or Scholasticism.*

Due to the complex nature of his philosophy (it assimilated various ideas of previous centuries, including the classic Greek philosophy of Plato and Aristotle), the different parts of the puzzle are separated, and the following cluster of ideas in his ontology are described and evaluated.

Aquinas accepts a hierarchy of being from (1) pure matter (an abstraction) below to (2) all created things consisting of matter and form up to (3) God as pure form/essence/law.

A dualistic distinction is made between a highest, transcendent part (God) and a non-transcendent (creation). An interlocking of form and matter consists in this one chain of being. In his philosophy, Aquinas confines himself to the existing creation (not its origin or genesis), which is predetermined by the exemplars in God (see the previous chapter).

In the Summa Contra Gentiles *Aquinas neither accepts individualism nor universalism but thinks partially in a universalistic manner. However, he does not propose a horizontal type of partial universalism (the theory of macro-micro cosmos) but a vertical type (the form-matter theory). The universal has a place above the individual. God, therefore, is also the universal being for Aquinas.*

Aquinas' dualistic distinction between God and creation (in one ontic chain of being) is explained by two doctrines in his Summa: *analogy and participation. According to the first, God and the world are simultaneously different and similar. According to the second, created beings exist and therefore resemble God and aspire to return to and participate in Him. The higher the chain of being a creature is, the more apparent its likeness to God and its participation in the divine nature.*

1. Introduction: Reference, Focus, Sources and Lay-Out

BY WAY OF INTRODUCTION, the author explains (1.) how this chapter relates to the previous two; (2.) which aspect of Aquinas' philosophy in the *Summa Contra Gentiles* (abbreviated as SCG) will be investigated; (3.) the sources to be used; as well as (4.) how the investigation will proceed.

1.1 Reference

Chapter one already explained why studying the philosophy of Thomas Aquinas (1223/5-1274) is still relevant today. It was explained how his SCG (ca. 1261-1264) originated as his main philosophical work. Subsequently, the synthetic direction of his philosophy was investigated. Chapter two discussed the "heart" of Aquinas' philosophy, concerning its *structure* and his idea of law.

His nomology was seen as a significant key to his whole system since the law exists before created things *in God*, is created *into the things* by God, and is present *in the human mind* by abstraction. The fact that Aquinas places the laws or archetypical ideas in the intellect of God indicates the Platonising feature, which is still typical of Aquinas' interpretation of Aristotle in the SCG (cf. Vollenhoven, 2011: 94).

1.2 Focus

This chapter will focus on Aquinas' cosmology, followed in the subsequent chapters by a contribution on his anthropology and epistemology, as well as a chapter on his doctrine of God's providence.

1.3 Sources

As in the previous two chapters, this one also links up with previous research (cf. Van der Walt 1968 and 1974), while new insights and sources are included. However, there is a minimum amount of reference to secondary sources since the author wishes to hear Aquinas himself and not the interpretation of others. For the original Latin text of the SCG, an edition of 1935 was used (cf. S. Thomae Aquinatis, 1935). The English translation quoted in this chapter follows the Doubleday edition (cf. Thomas Aquinas, 1955-1957). The references given with the quotations are first to the specific book in Roman numerals, followed by the page number(s) of the particular translation in Arabic numerals (e.g. I, 150). Since Book 3 of the SCG was translated in two parts, these are given as IIIa and IIIb.

1.4 Lay-out

The following facets of Aquinas' cosmology will be dealt with: (1.) His hierarchical ontological thinking. (2.) His purely cosmological philosophy. (3.) His ontic dualism. (4.) Partial universalism. (5.) The analogy of being. (6.) Participation (cf. Van der Walt, 1974: 248-268).

These facets together form like a magnet, a cluster of ideas that attract and strengthen one another. (The way Aquinas uses concepts like *universalia, analogia entis, participatio* and the like in his different works can easily be looked up in the *Thomas Lexicon by* Schütz, 1895).

The first idea in this cluster is *A Hierarchical Ontological Philosophy*.

2. A Hierarchical Ontological Philosophy

Ontological thinking (from the Greek: *ontos* = being + *logos* = philosophy) attempts to fathom the being of existing things scientifically. However, the concept "being," which the Greeks already turned into a philosophical term, should be handled with caution. It is a concept of appreciation – it indicates the real, best, highest existence, the true reality. (Nonbeing is its opposite). Therefore Aquinas and many other Christian philosophers thought that calling God the highest "Being" would show particular deference to Him.

2.1 Risks Attached

However, the risk attached to this is that one could regard God as a part – albeit the highest part – of one being or reality. This is why Reformational philosophers like Vollenhoven would not speak of a philosophical ontology that would include God. Of course, Aquinas tried to evade this risk by propagating a *hierarchy of being*. However, the difference between God and his creation remains merely one of relative degrees.

A hierarchy of being entailed numerous other hazards, such as a high degree of rigidity: God determines (by way of divine exemplars in the created things) all of creation. A hierarchy of being also leads to a hierarchy of authority and power in church and society. It is supposed that God "delegates" his (nota bene: divine) authority to human beings. Or human authority is supposed to be "derived" from God's authority, meaning that questioning human authority entails disobedience or rebellion against God Himself. As a consequence of Aquinas' hierarchy of being, making a mere relative distinction between God and man, he could not distinguish between infallible divine authority and fallible human authority.

2.2 God's Being to be Fathomed

Being (*ontos*) to Aquinas is the most important thing to be known philosophically. His idea of God is theo-ontological. He even attempts to fathom God's being theologically and philosophically! Venter (1988: 158 et seq.) approaches the basic concepts of Aquinas' ontology in detail from the perspective of the following four combinations: act-potential, form-matter, substance-accidence and essence-existence (also cf. J.J. Venter, 1985: 11-12). However, I merely mention that Aquinas holds a hierarchical ontology, an order of being which escalates from the pure matter at the very bottom, via things consisting of both form and matter, to pure form at the top of the ladder (God).

2.3 Relativism of Being

However, Venter rightly asks: "Does Thomas succeed in distinguishing between Creator and creation? Does not a division of being based on degree lead...to the radical difference between God and creature being gradually bridged so that God and matter are merely the two endpoints of one continuous line?" (Venter, 1988: 162). Aquinas himself realizes the problem when he teaches that God *is* being, while creation only *has* being. But did he succeed in solving the issues implicated? Now we will discuss a second aspect in the whole ontological cluster of Aquinas' philosophy.

3. Purely Cosmological Philosophy

In created reality, there is constancy and change, a static and a dynamic side. Specific things for instance, God's ordinations and his central law of love, do not change. On the other hand, creation also reflects development, progress, change, coming into being and passing away.

3.1 Two Viewpoints

When a philosopher does not see the constant, he/she is biased and quickly lapses into relativism. However, he who emphasizes the constant and regards change as merely secondary holds a very rigid view of reality.

These different views are closely connected with the issue of origin. *Cosmogonic* thinking emphasized its *genetic development*. On the other hand, *purely cosmological* philosophy (or structural thinking) tried to limit the knowledge it pursued to the *existing,* more or less static universe. The latter view was also the one held by Aquinas (cf. Vollenhoven, 2005a:

415).

The variety of Aquinas' philosophical elements would support and strengthen this static, predetermined view of the universe. Among these were the following facets.

3.2 The Role of the Idea of Law

Concerning Aquinas' view of the universe, it becomes evident that his idea of law played a crucial part. The exemplars, essences or archetypes (cf. previous chapters) *have existed* since all eternity in God. (This is the reason why Aquinas called them *rationes sempiternas)*. Aquinas does not attempt to explain their origin or inception but regards it as evident due to his acceptance of a Neo-Platonic idea of law taken over from Augustine. That God created the things and created them to imitate or reflect God (as a consequence of the divine laws created into them) still does not give a *scientific* explanation of their coming into being. It is clear from Book II, in which Aquinas deals with his viewpoint on creation, that he is not concerned with the *process* of creation but with the *product.*

Book III consists of three main parts; in Chapters 6-38, Aquinas deals with the *origin;* in Chapters 39-45, Aquinas writes about *the distinction,* and in Chapters 46-101, he discusses the *nature* of the creatures. The first central part of this book, therefore, deals with the origin of things. However, it is not a *scientific* account of the coming into being of things. It merely departs from the Scriptural truth about creation. Aquinas offers his Aristotelian-coloured philosophical interpretation of the Scriptures.

Aquinas is correct insofar as he only philosophizes about the *existence* of creation and does not want to *speculate* on the issue of its *origin* – one ought to accept this in faith. However, the defect in his purely cosmological viewpoint is that he only has room for his (nomolised) universe in his philosophy. God is the object of study only in his sacred theology. My view is that truly Christian philosophy should not exclude acknowledgement of the existence of God, especially in the discussion of created things.

3.3 The Light of the Scriptures for Philosophy

Aquinas, in his philosophy, confines himself to the sphere of nature (or what he calls the "world"). For this, he regards three biblical facts of particular significance, namely creation, sin and redemption. From the SCG, it becomes evident that this perspective appears in the work of Aquinas in the following order of importance: creation, redemption, fall.

In Book II, he deals with the creation, expressed in philosophical terms. In a part of Book IV, he deals with Christ and the redemption of human beings employing the sacraments and the final deliverance at the resurrection. Aquinas does not deal with the fall in a separate book or part of a book of the SCG, merely mentioning it in passing in a few instances. Mostly he does not speak about *sin* either but about *evil*.

Aquinas' rejection of the *radical* deprivation of creation as a consequence of Adam's disobedience is the reason why the fall does not fill such an essential part in his philosophy. The fall brought about the loss of the "supernatural part" of a human being. The supernatural gift that Christ merited restored this lost "supernatural part" of a human being. The domain of nature has, however, remained (to a great extent) untainted. Therefore, in Aquinas' opinion, the human mind was not *obfuscated* by sin but merely *weakened*.

3.4 A Philosophy of Creation?

In the light of Aquinas' purely cosmological thinking, one could characterize his philosophy as a "philosophy of the creational idea." Some commentators of his philosophy (cf. Van der Walt, 1968:78, 79) therefore regard the idea of creation as the basic notion of his philosophy (In his theology, he is primarily concerned with the Creator and his philosophy with creation).

In my own interpretation, Aquinas' emphasis on the existing creation (as a product) and his cosmological position regarding origins are consequential to my interpretation of his philosophy. It is just a facet of the cluster of his ontology and not the central idea. Behind the emphasis laid by Aquinas on the Creator and creation once again lies his concept of law. Aquinas' Creator God is a Law-God – because creation lies locked up in Him as laws which have been reified (cf. Aquinas' viewpoint of exemplars in the second chapter). The other way round, the universe constantly reminds us of its creational character – since it bears the image or vestiges of its Creator.

3.5 A Static View of Creation

While God's creation originally meant to develop and unfold, a purely cosmological viewpoint means a static view that depreciates these dynamics. It leaves no room for development and change but emphasizes the eternally unchangeable versus the temporary (cf. Vollenhoven, 2000: 330-332). The influence of the eternally static, immovable deity of Aristotle (who simultaneously directs creation) emerges in the work of Aquinas.

3.6 The Positive Side

Despite the above critique, Aristotle's emphasis on visible reality (in contrast to Plato's emphasis on an invisible world of ideas) in another respect did influence the good (cf. Hart, H. et al., 1974: 85).

Aquinas criticizes the Neo-Platonic, Augustinian philosophers of his time for disregarding or disparaging creation and their resulting unworldly focus on God alone. On their part, they blamed Aquinas for being "worldly-minded." Aquinas distinguishes (in my opinion correctly) between three meanings of the word "world" in the Scriptures: (1.) all things created by God, (2.) creation as reality fallen into sin and (3.) creation as delivered by Christ (cf. his *Commentary on the Gospel of John*, 1: 5). Both the first and third meanings are positive. His comment on the conservative Augustinians is also applicable: "They hold a plainly false opinion who say that in regard to the truth of religion it does not matter what a man thinks about creation so long as he has the correct opinion concerning God. An error concerning the creation ends as false thinking about God" (II, Ch. 3).

Elsewhere in Aquinas' work, it becomes clear that he would also subscribe to the opposite statement, namely that a wrong idea about God would lead to the wrong idea of creation.

4. An Ontological Dualism

In the first chapter, the discussion has already focused on Aquinas' nature, grace dualism. But he also teaches a dichotomy *within* creation (cf. Vollenhoven, 2005a: 415), answering the fundamental question of how reality initially looked. Was it originally a unity or duality?

4.1 Two Different Theories

Since Greek antiquity, some philosophers thought in a monistic and others in a dualistic way. Monism departs from the original unity of everything. Initially, there was only one "something" from which the later plurality emerged. Consistent monism would teach that the deity/God and the world are one in their origin since both are supposed to be offshoots of a still more profound original unity. Therefore, there is no essential difference between God and the universe (Pantheism is an example of this philosophy).

Dualists, however, choose a different point of departure. Initially, there was a duality, two roots or origins of everything. Vollenhoven concisely summarizes these two original Greek theories:

> Monism (Greek for *monos*, alone, unique) is a philosophical theme that sees god and world as a unity, denying the creation. In this monism stands in contrast to dualism which, likewise denying the creation, takes God and the world as originally given eternal counterparts" (2005a: 265).

Seeing that Aquinas was a Christian, he could not accept monism but chose dualism within a hierarchy. From his dualistic view, where monism had to explain the origin of the diversity (they see it as divergences from the unity), Aquinas had to explain the harmony between the duality (the transcendent God and non-transcendent universe). This philosophical tension leads to the age-old debate on God's so-called immanence and transcendence: God is present *in* the universe, but not wholly (this would land one in pantheism); God is also *above* the universe, yet not fully (this would land one in deism). Aquinas attempts to retain the balance between transcendence and immanence, employing his idea of law and teaching the analogy based on his law idea.

This teetering, of course, is rooted in an erroneous ontology, where there is no *radical* distinction between God and his creation. The spatial and other facets of creation would also apply to God! Up to the present day, theologians are struggling with this false issue of God's (so-called) immanence versus his (so-called) transcendence (cf. Kruger, 2011). And, of course, one can never find correct answers to wrong problem statements.

4.2 Influence of His Idea of Law
Aquinas' particular idea of law, therefore, results in a dualist philosophy. This plurality was primarily due to the plurality of the exemplars of the things in God since all eternity.

Also, regarding the situation after creation, Aquinas' viewpoint is dualistic. As indicated, Aquinas focuses attention on two things: the Creator and the creation. Although he does not use the designations "transcendent" and "nontranscendent" for Creator and creation, it emerges from the whole of his philosophy that God is the transcendent and creation the non-transcendent. For instance, he says: "God transcends all sensible things ... His effects ... are sensible things" (I, 85). God, who the senses cannot detect, transcends observable reality.

When dealing with his telos-doctrine of purpose (cf. Chapter 5), it will also become evident that Aquinas (in line with Aristotle's dualism) accepts a view of a transcendent, immovable God who draws all non-transcendent things like a magnet back to Him as their highest goal.

4.3 Comment
Both monism and dualism – at least in their original forms – are equally far from Scriptural Revelation. It is as unbiblical to look for a more profound unity behind God and the universe (in a monistic way), thereby attributing something divine to the universe, as to teach (in a dualist way) that the universe, as the second root of reality, has an independent existence next to God. Philosophical speculation on the original state is wrong, for the Scriptures reveal (and one has to accept this in faith) that (1) God

is there from all eternity, that He (2) created a rich diversity and that He (3) laid down his law for creation. A fourth important facet of Thomas of Aquinas' philosophy in the SCG is the following.

5. Partial Universalism

A philosopher has to answer the question of the relation between the general (universal) and the particular (individual) since the existence of neither can be denied. There is this unique tree, but we also speak about "tree" in general, meaning a particular kind of plant. Formulated differently: One can distinguish between the "it" (individuality) and the "what" (universality) of something. Both are *facets* of the *same* created thing. However, the history of philosophy and the various theories did not see it like this. In Aquinas' time, it was one of the most debated problems (cf. Venter, 1985: 47-64 and Van der Walt, 1986: 243-254).

5.1 Different Theories

The history of philosophy (cf. Spier, 1959: 12) shows how philosophers gave preference to either the universal or individual. The universalists held that the universal is the most important, while the individual is of secondary importance since it merely emerges from the universal. When applied at a social level, such philosophers would regard societal relationships (e.g. church, school, government) as more important than their members.

Individualists taught the exact opposite: the individual is the actual, the true. The particular comes first. When applied to society, they would say that a societal relationship merely exists as a cluster of separate individuals. As it usually happens in philosophy, we also find a reconciling position situated between the two, that of the partial universalists. Both the universal and the individual have a certain independence and exist *next to* each other.

However, there were differences within this group, for according to one theory (the macro-micro cosmos doctrine), the universal is *more significant* than the individual. According to another theory (the doctrine of form-matter), either the universal or the individual is the *higher*. Therefore, the first-mentioned theory can also be called *horizontal* partial universalism, while the latter can be labelled as *vertical* partial universalism. Aquinas was, as will become clear, a *vertical* partial universalist.

But even vertical partial universalists do not all agree. To the empiricists, the universal is situated in the lower (matter) and the *principium indivuationis* in the higher (form). In contrast to this, the intellectualists place the universal (form) in the higher and the *principium indivuationis* in the lower (matter) (cf. Vollenhoven, 2005a: 330-332). As will now become clear, Aquinas was an advocate of the latter, the intellectualist theory.

5.2 The Doctrine of Form and Matter

In several instances in the SCG, it is distinctly put that the form is universal. Therefore, form has to be individualized by matter. "... every form ... is individuated by matter ..." (II, 232). Aquinas' view that form is universal is also valid for the human intellect: "... the intellect is individuated by that matter which is the human body and of which the intellect is held to be the form" (II, 232).

Thus, Aquinas does not adhere to either a universalistic or an individualistic viewpoint. He does not see the universal and individual next to each other as do the partial universalists with their macro-micro cosmos. The universal and the individual occur (like the higher and the lower components) in the same thing: "universal and singular are differences or essential attributes of being" (I, 214). Aquinas holds a partial universalism in his doctrine of form-matter.

5.3 Once Again His Idea of Law as The Key

Nevertheless, he remains a partial *universalist*, for the universal is still the more important to him, understandably against the background of Aquinas' idea of law. The (universal) form to Aquinas, as we have already seen (cf. second chapter), is the law. Since the law is everything to him, the universal will also be more important than the individual. For instance, he says: "The good of the species is greater than the good of the individual, just as the formal exceeds that which is material" (II, 138). Elsewhere he says: "it is clear that singulars exist for the sake of the universal nature" (IIIa, 251).

5.4 Comment
First, I reiterate that the universal (e.g. being human) and the individual (this specific human being) are not "things" or (as in the work of Aquinas) *parts* of things, but *facets* of every created thing. Secondly, these concepts cannot, the way Aquinas does, be applied to God either. Aquinas sees God as the universal mover, who brings individual creatures in motion. Therefore, Aquinas' understanding of God had significant implications on how he viewed the relationship between God and human beings (more on this in the fifth chapter).

A fifth important characteristic of the philosophical cluster of the *Doctor Angelicus* now asks for our attention, *Analogy of Being*.

6. Analogy of Being
One would have to deal first with Aquinas' doctrine of participation (cf. sec 7 below) since his doctrine of analogy explains in *which way* the cosmic being has a part in the divine. However, we keep this link in mind here.

6.1 The Heart of Aquinas' Philosophy?
An enormous amount has been written on the *analogia entis* doctrine *of Aquinas* (cf., e.g. Habbel, 1928; Klubertanz, 1960; Lyttkens, 1952; McInery, 1961 & 1968; Phelan, 1943 and Venter, 1985: 17 et seq.). Some secondary sources regard it, albeit not the key to his philosophy, then still something lying near the heart of his philosophy or running through it like a golden thread (cf. Van der Walt, 1968: 85 et seq.). However, I am of the opinion that Aquinas' doctrine of the analogy of being is only one of the implications of his idea of law – which forms the heart of his philosophy. We find the *analogia entis* doctrine of Aquinas mainly in Chapters 29 to 34 of Book I. The heading of Chapter 29 already reveals: "On the resem-

blance (*similitudo*) of the creatures to God."

The preceding chapter (2) has given enough attention to the meaning of *similitudo* to see the relationship between Aquinas' doctrine of the *analogia entis* and his law-idea.

6.2 Likeness in Difference

In Chapters 29-34, Aquinas deals with the question of how we can get to know God. One can, according to Aquinas, know God from His effects since the cause brings forth something similar to Himself. Therefore, Aquinas first emphasizes the likeness between God and the creation and explains it by way of an image:

> Thus, the sun causes heat among these sublunary bodies by acting according as it is in act. Hence, the heat generated by the sun must bear some likeness (*similitudo*) to the active power of the sun, through which heat is caused in the sublunary world; and because of this heat the sun is said to be hot, even though not in one and the same way. And so the sun is said to be somewhat like those things in which it produces its effects as an efficient cause (I, 138).

Apart from the similarity, there is, however, also a dissimilarity:

> Yet the sun is also unlike all these things in so far as such effects do not possess heat and the like in the same way as they are found in the sun. So, too, God gave things all their perfections and thereby is both like and unlike all of them (I, 138).

"Both like and unlike ..." Now, Aquinas has given us the heart of his doctrine of *analogia entis*.

However, there is a significant difference between God and the creatures because it is a "one-way likeness" (compare I, 139): the creatures look like God, but God does not look like His creatures. The creatures receive from God that which causes them to resemble Him. A stone imitates God, but God may not be called a stone (cf. I, 142).

6.3 His Idea of Law as Background Again

Against Aquinas' peculiar law-idea, the likeness and difference between God and the creatures are pretty understandable. Creatures can exhibit *likeness* to God since they received from God what causes them to resemble Him, namely the exemplars. However, they *differ* from God since they are not like God, pure law. Although their exemplars are implied in the god-law, the exemplars still are not identical to the law-god. As a consequence of the exemplars being law in the creatures, there is *likeness* to God (who is law), but due to not-being-God, there is a *difference*.

Concisely put: to Aquinas, *analogia entis* is possible because the *entis* (being) to him is a law-being, as indicated in the second chapter. His analogy of being rests on his analogy of law: his analogy of being is an analogy of law.

6.4 Epistemological Implications

According to Aquinas, the doctrine of analogy is possible, apart from a supernatural theology (derived from the Scriptures) and a natural knowledge of God. Since God and the created things are not the same, nothing may be said of both of them in a univocal (*univoce*) way.

Since there is also a likeness of God and the world (Aquinas as a dualist accepts one being with a higher, divine and with a lower, non-transcendent part), we may not speak of them only in purely equivocal terms either (*pure aecquivoce*). Names for God and His creatures have, however, to be used analogically (*analogice*): "Therefore, it remains that the names said of God and creatures are predicated neither univocally nor equivocally but analogically, that is, according to an order of reference to something" (I, 147).

In a nutshell, this is Aquinas' famous *analogia entis* doctrine. God and his creatures are in an analogical relationship: They are *similar* while they *differ*.

6.5 Application

It seems evident that Aquinas would apply his viewpoint of analogy in many fields. Here are two examples. *The First example* highlights that which forms the foundation of Aquinas' proofs of God's existence. Although the docrine of analogy can hardly be maintained, his natural or philosophical theology cannot do without it. *The second example* is how his doctrine of analogy also determines his anthropology. Aquinas explains the biblical idea of image-bearing humanity in light of His doctrine of analogy. As far as His intellect is concerned, human beings resemble God, but they differ from Him as far as his body is concerned. Of course, this is not at all what the Bible means by the image of God (cf. Van der Walt, 2010).

I confined myself to pointing out that the doctrine of analogy does not apply to God or human beings. It is only acceptable within a (dualistic) *relativism* of being in which the biblical message of their *radical* ontological distinction is not duly recognized. This ontological merging between God and his creation becomes even more distinct in the following (sixth) facet of the philosophy of Aquinas.

7. Participation

The idea of participation or "having-part-of" is the last consequence of Aquinas' particular notion of law. On this, too, many chapters and books have been written (cf. e.g. Fabro, 1961; Geiger, 1942; Henle, 1956 and Krämer, 1967).

In my interpretation, it becomes evident from Aquinas' doctrine of participation that he (as a result of his nomolising of both God and the universe) does not distinguish *radically* between Creator and creature. Creatures, also having a part of God, are, therefore, to a degree divine in nature (cf. Venter, 1985: 15 and 1988: 163). There is a participatory and distinct link between Aquinas' doctrine of exemplars and his doctrine of likeness (a point of discussion in the previous chapter). To Aquinas, *exemplar* and *similitudo* mean the same thing.

7.1 The Link with "Exemplar" and "Similitudo"

As a consequence of Aquinas' law, which is an exemplar and likeness in God and also in the creatures, the creatures can have a part in it. For instance, Aquinas states:

> Since, then, that which is found in God perfectly, is found in other things according to a certain diminished participation, the basis on which the likeness is observed belongs to God absolutely, but not to the creature (I, 139).

Here, Aquinas deals with the good in God, whose essence is good and not through participation in the good like the creatures:

> God is good through His essence, whereas all other things are good by participation...Nothing, then, will be called good exept in so far as it has a certain likeness of the divine goodness. Hense, God is the good of every good (I, 156).

The following words of Aquinas do not need any additional explanation to prove that his idea of law renders his doctrine of participation conceivable:

> Being itself belongs to the first agent according to His proper nature, for God's being is His substance, as was shown in Book I. Now, that which belongs to a thing according to its proper nature does not belong to other things except by participation, as heat is in other bodies from fire. Therefore, being belongs to all other things from the first agent by certain participation (II, 155).

7.2 The Difference Between the Doctrine of Similitudo/Exemplars and Participation

Similitudo to Aquinas means the same as *exemplar*. However, the doctrine of participation is not the same as Aquinas' doctrine of exemplars.

One could perhaps formulate the difference between the doctrine of participation and that of the exemplars as follows. In the doctrine of exemplars, the direction from above to below is essential: God creates the *exemplar* in the creature. According to the doctrine of participation, the creature has a part in God due to the exemplar in him. Hence, the direction from below to above is important. Therefore, the doctrine of participation is the *result* of the doctrine of exemplars.

7.3 A Platonising Trait

Several authors on Aquinas' philosophy (cf. Geiger, 1942, Fabro, 1961 and Van der Walt, 1968: 85-92) laid a connection between the doctrine of participation and the Neo-Platonism of Augustine and others because Augustine, as a Christian, transferred Plato's ideas or laws to the mind of God (*in mente Dei*). Aquinas accepts this idea of exemplars in God but expands it by teaching that God also creates the exemplars *for* the things *into* the things themselves.

Venter (1988: 163, 167) rightly links Aquinas' doctrine of participation with both Aristotle and Plato. According to Aristotle, a consequence has a part in its cause. But also, the Augustinian doctrine (of the Platonic ideas in God) was taken over by Aquinas so that the things in their archetypical examples (exemplars) have a part in God.

7.4 A Full Circle

This originally Neo-Platonic characteristic in the work of Aquinas occasioned him as a Christian to view reality as the dynamics of two simultaneous but opposite motions. First, the step-by-step emancipation (*exitus*) from the One or the Origin (God) to an ever-increasing cosmic diversity. But at the same time, there was, in the second instance, a return (*conversio*) to the Origin. To human beings, the return means that they detach themselves from the material, the natural, to become spiritual and divine.

Aquinas combines this originally Neo-Platonic circulation idea of *exitus* and *reditus* with the Aristotelian cause (form or principle) and effect. (For detail cf. Aertsen, 1991: 105 et seq.) He writes:

> An effect is most perfect when it returns to its principle; thus the circle is the most perfect of all figures, and the circular motion the most perfect of all motions, because ... a return is made to the starting point. It is therefore necessary that creatures return to their principle in order that the universe of creatures may attain ultimate perfection (Book II, Ch. 46).

According to Aquinas' teaching on nature-grace (cf. Chapter 1), two realms have to be distinguished in a human being. Therefore, a human being has both a natural and a supernatural purpose. Grace alone can bring about complete perfection. However, Aquinas does not understand the correct biblical view; grace as forgiveness of sins restoring the religious relationship with God.

To him, grace means the supernatural perfection of a human being, the fulfilment of a human being's ontic incapacity to close the second part of the circle (the return to above) by himself. (Chapter 1 illustrated that grace not only *supposes* nature but also *perfects* it.)

8. The Implications of Aquinas' Idea of Law
I have already mentioned (in Chapter 2) that, in my opinion, this cyclic motif cannot be the primary key to the philosophy of Aquinas the way Aertsen (1991) claims. Still, his idea about law goes more in-depth. I will now merely point out the deterministic implications of Aquinas' law-idea.

8.1 Serious Reservations
With the aid of his doctrine of exemplars, Aquinas reaches the intellectualist conclusion that God knows everything (in their exemplars in his mind) and thereby determines the "contingent" events of the future. Does it not follow from this that what God knows in Himself *inevitably has to take place*? But if all events on earth are inevitable, is there any freedom and responsibility left for a human being? Does it not also conflict with the biblical notion of a personal, religious relationship between God and human beings?

8.2 Already Queried By His Contemporaries
The present author is not the only one asking these questions; during and after his lifetime, Aquinas' critics also raised questions. Several rejected his intellectualistic determinism (i.e. that the intellect of God is supposed to determine everything). They emphasized to the contrary (in a voluntaristic manner) the importance of God's free will and, in some instances, also of human beings.

But the ideas of Aquinas did not disappear from the scene. Suarez

(1548-1617), a later Roman Catholic scholar, followed Aquinas in his Aristotelianising ideas while making some modifications. For instance, he rejects Aquinas' determinism. Instead, he proposes the following. God knows from all eternity (therefore retaining the original law-idea) what the individual human being will choose but intervenes in His grace to prevent the direction the human being chooses, causing him/her to deviate from it.

8.3 Even Protestant Philosophy Influenced
Subsequent Lutheran and Protestant Scholasticism (of circa 1650-1700) linked up with this Roman Catholic Scholasticism to create its orthodox theology. The spirit of Aquinas' determinism was still present at the Synod of Dordt (1618-1619), influencing the decisions and understanding of the relationship between divine sovereignty and human responsibility (in election and rejection). Even the Reformed theologian Herman Bavinck's theology was closely related to Aquinas' and Suarez's (cf. Vollenhoven, 2000: 257).

9. Summary
Aquinas' philosophy is a complex system that cannot easily unravel, resulting in many philosophical trends throughout the several centuries, converging as it worked into a synthesis. In the two previous chapters and this third one, the author has attempted to take apart the puzzle pieces to understand his philosophy better. As we said at the onset (cf. 1.4), the different elements of the philosophy of the SCG are, however, not to be disconnected. They are connected, support one another, and form one complex or "cluster" of ideas. The following result is a hierarchical, static view of creation, determined from above.

Looking back and in summary, the Thomistic puzzle contains the following elements.

9.1 Direction and Idea of Law
Regarding the normative direction of Aquinas' philosophy, *firstly*, his syn-

thesis between the Word of God and Greek philosophy through a method of nature and grace (the supernatural) becomes more apparent all the time. It also becomes evident that his interpretation of Aristotle on specific points shows marked Platonising features.

In the *second instance*, it became even more evident (in the previous two chapters) how Aquinas' law idea pervades his whole view of reality. Without it, one cannot gauge his concept of God and his view of the universe with sufficient thoroughness.

9.2 View of Reality

In the third instance, the contours of his view of reality or ontology also emerged more clearly. His ontology looks like this: He departs from one existence (being), composed hierarchically of (1.) pure matter (an abstraction) right at the bottom, (2.) after that everything (matter, plant, animal and human being) consists of form (or law) and matter, which (3.) finally ends right at the top with God (as pure form/law). The exemplars/similarities/rational germs (cf. previous chapter) therefore exist in God, in the things and (by abstraction) in the mind of human beings.

However, in the one chain of being or the existing reality, he distinguishes a transcendental (God) and a non-transcendent (creation). He, therefore, holds an *ontic dualism*.

In his philosophy, he confines himself in a *purely cosmological way* to creation as it exists today, the development (genesis) of which is underrated since it is determined by (exemplars in) God.

He neither regards the universal nor the individual as primary, but he occupies a middle position in his partial universalism that seeks to recognize both. However, according to Aquinas, these two are positioned *vertically* one above the other: the universal (form) is the higher, and the individual (matter) is the lower. Thus to Aquinas, God is the most universal, most important being.

Aquinas distinguished between his transcendent God and the non-transcendence of creation, demonstrating futher relativization (the two already form one being from the beginning). Aquinas' doctrine of analogia entis emerged from this distinction, a simultaneous difference and likeness between God and creation. That God and the created things are not radically different becomes even more evident from his *doctrine of participation*. Therefore, the higher and nearer to God in the hierarchical order of being, the more distinctly created things (especially human beings) have a part in Him, becoming "Divine." As in a circle, everything emerges from God and again returns to Him.

The foregoing complex of ideas has significant implications for Aquinas' anthropology and epistemology, dealt with in the following (fourth) chapter.

CHAPTER 4
THE THOMIST ANTHROPOLOGY AND EPISTEMOLOGY

THIS CHAPTER FURTHER INVESTIGATES *and questions the anthropology and epistemology of the famous Medieval theologian-philosopher Thomas Aquinas (1224/25-1274), as explained in his* Summa Contra Gentiles. *The doctor, Angelicus, was a very influential thinker in Catholic circles and Reformed scholastic theology (± 1550-1700) and afterwards up to its present revival in our time. His ideas even partly influenced two founders of a Reformational philosophy in the thirties of the previous century, viz. Stoker and Dooyeweerd.*

The three previous chapters discussed Aquinas' primary direction of thought (synthesis philosophy), his idea of law, as well as the cluster of ideas comprising his ontology or view of reality (God and cosmos). This chapter will offer evidence on how Aquinas' ontology determined his anthropology. Also, this chapter will detail how his anthropological views, in turn, influenced his epistemology. Furthermore, this chapter will give special attention to the role of (what the author indicates as) Aquinas' nomology or his view of law (in God, in the creation and conceptualized in the human intellect).

This chapter develops through the following stages: (1.) The origin, composition (of soul and body) of mankind is explained. (2.) The nature of the intellective soul (a separate, independent, immortal, supra-temporal substance) is investigated. (3.) Followed by Aquinas' distinction between a practical and speculative intellect. (4.) The speculative intellect, through a long and complicated process, finally arrives at scientific knowledge of a thing's form, essence, or law. Correspondence is reached between what is known outside the mind and its logical duplicate in the human intellect. (5.) Apart from this natural, rational or philosophical knowledge of the cosmos, Aquinas, as a Christian thinker, also accepted (in his theology) faith as a means to acquire knowledge of the supernatural world (God included).

1. Introduction
A FEW REMARKS BEFOREHAND on: (1.) The contribution of and link with the previous three chapters, (2.) a limitation, (3.) sources used, and (4.) an outline of the layout.

1.1 Link
Aquinas' view on reality as a whole (cf. second and third chapters) determines his anthropology, as we will be dealing with in this chapter. On the other hand, his anthropology can also further elucidate some facets of his ontology. A person's anthropology, in turn, also determines the epistemology that he/she holds – a second important point of investigation in this chapter.

1.2 Limitation
Of course, we will not be able to deal with Aquinas' anthropology in full here. Nevertheless, it does offer the philosophical point of departure for his different theological viewpoints.

One example is his teaching on the biblical revelation that a human being is the image and likeness of God, on which many books have been written (cf., e.g. De Grijs, 1967 and Scheffczyk, 1969: 206-330). However, the way Aquinas understands this information from the Scriptures is also clearly determined by his philosophical nomology. According to the exemplar in Himself, God creates a human being analogous to Him. *Imago* (image), therefore, denotes the rational human nature which exists in all people, while *similitudo* (likeness) denotes the supernatural image of grace (cf. Van der Walt, 2010a: 330-331).

Although this explanation (of a dual image) is not what the Scriptures teach, it is still accepted today even by some Reformed theologians. To exhibit the image of God, however, does not mean having something divine *in* one. According to the Scriptures, a human being reflects the image of God to the extent to which he/she obeys God's central law of love.

1.3 *Sources*

At the onset, the author again reminds readers that reference to secondary sources is kept to a minimum. Such sources primarily consist of philosophical interpretations of Aquinas, while the author wants to listen to the *original* Aquinas in his *Summa Contra Gentiles* (SCG). For the original Latin text, an edition of 1935 was used (cf. *S. Thomae Aquinatis, 1935*). The English translation cited is the Doubleday edition (cf. Thomas Aquinas, 1955, 1957). The references given with the quotations consist of first the number of the specific book in Roman numerals and then the page numbers of this translation in Arabic numerals (e.g. II, 55). Since Book III of the SCG was translated in two separate volumes, these are referred to as IIIa or IIIb. As mentioned in previous chapters, this chapter expands on the author's earlier, still unpublished research – with more recent literature and his own insights (cf. Van der Walt, 1968 and 1974).

1.4 *Lay-out*

The following facets of Aquinas' anthropology in the SCG will be dealt with here: (1.) how a human being (significantly his highest, intellective soul) originates; (2.) the relation between soul and body; (3.) the soul as an independent, immortal substance and (4.) finally the capacity of the soul from which also (5.) Aquinas' epistemology is derived.

2. The Origin of Human Beings

According to Aquinas, human beings (like all creatures) consist of form and matter; the former (the form) is also called the soul. His dualistic ontology (cf. previous chapter) also leads to a dichotomy in his anthropology: the human being consists of two separate parts. In turn, the soul itself has three distinct parts.

2.1 Three Parts of The Soul

The intellective (rational) part of the soul distinguishes human beings from animals: "Now, it is with respect to the intellective soul that we are said to be *men*; to the sensitive soul, *animals;* to the nutritive soul, *living beings"* (II, 173).

Human beings possess all three parts of the soul, while animals have only two parts, and plants have only one part soul. Aquinas writes:

> The vegetative soul, which is present first (when the embryo lives the life of a plant), perishes, and is succeeded by a more perfect soul, both nutritive and sensitive in character, and then the embryo lives an animal life; and when this passes away it is succeeded by the rational soul introduced from without, while the preceding souls existed in virtue of the semen (II, 304).

Aquinas' intellectualism is already quite clear: a human being is primarily an intellectual, noetic being. Neither is the human embryo human before the intellect has entered it *from outside.*

Since the intellective soul makes a man a human being, Aquinas focuses almost exclusively on this. How does such a soul originate? In Book II, Chapters 83-89, Aquinas explains his point of view in this respect. First, he says how the intellective soul *does not* come into a human being (Chapters 83-86) and afterwards how it *does* happen (Chapters 87-89). However, even how, according to Aquinas, it does *not* happen, reveals much of his point of view.

2.2 How the Soul Does Not Originate

It is noteworthy that Aquinas criticizes Plato (Ch. 83) because the latter taught a pre-existence of the soul. Thus, according to Aquinas, the fact that the *exemplar* of man's intellective soul exists from all eternity in the Law-god still does not imply the soul's pre-existence. (Evidently, it is only the *exemplar* and not the intellective soul itself which exists from eternity in God.) Nor can Aquinas accept Plato's viewpoint that a human being is "a soul enclosed by a body" (compare Chapter 83). Likewise, Origen, (who taught in line with Plato) viewed that all souls exist from eternity and are united with bodies as prisons to punish them for their sins. Aquinas finds this unacceptable (cf. Chapter 83).

Book III, Chapter 85 demonstrates why the souls cannot be made of God's substance either.

Those who appeal for this to Genesis 1:26 err, according to Aquinas. The image of God is not a part of the substance of God in a human being: "The breathing of which Genesis speaks signifies the pouring forth of life from God into man according to a certain likeness, and not according to unity of substance" (II, 290). It is clear why Aquinas could not accept that the human (intellective) soul is made of God's substance or being. The *exemplars* of the various human souls lie in the divine intellect, but they are not identical.

The intellective soul is, according to Aquinas, definitely not transmitted with semen either. Chapter 86 states that the semen does transmit the body (the vegetative and sensitive parts of the soul) but not the intellective soul:

> Now, the nutritive and sensitive soul cannot operate independently of the body, as we have seen before. On the other hand, as we have likewise pointed out, the intellective soul does not operate through any bodily organ. Therefore, the nutritive and sensitive souls are brought into being through the body's engendering; but not the intellective soul. The transmission of the semen has as its aim the body. It is therefore through the transmission of the semen that the nutritive and sensitive souls begin to be; but this is not true of the

intellective soul (II, 291).

2.3 Each Soul is Created by God Himself

Aquinas' point of view is that the intellective soul can only come into being by a creational deed, and since only God can create, the intellective soul can only owe its origin to Him. "The soul is created immediately by God alone" (II, 294. Cf. also p. 305, 306). Hence we can call Aquinas' viewpoint in this regard creatianism – in opposition to the perspective of the traducianists who believe that the semen transmits the soul. (Creatianism is not to be confused with creationism, the belief of some Christians that God created the world in six days of 24 hours.)

Aquinas interestingly appeals to particular texts to support his viewpoint, also used today for the same purpose by some Reformed theologians. Amongst other verses, he quotes Psalm 33:15: "He who forms the hearts of all" (II, 284) and Genesis 2:7: "... the LORD God formed the man from the dust of the ground and breathed into his nostrils the breath of life" (II, 295). It is striking that he does not quote the last part of the verse as well ".... and the man became a living soul" (KJV). Because the "living soul" presented a problem to him. According to Aquinas, the soul *is* something living; it cannot, therefore, *become* living.

2.4 Arguments Employed Against the Creation of Aquinas

It is interesting to investigate the controversy between Aquinas and his traducianist opponents (as we find in Chapters 88 and 89). Because both sides are busy with a false issue, namely how the soul comes into the body, both could find arguments – even from the Bible – and still offer no definitive solution to the problem. Some of the most intriguing speculations are given here to show how the debate gives rise to clever arguments.

One argument is that a human being (according to Aquinas) has one soul with three parts. How can it be possible that two parts of the soul are transmitted with semen, and the third part is not transmitted? Aquinas, however, received criticism for his creatianism (compare arguments 6, 9,

10 and 12) because the soul and the body were supposed to originate *one after the other*. Aquinas offered a clever answer to this:

> It follows that the human body, so far as it is in potentiality to be soul, as not yet having one, precedes the soul in time; it is then, not actually human, but only potentially human. However, when the body is truly human, as being perfected by the human soul, it neither precedes nor follows the soul but is simultaneous with it (II, 306).

Another argument against Aquinas' creatianism is that God would create sinful souls – for according to the Scriptures, all people are sinners from birth. One could also say that God cooperates with adulterers by (willingly) supplying a soul for that consequence of their sinful deed. To this, too, Aquinas devised an answer:

> Regarding the *fifth objection,* there is nothing incongruous in God's co-operating with adulterers in the action of nature; for it is not the nature of adulterers that is evil, but their will, and the action deriving from their seminal power is natural, not voluntary. Hence, it is not unfitting that God should co-operate in their action by bringing it to its final completion (II, 306).

Furthermore, people *denounced* Aquinas with Genesis 2:2 where it says that God completed his work of creation and rested. Therefore, God cannot make new souls daily (cf. II, 273). To this, Aquinas answers: "God's resting must be understood to refer to cessation from forming new species, but not new individuals" (II, 286).

As already noted, Aquinas asserted (cf. again II, 304) that a human embryo has only a vegetative and a sensitive soul (like plants and animals). The human embryo only becomes a human being when God from outside also creates a third (intellective) soul. However, as far as we could ascertain, nowhere does Aquinas say *when God* does this. Is it after some months or only at birth? Would abortion then be permissible before the entrance of an intellectual soul? Aquinas also argues against the traducianists who believe that the soul is transmitted with semen (from the male).

That would mean that out of something mortal (the body), something immortal comes forth, and that with every seminal discharge at which no conception takes place, rational souls would be multiplied and lost, while the soul remains immortal (cf. II, 301). We confine ourselves to these few snatches from the futile dispute (because it concerns itself with a false issue) between creatianism and traducianism. (For a more biblical view of concepts like "body," "soul," "spirit," "flesh," etc. cf. Van der Walt, 2010b.)

3. The Relationship Between Intellective Soul and Body

The intellective soul is the *exemplar* that God creates into a human being. Chapter two already demonstrated that the *exemplar* which God creates is the form of the creature.

3.1 Form and Matter

The relationship between the soul and body in a human being, according to Aquinas, is that of the difference between form and matter:

> Now, that the soul is united to the body as its proper form is proved as follows. That by which something becomes a being in act from a being in potency is its form and act. But it is through the soul that the body becomes a being in act from being potentially existent, for living is the being of the living thing. Now, the seed before animation is living only in potency and, through the soul, becomes living in act. Therefore, the soul is the form of the animated body (II, 172).

Elsewhere: "Nothing, therefore, prevents an intellectual substance from being the human body's form, which is the human soul" (II, 205).

Since Aquinas, according to his partially universalistic view, sees form and matter as the higher and lower components of the same thing (cf. previous chapter), the relationship between soul and body is also higher and the lower, emerging very clearly in the SCG: "... these (bodily) pleasures are not agreeable to man by virtue of what is noblest in him, namely, his understanding..." (IIIa, 111). The sensitive part of a human being, which he shares with the animals, is in opposition to the higher intellect (cf. IIIa,

120). Note once more his intellectualism. The following more or less summarizes Aquinas' thoughts in this regard:

> Moreover, that man's highest good does not lie in goods of the body, such as health, beauty and strength, is clearly evident from similar considerations. For these things are possessed in common by both good and bad men; they are also unstable; moreover, they are not subject to the will (IIIa, 119).

3.2 Significant Implications

Since Aquinas' dichotomist anthropology considers the soul more important than the body, it also results in the "spiritual" or "eternal" things being more important to him than the "bodily" or "temporary." Voluntary poverty (Aquinas was a member of the Dominican mendicant order) meant expressly to free a person from what is worldly so that he can devote himself to the eternal (cf. III, Ch. 133, 134). For this reason, celibacy is better than marrying (Aquinas was also a monk), for sexual desire is something lower and therefore less good (cf. III, Ch. 137).

Aquinas viewed sin as the lower, sensitive part of the soul that rises all desires; sin does not come from the intellect (cf. IIIb, 105, 112). Sin means yielding to one's lower passions and inclinations. Therefore, redemption does not mean that the Holy Spirit regenerates one's heart.

Christ is supposed to have come into this world "...to change men from love of bodily things to love of spiritual things" (IV, 245). Aquinas' ontology and dichotomist anthropology, here, display the unbiblical implications of his dualism.

Besides, it is most evident why some describe Aquinas as an *intellectualistic* philosopher. To him, the intellect is the most important and unblemished. However, he was not yet a *rationalist* – rationalism would only appear on the scene from approximately 1600 AD.

4. The Intellective Soul: An Independent, Immortal and Supratemporal Substance

Corresponding with his teaching on form and matter, the soul is the higher and the bearer of life. The semen, which only exists potentially, becomes alive in the act (cf. III, 172). Therefore, the exemplar that God creates into a human being acts in a helping or assisting capacity. Without it, a human being cannot exist. God, who Himself is pure act, causes man to exist employing the *exemplar*, and He creates the human being. This idea is called the subsistence theory of Aquinas. Berger (1968) gives a good account of how this concept of substance originated in Greek philosophy (Plato and notably Aristotle) and (on p. 107-159) how Aquinas adapted it. And more recently, Ter Horst (2008) offers a critical appraisal of Aquinas' doctrine on substance.

4.1 The Intellective Soul as a Substance

Therefore Aquinas calls the soul the *substantial* form (*forma substantialis* – compare for instance II, 158, 204 and 213) of the human composition. In many instances, he indicates the human intellective soul as *substance* (*substantia intellectualis*). (Compare the headings of Chapters 47, 53, 55 and 56 of II.) In not one single instance, however, does Aquinas call the body (*corpus*) a substance.

But if one sees the intellective soul as a separate substance, the *corpus* should be something as well–even if it is not called a substance. So Aquinas keeps wrestling with the problem of how the unit of a human being originates from two independencies. However, if one starts with a dichotomy, it is impossible ever to reach an integral view of being human.

4.2 The Intellective Soul is Immortal

The intellective soul as substance is also immortal. It is a *forma substantialis* (a form of the substance human being) and a *forma subsistens* (a subsisting form with continued existence). As an intellectual substance, it is indestructible: "It has been shown, however, that no intellectual substance is composed of matter and form. Therefore, no intellectual substance is corruptible" (II, 158). Further: " intellectual substances subsist and are and live; and they have life unfailing and undiminishable, being free from universal corruption, free from generation and death" (II, 164).

Elsewhere he says: "when bodies perish, the intellect retains its substantial character " (II, 312).

Only the human intellective soul keeps on existing after death. In Chapter 82 of Book II, Aquinas states that "the souls of brute animals are not immortal." While the (sensitive and vegetative) souls of animals die with their bodies, about man, he says: "man alone has a subsistent soul, that is, a soul having life in itself" (II, 268).

4.3 Comment

However, the Bible does not teach that a human being *has* a soul, much less than the soul in itself possesses *immortality*. God alone is immortal. According to the Scriptures, a human being (please note not the soul) *receives* immortality only after being raised (by God). (For more detail, compare Van der Walt, 2010b: 159-289). On this point, Aquinas could not accept Aristotle, who taught that the human soul perishes at the time of death. However, he does not directly oppose Aristotle but criticizes his Averoistic followers (cf. II, 258).

From the preceding, it emerges very clearly that Aquinas' idea of law plays a decisive part. After the death of animals, the *exemplar,* created into them by God, perishes.

However, this *exemplar* continues existing (as a "separated form") after the death of a human being, individually, apart from its *exemplar* in God.

According to Aquinas, however, the form needs the matter to be individualized. Therefore, one could ask how the human soul can still exist after being severed from the body at death? He attempts to solve the issue (cf. II, Chapter 75) by saying that, although the soul, when it originates, is dependent on matter (body), it needs not lose its individuality at the destruction of the body. Since the soul has independent existence (a substance), it retains the individuality acquired at its origin even after the separation from the body at death.

4.4 A Supra-Temporal Soul

Aquinas even claims that the soul, apart from being immortal or everlasting, is also supratemporal. For instance, he says: "the human soul ... is situated in the boundary line between corporeal and incorporeal substances, as though it existed on the horizon of eternity and time" (II, 265. Cf. also IIIa, 201). He speaks of "... the intellect, whose being does not come under time" (IIIa, 201). Elsewhere he says: "the mode of an intelligent substance consists in the fact that its being is above movement and consequently above time, whereas the being of every corruptible thing is subject to motion and time" (II, 162).

But supra-temporality of the intellective soul does not mean that it is eternal (*aeternus*) like God, merely that it is "everlasting" (*perpetuus*) (cf. II, 286). In Aquinas' dualistic ontology of a transcendent, eternal God and a non-transcendent, temporary world, the human soul, therefore, takes up an intermediate position. It is neither eternal (*aeternus*) nor temporary (*temporaliter*) but supra-temporal (*aevernus*). This idea was later also supported by Dooyeweerd in the form of a supra-temporal heart (Cf. Van der Walt, 2014: 116 ff.).

4.5 Subsistence Theory

So clearly, Aquinas holds a substantialist anthropology. We denote his anthropological viewpoint, designated as "subsistence theory," the *anima intellectiva* (not the vegetative and sensitive souls), seen as a substance or a subsistent form. It is created into the body by God to assist or quicken it. After the body's death, it continues to exist as an individualized form or substance (also compare Vollenhoven, 2011: 92, 93).

Above, we have already mentioned the excellent work by Berger (1968) for more particulars on the history and meaning of the concept "substance." He demonstrates clearly (p. 71 et seq.) that Aristotle is the source of the idea of substance voiced by Aquinas (p. 71 et seq.).

Substantia and *accidentia* are the two distinguished categories in Aquinas' work (the latter are the former features).

The concept of "substance" is not as innocent as it appears. It means something (a thing) that *can exist independently*. However, it is a question of whether such an idea is biblically justified since the Bible distinctly teaches that God created everything, which remains wholly dependent on Him (cf. Spier, 1959: 96). Aquinas' *anima intellectiva,* regarded as something existing independently and naturally having immortality, therefore, has to be queried. God alone is immortal (cf. 1 Timothy 6:16), and He *bestows* immortality on a human being – only *after* the resurrection (1 Corinthians 15:53 , 54).

The capabilities of the intellective soul will be the next topic of discussion because Aquinas' epistemology cannot be comprehended without it.

5. The Abilities of The Intellective Soul

Aquinas distinguishes between a speculative and a practical intellect (cf. II, 318). In the speculative intellect, reason plays the most important role, and in the practical intellect, the will is most important.

5.1 Intellect and Conduct

The relation between the two intellects (speculative and practical) is between the inner and the outer man: reason is connected with intellect and the will with action. The intellect comes before the action, or the action is a consequence of the intellect. The other way round, however, it is the will that sets the intellect into motion. Aquinas describes the interaction as follows:

> Again, among moving powers in beings possessing an intellect, the first is found to be the will. For the will sets every power to its act; we understand, because we will ... The will has the role because its object is the end; although it is also a fact that the intellect, though not in the manner of an efficient and moving cause, but in that of a final cause, moves the will by proposing to it its object, namely, the end (I, 241).

In the preceding age-old speculations on the primacy of the human intellect or will, Aquinas thinks in an intellectualist manner. Aquinas writes:

The intellect apprehends the forms of things in a more universal mode than that in which they exist in things; and for this reason, we observe that the form of the speculative intellect is more universal than that of the practical intellect. (II, 318).

In dealing with the speculative intellect, Aquinas further distinguishes between the *intellectus agens* and *intellectus possibilis*. Below we will look into the function of each of these. We first deal with another Thomist distinction.

5.2 Intellect and Faith

Employing speculative intellect, where reason is vital, Aquinas could obtain knowledge of the things the senses can detect. Reason has the domain of nature as its field of investigation (on the theme of nature-grace, see again Chapter one).

Earlier, we also mentioned (cf. again Chapter one) that Aquinas also saw faith (a supernatural gift of grace from God) as a faculty of knowing. Through faith, one can obtain knowledge of the things that are not perceptible to the senses. Faith, therefore, offers knowledge in the domain of grace (cf. Lais, 1951 and Niede, 1928).

In what follows, I will give special attention to how knowledge in the domain of nature is acquired through the intellect (cf. also Neumann, 1963 and Siewerth, 1933). The following facets will also be discussed: (1.) knowledge of the universal or law; (2.) "empiricism"; (3.) *phantasma;* (4.) *intellectus agens;* (5.) *intellectus possibilis;* (6.) his theory of correspondence; (7.) knowledge acquired by faith in God's revelation. We remark in passing that not all facets of Aquinas' epistemology will be covered. Still less, the complex problems in this area during the Middle Ages in general (cf., e.g. Venter, 1985: 81).

6. Knowledge of the Universal Form of Law

Aquinas, obviously, thinks in an intellectualist manner. I repeat the quotation under the previous section: "the intellect apprehends the forms of things in a more universal mode than that in which they exist in things;

and for this reason, we observe that the form of the speculative intellect is more universal than that of the practical intellect " (II, 318).

6.1 Difference Between Two Kinds of Knowledge

The difference between practical and speculative (scientific) knowledge is explained as follows:

> Speculative knowledge and the functions that pertain to it reach their perfection in the universal, while the things that belong to practical knowledge reach their perfection in the particular. In fact, the end of speculative cognition is truth, which consists primarily and essentially in immaterial and universal things; but the end of practical cognition is operation, which is concerned with singulars. So, the physician does not heal man as a universal, but, rather, this individual man, and the whole science of medicine is ordered to this result ... Besides, speculative knowledge is perfected in the universal rather than in the particular, because universals are better known than particulars (IIIa, 252. cf. also I, 215).

Where practical knowledge, therefore, concerns individual, tangible things, the speculative searches for the universal, the abstract: "Scientific knowledge ... consists in the assimilation of the knower to the thing known. Now, the knower is assimilated to the thing known, as such, only with respect to universal species; for such are the objects of science" (II, 187).

Elsewhere: "it is the nature of the intellect to grasp universals" (II, 145. cf. also p. 148).

Thus, the intellect does not stop with the external, as do the senses: "there is a difference between intellect and sense, for sense grasps a thing in its exterior accidents, which are colour, taste, quantity and other of this kind, but intellect enters into what is interior to the thing" (IV, 86, 87).

6.2 Knowledge of The Laws

Therefore, it is clear why Aquinas is concerned with knowledge of the forms or laws in scholarship. Aquinas writes: "forms are made understood in act by abstraction from matter ... the intellect deals with universals and not with singulars, for matter is the principle of individuation" (I, 171).

Further: "a material thing is made intelligible by being separated from matter" (I, 176). Elsewhere: "the intellect understands things by those forms of theirs which it has in its possession" (II, 147). To Aquinas, the law was most dominant in his teaching on reality. His nomology also determines his epistemology. One, for instance, is concerned with knowledge of the law in scientific work.

7. "Empiricism"

But in some way or other, the knowable things have to enter the human intellect, which happens through the senses (Aquinas distinguishes five senses – cf. I, 215). Thus in his intellectualism, he does not yet neglect – like many later rationalists – the sensory factor, an Aristotelian emphasis.

7.1 Sensory Perception

Sensory observation is indispensable for reasonable knowledge: "our act of understanding takes its beginning from the senses" (IV, 86). He says the " intellect, taking the origin of his knowledge from the senses, does not transcend the mode which is found in sensible things" (I, 140). Or: " intelligibles are taken from sensible things" (II, 314). Elsewhere: "it is natural for man to receive knowledge through his senses, and ... it is very difficult to transcend sensible objects " (IIIb, 131).

7.2 Natural Sensory Knowledge of God

Even knowledge about God using reason arrives through sensory observation: "the knowledge of God which can be taken in by the human mind does not go beyond the type of knowledge that is derived from sensible things" (IIIa, 161). Aquinas' thinking, here, is most significant for understanding his natural theology and proofs of God's existence.

Since Aquinas (when it concerns rational knowledge) departs from the empirical, sensory perception, his viewpoint is labelled "empiricism." However, it is written in quotation marks since Aquinas did not (like Aristotle) teach that knowledge can exclusively be obtained in this way but by faith.

7.3 The Beginning of the Process of Knowing
Aquinas does not present the process of knowing as if the intellective soul directs itself at the knowable. Instead, he claims that the knowable enters the intellective soul through the ingression channels of the different senses (sensitive intellective soul). Therefore, the first step in the process of knowing is that the form of the knowable thing is impressed as something perceptible on the senses as *species sensibiles impressae*.

8. "Phantasma"
In the next step, the *species sensibiles impressae* as *phantasmata* enter the imagination (*imaginatio*), memory (*virtute memorativa*) and intellect (*virtute cogitativa*). Memory and intellect are called virtues (*virtutes*) because not all people possess them. For instance, Aquinas says: "not all are possessed of the requisite act of cogitative power (*virtute*), but only those who are instructed and habituated." For this reason, not all humans comprehend "the things whose phantasms they have" (II, 241). All have the imagination.

8.1 A Subsequent Step Needed
The *phantasma* is another step removed from the knowable. For instance, Aquinas speaks about: "the phantasm, which, in the order of objects, is higher than the sensible thing existing outside the soul" (II, 326). The *phantasma* is a likeness of the knowable in the one who knows.

8.2 Not Yet Sufficient
Through the intellect and memory (cf. II, 246, 247), the *phantasma* has to be prepared further for the intellective soul:

> To enable us to understand, the soul needs the powers which prepare the phantasms so as to render them actually intelligible, namely the cogitative power and the memory-powers which, being acts of

certain bodily organs and functioning through them, surely cannot remain after the body perishes (II, 261).

Elsewhere, too, he speaks of "the powers of cogitation and memory, by which the phantasms are prepared" (II, 265). The *phantasmata* are now changed to *species sensibiles expressae*. They, therefore, retain their sensory character.

Up to this point, the process of knowing has not progressed further than the sensitive. To a certain extent, the phantasma still has the material and individual character of the knowable things outside the intellect. However, the intellective soul does not concern the individual like the sensitive soul but the universal. "The human soul is cognizant of singulars and of universals through two principals, sense and intellect" (II, 340).

Therefore, the next step in knowing is to the intellective soul, where the *intellectus agens* abstracts the universal.

9. "Intellectus agens" and "Possibilis"

The *intellectus agens* and *possibilis* are positioned towards each other in the relation of form (actual) and matter (potential). Aquinas writes:

> The intellective soul is a nature in which we find potentiality and act, since sometimes it is actually understanding, and sometimes potentially. Consequently, in the nature of the intellective soul there is something having the character of matter, which is in potentiality to all intelligibles – and this is called the *possible intellect;* and there also is something which, in the capacity of an efficient cause, makes all in act – and this is called the *agent intellect*. Therefore, both intellects on Aristotle's showing, are within the nature of the soul, and have being separate from the body of which the soul is the act (II, 250).

9.1 The Role of the Active Intellect

The *intellectus agens* is making the *phantasma* or *species sensibilis expressae* into a truly intelligible species: "there is in the soul an active power *vis-à-vis* the phantasms, making them actually intelligible; and this power is called the *agent intellect* " (II, 247). Elsewhere: "the function of the agent intellect is to make phantasms actually intelligible" (II, 240).

9.2 *Illumination*
The *intellectus agens* illuminates the *phantasma*. For instance, Aquinas writes about "a phantasm which the agent intellect has illumined" (II, 242), and elsewhere he says about the *intellectus agens:*

> So, the function of that intellect is to make that which is intelligible proportionate to our minds. Now, the mode of intellectual light connatural to us is not unequal to the performance of this function. Therefore, nothing stands in the way of our ascribing the action of the agent intellect to the light of our soul, especially since Aristotle compares the agent intellect to a light (II, 248).

This teaching of Aquinas, namely that the *intellectus agens* illuminates the *phantasmata,* reveals the influence of Plato's teaching on illumination.

In the work of Plato, however, the illumination was only applicable to the intelligible world (this type of illumination will become apparent when we come to Aquinas' knowledge by faith in God's revelation). In the work of Aquinas, one could, therefore, speak of a distinct Plato-and-Aristotle-interpretation. Thus, not only in Aquinas' ontology in the SCG does one find a clear Platonising tendency (the ideas in the divine intellect) but also in his epistemology.

I leave aside whether the human intellect can play such an illuminating and even revelatory role. To my mind, only *God's* revelation and Spirit can have such a character.

9.3 *Abstraction*
When one is illuminated to *phantasma*, the universal form can be abstracted from the *intellectus agens* (cf. II, 243). Elsewhere, Aquinas also makes reference to the *quidditas* (being) instead of the universal form or species: "the species ... which is the *sign of a thing's quiddity* (II, 321). Or: "which quiddity our intellect is naturally capable of abstracting" (IIIa,

134). The *intellectus agens,* thus, first makes the *phantasma* intelligible.

The *species sensibilis expressae,* which is accepted as the *species intelligibilis impressae* by the *intellectus possibilis,* now becomes *species intelligibilis.* Aquinas repeatedly speaks about "the intelligible species received into the possible intellect" (II, 245). Elsewhere, he discusses the "phantasms which the agent intellect has illumined ... impress their likeness on the possible intellect" (II, 242).

10. "Intellectus Possibilis"
The *intellectus possibilis,* which, as we have seen, is a potential, is now actualized by the essences or *species intelligibiles impressae* coming from the *intellectus agents* (compare II, 245).

10.1 Knowledge of the Essence
The result of actualizing the *intellectus possibilis* is the comprehension of the knowable. Finally, one can conceive the knowable (the concept of law) by the *intellectus possibilis,* which forms for itself a specific intention of the comprehensible thing.

10.2 Intentionally Oriented
Since "species" (the intellect and the principle of understanding) are in the likeness of objects, it, consequently, follows that for Aquinas, the intellect forms an intention: "Like that thing, since such as a thing is, such are its works. And because the understood intention is like something, it follows that the intellect, by forming such an intention, knows that thing" (I, 189).

The result of knowing is that one reaches a "word" or concept: the intellect brings forth the word. The "intention understood" is nothing other than the word or result of knowing. For instance, Aquinas says:

> Now, I mean by the intention understood, what the intellect conceives in itself of the thing understood. To be sure, in us this is neither the thing which is understood nor is it the very substance of the intellect. But it is a certain likeness of the thing understood conceived in the intellect, and which the exterior words signify. So, the

intention itself is named the "interior word," which is signified by the exterior word (IV, 81. Cf. also IV, 83, 84, 85 and 87).

10.3 Knowledge not yet Apriorised

The above quotation shows that Aquinas did not yet hold the (later) rationalist teaching of an immanent logical object, also emerging from the following:

> In the act of understanding, the intelligible species received into the possible intellect functions as the thing by which one understands, and not as that which is understood, even as the species of color in the eye is not that which is seen but that by which we see. And that which is understood is the very intelligible essence of things existing outside the soul (II, 234).

After all, these very intricate steps in the process of knowing there followed the test of the sum total.

11. Agreement

Aquinas remarks on the word or concept, where he expresses the result of knowing: "the word conceived in the intellect is the image or the exemplar of the substance of the thing understood" (IV, 87).

Here, the *exemplar* which existed *ante rem,* in God, which He created *in re,* into the thing, is now also *post rem* in the knowing mind. Spier aptly summarises it as follows: "All abstraction [in the work of Aquinas] is a deeper reaching down to the form, to the divine idea, realized in the creature. Thus we know the *universalia,* that is *ante rem, in re* and *post rem"* (1959: 101).

11.1 A Likeness of Reality

Therefore, Aquinas uses the well-known word *similitudo here.* He writes: "understanding remains in the one understanding, but it is related to the thing understood because the above mentioned species, which is a principle of intellectual operation as a form, is the likeness of the thing understood" (I, 188). The species "is the likeness of the external thing" (I, 188).

11.2 Correspondence

Understandably, Aquinas maintains the theory of correspondence (agreement: the criterion for the result of knowing), recognizing that the *exemplar*, which is now not only in the thing but also in the mind of the human being, emerging in the following quotation: "the truth of the intellect is 'the adequation of intellect and thing' (*adequatio rei et intellectus)*" (I, 201). Later Aquinas says:

> There is truth in our intellect because it is adequated to the thing that the intellect understands ... the truth of our intellect is measured by the thing outside the soul, since our intellect is said to be true because it is in agreement with the thing that it knows (I, 208).

11.3 Determinative Role of the Doctrine of Exemplars

Aquinas' theory of correspondence boils down to the fact that the *exemplar* or law within the intellect must correspond with the *exemplar* or law outside the intellect.

The *exemplar* also applies to God's knowledge of things. However, the order is reversed: the things should correspond with God's intellect and not his intellect with the things, seeing that the *exemplar* of the things exists from eternity in God's intellect and only later comes into created things. The *exemplar* in human beings does not exist beforehand in their intellect but is initially situated in these things (Compare I, 208).

Tol (2010: 8, 48) rightly describes this classic scholastic in epistemology as the *similarity* or *harmony between* two kinds of rationality, namely, an objective and a subjective. Tol observes:

> One order is that of the 'objective rationality' that holds for the nature of things, as secured in the *ideas* of distinctive being, and the other order is that of 'subjective rationality' in the human being, who attempts to make its *conceptual* understanding more adequate

by increasing the harmony of that conceptual understanding with the objective order.

12. Knowledge by Faith

In the way described above, reason can also reach the knowledge of God since there is a conformity between the *exemplar* of the creature (which is known) and its *exemplar* in God (compare Aquinas' teaching on the *analogia entis* and his participation doctrine as presented in the previous chapter). This knowledge of God is shown in Aquinas' natural theology. The fall into sin did not affect this natural domain (cf. Stinson, 1966). Apart from the reasonable knowledge of sensory things (the domain of nature) to him as a Christian, there is also the knowledge of God's revelation by faith (the domain of grace). (Cf. IIIb, 236, 237; Lais, 1951 and Niede, 1928.) I want to draw attention to his teaching of illumination when it comes to knowledge by faith. In this respect, the Platonising feature of Aquinas' philosophy in the SCG surfaces again.

13. The Value of the Preceding Research

Concluding four chapters on Aquinas (who died almost 740 years ago) and his philosophy, any reader who has read thus far, will be inclined to ask whether this is not merely "raking up the past."

I again refer the reader to the introductory part of the first chapter to answer this. (1.) His philosophy all through the ages had a significant influence on Roman Catholic thinking. (2.) He also influenced Reformed Orthodox theology (from approximately 1550 to 1700) via the Thomism of Suarez and Zaberella. (3.) In the third instance, Thomism influenced eminent Reformed theologians like Bavinck and Kuyper (they hold the same philosophical conception as Aquinas did in the final phase of his development) (cf. Vollenhoven, 200: 257). (4.) In the fourth instance, the philosophy of Aquinas played a particular role even in the origin of a Reformational philosophy towards the thirties of the previous century (cf. Van der Walt, 2014). Vollenhoven (according to Tol, 2010: 75-200) initially also held the kind of scholastic law-idea and epistemology found in Aquinas' work but later dissociated himself from it. However, it would seem as if neither Dooyeweerd nor Stoker were free from the influence of Aquinas and his Thomist followers. (5.) Lastly, this kind of synthesis philosophy is reviving today among Reformed theologians and philosophers, for example, in Radical Orthodoxy.

Therefore, the value of these four chapters is as follows: getting to know Aquinas enables us to comprehensively understand our own Reformed theological and philosophical tradition.

CHAPTER 5
DIVINE PROVIDENCE IN THE PHILOSOPHY OF THE "DOCTOR ANGELICUS"

THOMAS AQUINAS, THE DOCTOR ANGELICUS *(angelic doctor), devoted an exceptionally substantial part of his* Summa Contra Gentiles *(the entirety of Book 3, the most significant part of all four books) to the question of how one should understand God's providence. His ideas in this regard had a remarkable and long-lasting influence on both Catholic and Protestant theologies – the Reformed tradition included. Since this is one of those insoluble, enigmatic, but simultaneously unavoidable, practical problems, it remains a topical issue today. From various theological perspectives, many volumes already dealt with the matter. This chapter, however, aims at revealing the deeper philosophical presuppositions of Aquinas' doctrine of providence. It provides the results of a careful reading of* his Summa Contra Gentiles, regarded as his main philosophical work.

The chapter develops as follows: (1.) As an introduction, Aquinas' ideas about God are reviewed. (2.) The next section explains the fact of God's providence. (3.) The third part investigates how He executes his providence. (4.) Then, the general relationship *of God's providence to humankind is discussed. (5.) The following section focuses on human freedom, prayer, evil and predestination. (6.) The chapter approaches the difficult issue of God's predestination in election and reprobation after more than seven centuries since Aquinas wrote his Summa Contra Gentiles. (7.) The chapter closes with a few conclusions.*

1. Introduction: Topicality, Links, Lay-out and References

AT THE ONSET, IT is necessary to say something about the following: (1.) the lasting topicality through the ages of the subject treated; (2.) the fact that this contribution links up with four previous chapters on the philosophy of Aquinas and spells out the practical implications of his philosophy; (3.) the layout of the investigation, and (4.) the sources used.

1.1 Topicality

The relationship between a deity/God and a human being is a problem as old as mankind itself. It remains a problem in pagan and other non-Christian religions and Christianity up to the present. Therefore, the work of God/a god proves to be an *insoluble* problem and is (at the same time) an *unavoidable* issue. The relationship between God and human beings confronts them possessing the innate compulsion to think about it.

On my bookshelf, my eye falls on, amongst others, the work of Berkouwer (1950), a well-known Reformed dogmatician. The first chapter deals with the crisis in the belief in providence during the middle of the 20th century. Most probably, the situation has not changed much at the beginning of this century.

The famous Medieval Christian philosopher Thomas Aquinas (1224/5-1274) also thought intensely about God's providence. In his reflection, he used the Bible and even Aristotle's philosophy to reach clarity on this issue. It could be worthwhile listening to him.

Christians from the Reformational tradition may think that they cannot learn anything from this theologian-philosopher. Is he not the *doctor Angelicus* of the Roman Catholic Church? He truly is, but one should remember that his ideas also had a far-reaching influence on Reformed theological thinking. It would even seem as if Reformed theologians and philosophers today want to return to Aquinas for guidance via the Reformed Orthodoxy of the sixteenth and seventeenth centuries (cf. Chapter 1). However, Klapwijk (1994: 94) writes on this kind of conservatism and repristination:

> It refuses to investigate contemporary issues and ruminates on its past. Symptoms of such conservatism can be recognized in the reprinting of the 'ancient authors,' in the attention given to the *Synopsis Purioris Theologiae* and the tendency to fall back on Groen van Prinsterer, Kuyper, Schilder, etc. They certainly are worthy of our full attention but do not need a halo or the mantle of a prophet. [Translated from the Dutch.]

1.2 Links

This contribution links up with the four previous chapters. In these, we dealt with Aqunias' synthesis philosophy (between the Scriptures and especially Aristotle), his idea of law, ideas about reality, anthropology and epistemology. This chapter brings us to an application or the implications of the previous chapters. In the light of his whole philosophical system, how does Aquinas see the relationship between God and cosmos and, in particular, the human being?

In the previous chapters, we repeatedly pointed out that Aquinas' idea of law (nomology) plays a central role in his whole complex of ideas. Is it also decisive in the case under consideration?

1.3 Lay-out

Aquinas treats the issue on which we now focus primarily in Book III of his *Summa Contra Gentiles* (Book I deals with God, Book II with creation and Book IV with redemption). In this book, the topic is God's providence (*providentia*) and the human being's responsibility in predestination and reprobation (cf. Chapter 163).

The main lines of this chapter will run as follows: (1.) By way of introduction, we take a brief look at Aquinas' *idea of God* (actually his proofs of God's existence). (2.) Subsequently, we deal with the *fact* of God's providence in general. (3.) A third part will go into how God employs his providence. (4.) Subsequently, what the relation of God's providence in general entails *for a human being*. (5.) Then, the foregoing will be applied to the following four practical problems: human freedom, prayer, evil and predestination (election and reprobation) in their relation to God's providence. (6.) The investigation is taken further with some ideas on how Christians should currently think about the difficult issue of divine predestination in election and reprobation after more than seven centuries. (7.) The chapter is brought to a close with some conclusions and a view of the future.

1.4 References

As we mentioned in the previous chapters, references to secondary sources are kept to a minimum since the author wants to give the word to Aquinas, as expressed in his *Summa Contra Gentiles* (SCG). For the original Latin text, an edition of 1935 was consulted (cf. *S. Thomae Aquinatis,* 1935). The English translation quoted in this chapter is the Doubleday edition (cf. *Thomas Aquinas,* 1955-1957). In the quotes, reference is first made to the specific book of the SCG and then to the page number(s) of this translation (e.g. IV, 160). Since Book III was translated in two parts, these are designated as IIIa or IIIb. While adding new secondary sources, the author brings insights and corrections to previous ones; the author also uses prior (hitherto unpublished) research (cf. Van der Walt, 1968 and 1974).

The fact that the question of God's providence was a burning issue to Aquinas becomes evident from the volume of Book III of the SCG, which is devoted to it in totality. It is the most voluminous of all four books, which deal with God, creation, providence and redemption in that order (in the Doubleday translation Book III covers 546 pages altogether).

Aquinas' idea of God determines his thoughts on God's providence. Thus we cannot confine ourselves to Book III but will begin with Book I, in which his idea of God is explained.

2. Idea of God

As he explains it (in Book I), Aquinas' idea of God is fundamental to understanding his entire theology. We confine ourselves to pointing out just some significant aspects for an understanding of his teaching on providence.

In Book I, Aquinas' idea that God should regard as law clearly emerges. Furthermore, God is intelligent (cf. Chapters 44-59), meaning God's essence also includes his will (cf. Chapters 72-88). His will does not subtract from the freedom of the creatures or impose an absolute necessity on them. To Aquinas, God is also the ultimate good (cf. Chapters 37-41).

2.1 Proofs of God's Existence

Furthermore, we also find (in Book I) Aquinas' proofs of God's existence which are indispensable for understanding his teaching on providence. He gives four proofs of God in Chapter 13 of Book I. These four proofs of God correspond with proofs 1, 2, 4 and 5 of the well-known *quinque viae* of Aquinas' *Summa Theologiae* (Part I, Question 2, Article 3). Of these four proofs in the SCG, Aquinas took over from Aristotle the first three (cf. I, Ch. 13, p. 85-96).

2.2 The Various Substantiations

Aquinas bases his proofs of God on three principles. These principles are *laws of being*, so they are valid for everything that exists, including God. They are: (1.) that there is enough *reason* for existence, (2.) that there is a *cause* for existence and (3.) that the series from which something stems *cannot go on indefinitely.*

The proofs are the following: (1.) the proof from movement, (2.) the proof from cause, (3.) the proof of necessity, (4.) the proof of perfection and (5.) the proof of a final aim. All these proofs follow the same pattern: motion in creation indicates a first (immovable) mover (God); creaturely causes refer to a first (uncaused) cause; imperfection in the cosmos presupposes a perfect being, and so forth (cf. Van der Walt, 1968: 151-153 for particulars).

Aquinas also explicitly concludes at his account of the last proof (cf. I, 96) that there must be a being whose providence rules the world. Aquinas' teaching, in light of the evidence of God's existence, could be summarized as follows: God, being the first *cause* (compare the second proof) and *indispensable* Being (compare the third proof), *draws* all things (compare the first proof). which He created towards Himself as their ultimate *purpose* (compare the fifth proof), so that in Him as the absolute *perfect One* (compare fourth proof), they find their ultimate aim and perfection.

2.3 Comments

According to Aquinas, the following applies to each of these proofs: (1.) starting with sensory experience digested by natural reason; (2.) each proof would end with a being who is accepted as "god" by everyone. (3.) In his natural theology, however, Aquinas does not attempt to prove *what* God is *like* (this is the task of his supernatural or Christian theology), but merely *that* He exists. Yet each proof also contributes to the *contents* of his idea of God, for instance, as the first mover, uncaused cause, cause of perfection, etc.

In the ages following Aquinas, these proofs of God were severely criticized. On my bookshelf, I see all the following sources with one glance: De Vos (1971), Hick (1964), Krüger (1970) and Weischedel (1971 and 1972) (not the right moment to reiterate all the critiques). We, therefore, confine ourselves to some elementary remarks (cf. Venter, 1988: 181).

Where does Aquinas get the idea that God is everything that he deduces from each of his proofs of God? Not from the Bible but Aristotle. The biblical idea of God has been replaced by a heathen idea of a god or blended with it. It does not always emerge so distinctly that one, here, has to do with Aristotle's impersonal deity, directed at himself. However, when Aquinas calls God "absolute" (e.g. the absolute good), this term means that He can have no relationship with something/somebody who has relationships relatively dependent on that with which is in a relationship.

If God is the pinnacle of a continuous hierarchy of being beginning with the observable world, Is He not thereby included in the created world instead of being distinct from it? And if the radical distinction between God and His creation is upheld, are the proofs of Aquinas then still valid, or does he take a clear – but impermissible – leap between the finite and the infinite, the temporary and the eternal?

If one maintains the radical biblical distinction between God and His creation. In that case, it simply is inadmissible to call God a "cause," an "end," and so forth – all of the cosmic phenomena. What, then, are the implications of Aquinas' idea of God for his teaching on providence?

3. Providence as a Fact in General

As said, providence is the theme of Book III. First, God is the ultimate end of everything (Ch. 1-63). Subsequently, God, therefore, is also the Ruler of everything so that He can draw everything to Himself. Aquinas explains this in Chapters 64-163. However, he first deals with God's cosmic rule. He rules every creature (Ch. 64-100), and then with His particular rule, God rules intelligent creatures (i.e. human beings). It is here that Aquinas, due to his philosophy, runs into several problems. If God rules and determines everything by providence, how can one speak of a human being having *freedom?* Do man's *prayers* then have any sense? Is God then also the cause of *evil* or sin?

But we will say more about this below. We first confine ourselves to the *fact* that there is something like God's providence and subsequently *how* it happens or how God wields it.

One could summarize Aquinas' train of thought as follows: God, as the first cause, is also the ultimate end of everything and, therefore, draws everything (both intelligent and natural things) back to Himself as the supreme good, in which they find their absolute perfection and bliss (cf.

Chapter 2, 6.1.1).

3.1 Everything Directed at an End

Aquinas writes the following:

> Each of the things produced through the will of an agent is directed to an end by the agent. For the proper object of the will is the good and the end. As a result, things which proceed from will must be directed to some end. Moreover, each thing achieves its ultimate end through its own action which must be directed to the end by Him who gives things the principles through which they act (IIIa, 31, 32).

Everything acts, consciously or unconsciously, with a view to an end: "it makes no difference whether the being tending to the end is a knowing being or not. For just as the target is the end for the archer, so is it the end for the motion of the arrow" (IIIa, 34). This end idea is typically an Aristotelian idea in the work of Aquinas, which he has reworked on some points only to fit into his synthesis philosophy.

3.2 . Everything Pursues the Good

On this the *doctor Angelicus* writes the following:

> Again, the end is that in which the appetitive inclination of an agent or mover, and of the thing moved, finds its rest. Now, the essential meaning of the good is that it provides a terminus for appetite, since, the good is that which all desire. Therefore, every action and motion are for the sake of a good (IIIa, 38).

The role that the good plays in Aquinas' work is likewise due to Aristotle's philosophy. Therefore, the *Nicomachean Ethics* is quoted in the preceding quotation to support Aquinas' teaching on the good. Aquinas' synthesis "adapted" and identified the God of the Scriptures with the ultimate good.

3.3 Everything Pursues God

God is the ultimate good, so everything pursues Him as its ultimate end

(Ch. 17). However, God is not mentioned as the end in the sense that He did not exist before: "Therefore, God is not the end of things in the sense of being something set up as an ideal, but as a pre-existing being Who is to be attained" (IIIa, 74, 75).

3.4 Creaturely Perfection Means Deification

To pursue God as the ultimate end means to become like God:

> Created things are made like unto God by the fact that they attain to divine goodness. If then, all things tend toward God as an ultimate end, so that they may attain His goodness, it follows that the ultimate end of things is to become like God ... Moreover, all created things are, in a sense, images of the first agent, that is, of God, 'for the agent makes a product to his own likeness.' Now, the function of a perfect image is to represent its prototype by likeness to it; this is why an image is made. Therefore, all things exist in order to attain to the divine likeness, as to their ultimate end (IIIa, 76).

From this quotation, it emerges very clearly how Aquinas' philosophy and, in particular, his idea of law determine his natural theology concerning providence. Again, we here encounter his teaching (cf. Chapter 2) that God creates the things in His image (as a result of the exemplars/laws which exist in Him and which He creates into the things). Furthermore, we also find the idea (cf. Chapter 3) of the creatures' participation in God. Consequently, everything, in turn, strives to attain God. The nearer the creatures come to God in this pursuit, the more perfect – divine – they become.

3.5 God Himself the Mover

As the immovable mover, God Himself sets all things in motion to Himself as the ultimate end: "to rule or govern by providence is simply to move things toward an end through understanding" (IIIa, 210, 211). Once again, we have distinct proof that Aquinas' (natural) theology is determined by his synthesis philosophy, for in His Word, God is not revealed to us as an "immovable mover." However, to Aristotle, God was the immovable who, nevertheless, moves everything.

God moves everything through an act of understanding since, in Book I, Aquinas described God as intellect. Without a doubt, this reminds us of Aristotle's god, whom he regarded as the "intellect of the intellect." However, may a human being reduce God to something cosmic by speaking of his intellect?

3.6 Intellectual Creatures Pursue God Through their Understanding of God

Particular creatures (human beings) also possess an intellectual capacity. The intellect is the form of law that God created into them. Therefore, the fact that creatures have intellect brings them very near to the pure form/law viz. God: "Now, an intellectual creature chiefly becomes like God by the fact that it is intellectual, for it has this sort of likeness over and above what other creatures have, and this likeness includes all others" (IIIa, 99). This is valid of a human being as an intellectual substance: "the human intellect reaches God as its end, through an act of understanding" (IIIa, 99). Elsewhere: "The ultimate end of man is the knowledge of God" (IIIa, 102). And: "the ultimate felicity of man lies in the contemplation of truth" (IIIa, 123).

Is this really what the Bible teaches: an intellectualist union with God or rather childlike faith and obedience to His law?

3.7 Biblicist Eisegesis and Exegesis

To anyone with an elementary knowledge of the Bible, it will be apparent that what Aquinas is teaching here is not derived from God's Word. Then how does he reconcile the Aristotelian idea of god with the biblical concept of God? It becomes evident that his natural theology is not purely reasonable and "neutral" – he also attempts to support it with quotations from the Scriptures.

However, to a Biblicist method of eisegesis and exegesis, one cannot do this in any other way. As proof that God is the ultimate end, Aquinas, for instance, appeals to Proverbs 16:4: "The LORD works out everything for his ends..." and Revelation 22:13: "I am the Alpha and the Omega, the First and the Last, the Beginning and the End" (cf. IIa, 74).

3.8 Comments

We have to state that what the Scriptures here reveal about the end of God with things (Proverbs 16:4) may not be understood according to the Aristotelian teaching of an end as Aquinas does.

Aristotle was a heathen, and his idea of god was a pagan fabrication. As with all false gods (idols), there was no radical difference between his god and the cosmos. Cosmic concepts like cause, end and intellect could, therefore, be made to apply to his god. Furthermore, since there was no radical difference between him and his god, humans could also strive to become like gods. Such mysticism, however, is not biblical (cf. Van der Walt, 2015a, 2015b, 2015c and 2015d.).

If we depart from the Scriptural idea of the radical distinction between God and His creation, a temporary creature can never become eternal, never become like God. In the life hereafter, human beings will still be creatures and thus be "temporal."

A human being can never transgress the law (the impassable "border" between God and his creation) to become one with God mystically. This pagan idea of Aristotle to become like his god was the same sinful thought that caused Adam and Eve's fall in paradise (cf. Genesis 3:5). Therefore the pursuit of a human being may never be to become *like God* but once more to become a *child of God* who obeys the law. Instead of Aquinas' *ontological union* with God, the Bible teaches a *religious relationship* (a covenant) between God and humans.

So when the Scriptures speak about the/an end, one would have to be careful not to explain it in an Aristotelian-Thomist way, which also applies to the exegesis of Romans 11:36: "For from him and through him and to him are all things."

In my opinion, it is not a case that *above* human beings, there is an end by which they are drawn, but instead that God, through the work of His Holy Spirit, inspires people to live a life *here and now* that honours Him.

Being created as a child of God, a human being is destined for an all-inclusive vocation *on earth*. So it is not, as Aristotle claimed, that a human being has a supra-cosmic end to which his life leads. Human beings received the mandate for their lives *at the beginning* (cf. Gen. 1:26; 2:15), and this duty has to be fulfilled *here on earth*. Aquinas, in his word, focuses all attention on *heaven*.

The Word of God presents the new *earth* as our final home but that did not fit very well into his philosophy. Middleton (2014) shows what the Word of God really teaches about a new earth.

The next main point deals with the ways in which God wields His providence.

4. How God Wields His Providence

Having stated the *fact* of God's providence, we now move to *how* Aquinas pictured the rule of God by way of providence which he described: "to rule or govern by providence is simply to move things toward an end through understanding" (IIIa, 210, 211). How does this happen?

4.1 God Sets An Order For Things

Aquinas explains: "to govern things is nothing but to impose order on them" (IIIa, 212). The other way round: "to order the actions of certain things toward their end is to govern them" (IIIa, 213). Aquinas cites texts that call God, King and Ruler to confirm this idea. Aquinas, therefore, rightly sees God as the Law-giver. From what follows, it will become evident that his absolutization of the law and his nomolising of even God (cf. again Chapter 2) prevents him from holding a Scriptural view in this regard.

4.2 God is Omnipresent

Aquinas writes further: "God must be everywhere and in all things" (IIIa, 223); "wherever being is found, the divine presence is also there" (IIIa, 224). However, one should not misunderstand God's omnipresence (e.g. in a pantheist way):

But we must not think that God is everywhere in such a way that He is divided in various areas of place, as if one part of Him were here and another part (t)here. Rather, His entire being is everywhere. For God, as a completely simple being, has no parts... Instead, He is in all things in the fashion of an agent cause (IIIa, 226).

God's omnipresence should, therefore, be understood because He is the "agent cause" (*per modum causae agentis*). Here again, the Aristotelian *causa*-teaching plays a decisive role. God is not only the end cause (causa finalis) but also the working cause (*causa efficiens*).

As textual "evidence" for the omnipresence of God, Aquinas quotes amongst others the following: Jeremiah 23:24: "Can anyone hide in secret places so that I cannot see him? declares the LORD," or, "Do not I fill heaven and earth?' declares the LORD." And Psalm 139:8: "if I go up to the heavens, you are there; if I make my bed in the depths, you are there."

4.3 Comments

The concept of "omnipresence" (like the word "providence") does not occur in the Word of God. It should therefore be treated with caution: it could be of pagan origin.

The background to the teaching of God's omnipresence is that a human being in heathenism was regarded as autonomous and independent – detached from any bond with God. During early synthesis thinking the Christians (who had come to know the Word of God) did, however, realize that a human being can never be seen as autonomous, detached from God. So one way or another, God has to be brought into contact with human beings and thus be declared omnipresent.

In this way, however, God is quickly reduced to something cosmic, for a spatial term, which belongs to created reality, is brought to bear on Him. God is possibly called omnipresent to honour Him, for then He is elevated above the human being who is spatially limited.

However, in this way, one is thinking about God in terms of an earthly concept.

Aquinas' teaching on God's omnipresence is also connected to his dualistic ontology of God's cosmos. Since he knows the Word of God, he cannot detach God (as the transcendent) from His creation (the non-transcendent), for the Word of God teaches that He governs His creation. If Reformed theologians speculate on the transcendence and the immanence of God, it could be revealing that a dualist philosophy is their point of departure (for a recent example, cf. Kruger, 2011).

4.4 Primary and Secondary Causes

Following Aristotle, God executes His providence or rule, employing secondary causes (*causae secundae*). Something of this we already find in Chapter 21, where Aquinas states that things naturally strive to become like God in so far as they are the causes of other things.

Because the human being is also a cause, human beings resemble God, the primary cause. Recourse is taken to 1 Corinthians 3:9: "For we are God's fellow workers" (cf. IIIa, 83). This text, too, is, therefore, explained according to the Aristotelian *causa*-teaching. In Chapter 66, one finds more detail where Aquinas states that everything acts only through divine power. Amongst other things, he says: "Being is the proper product of the primary agent, that is of God; and all things that give being do so because they act by God's power ... the act of being is what secondary agents produce through the power of the primary agent" (IIIa, 219). In Chapter 77, Aquinas spells it out even more clearly that divine providence takes place through two causes (cf. chapter headings). Amongst other things, he says:

> So, He Himself through His wisdom must arrange the orders for all things, even the least; on the other hand, He may execute the small details by means of other lower powers, through which He Himself works, as does a cosmic and higher power through a lower and particular power. It is appropriate, then, that there be inferior agents as executors of divine providence (IIIa, 258, 259).

So there are two (intermediate) causes that (at different levels) carry out God's providence. According to Aquinas, God's providence concerns *all* creatures. He likes using the image mentioned above of the archer and the arrow. The archer intentionally aims his arrow at the target, but the arrow itself, albeit unintentionally, is also aimed at the target (cf. e.g. IIIa, 211).

4.5 God Rules By Means of Intellectual Creatures

Furthermore, it is understandable that God would exercise His providence through intentional, intellectual creatures as secondary causes (cf. Chapter 78), being possible due to a hierarchically constructed creation. The higher intellectual creatures are, the better equipped to be of service in God's rule because:

> An ability to establish order which is done by cognitive power, and an ability to execute it which is done by operative power, are both required for providence, and rational creatures share in both types of power, while the rest of creatures have operative powers only. Therefore, all other creatures are ruled by means of rational creatures under divine providence (IIIa, 261).

The intellectualism of Aquinas (cf. previous chapters) distinctly surfaces here. Not the will, but the intellect ultimately rules.

4.6 The Higher Ones Rule The Lower Ones

Aquinas' hierarchy of being also determines his teaching on providence when he writes: "in regard to the execution, He orders the lower things through the higher ones, and the bodily things through the spiritual ones" (III, 278). Elsewhere:

> Indeed, those who excel in understanding naturally gain control, whereas those who have defective understanding, but a strong body, seem to be naturally fitted for service, as Aristotle says in his *Politics*. The view of Solomon is also in accord with this, for he says: 'The fool shall serve the wise' (Prov. 11:29); and again: 'Provide out of all the people wise men ... who may judge the people at all times' (Exod. 18: 21-22) (IIIa, 273).

These words of Aquinas once again give clear proof of who speaks the final word in his teaching on providence: Aristotle does not concur with

Solomon, but Solomon's words are quoted because they are supposed to conform with the heathen philosophy of Aristotle. Thus God's rules are hierarchically from above to below: God, angels, heavenly bodies, human beings, animals, plants, and matter. The first four are all intellectual creatures, according to Aquinas.

4.7 Why Specifically by Intellectual Creatures?
The question now has to be answered why God rules the lower things through the intellectual creatures. The answer is quite interesting. Once again, it is connected to Aquinas' idea of law.

God, as already mentioned, exercises his providence by imposing order on things. God is pure form (essence/law). Therefore, Aquinas can say: "the first rational principle of divine providence is simply the divine goodness" (IIIb, 70). However, it has already become evident that apart from God being pure form (essence), the things (except for matter) also have forms derived from God. And these forms in things have a nomothetic character. Therefore, this solves Aquinas' problem completely. By employing the forms/laws in Himself and things, God can wield his providential rule, as evident from the following citation:

> Now, it is obvious that intellectual power is more cosmic than any operative power, for the intellectual power contains cosmic forms, while each power is operative only because of some form proper to the agent. Therefore, all other creatures must be moved and regulated by means of intellectual powers (IIIa, 262).

4.8 God's Rational Plan
Of course, a rational plan would be appropriate (cf. IIIa, 260, 261). Aquinas deals extensively with this *divinae providentiae ratio* in Chapter 97. The "rational plan" (from the Latin *ratio*) is nothing but the forms (laws), which God created into the things and which enable Him to rule them so that they can be aimed at Him as the ultimate end. Therefore, the foundation of Aquinas' teaching on providence is his particular law-idea (an absolutization of the law). Once more, it is evident that his (natural) theology

is determined by the philosophical angle from which he writes.

This idea of a predetermined rational plan in God's intellect would play an enormous role through all the ages of scholastic thinking, even among Orthodox Reformed theologians, who labelled terms differently (e.g. God's "eternal counsel" or "decree" according to which He is believed to have elected or rejected people since eternity). More disconcerting is that God, as Aristotle taught, is supposed to be immovable and cannot change his own "rational plan." On closer analysis, He is captive, subject to His counsel!

4.9 God Subjected to His Own Plan
A previous chapter pointed out how God is nomolised or subject to His law. For God and law is one – God is pure form, surfacing again in what Aquinas teaches on providence when (in Chapter 98); he states that God cannot act outside His providential plan. Thus God (as the Law-giver) does not stand "above" His law but is subject to His law.

4.10 Conclusion
Aquinas works with a nomolised god. His view of a nomolised cosmos prevents him from seeing the *religious* relationship between God and cosmos correctly but regards it as an *ontological* relationship.

However, if the *distinction* between God, law and cosmos is recognized, the covenantal *relationship* between God and creation can also be seen in the right way. Then it is clear that God, according to His law, rules the creation which is subject to it. God does not need intermediate, secondary causes to make His laws applicable. Neither is He subject to His own law/counsel. After this account of Aquinas' teaching on providence in general, we can subsequently deal with God's providence about human beings.

5. The Providence of God in Relation to The Human Being
First, we look at the issue which here confronts Aquinas and then at his "solution."

5.1 The Issue

As mentioned already, all secondary agents act through the power of the primary agent, namely God (cf. IIIa, 219). Texts from the Scriptures, like Isaiah 26:12, John 15:5, Philippians 2:13 (cf. IIIa, 222) and Proverbs 21:1 (cf. IIIb, 35), evidence that God does everything. However, this confronts Aquinas with several problems: "If God does everything through his power, does the creature then actually do nothing? Aquinas states the problem as follows: "if God produces the entire effect, then nothing is left of the effect for the natural agent to produce" (IIIa, 235).

Elsewhere he formulates the problem as follows:

> It may be made clearer that nothing escapes divine providence; also that the order of divine providence cannot possibly be changed; and yet that it is not necessary for all things to happen of necessity simply because they come about as a result of divine providence (IIIb, 53).

Please note that Aquinas states explicitly that God's providential plan is unchangeable (like God Himself). Thus God becomes his own prisoner, and His rational plan leads to a markedly deterministic view. How does Aquinas try to escape from his own philosophical net?

5.2 Aquinas' Solution to The Problem

In my opinion, he suggests several unsatisfactory solutions. For instance, he says that a distinction should be made between acts and the power by which it acts. A natural thing does act, but not without the power of God (cf. IIIa, 236). Aquinas adds further:

> It is also apparent that the same effect is not attributed to a natural cause and to divine power in such a way that it is partly done by God, and partly by the natural agent; rather, it is wholly done by both, according to a different way, just as the same effect is wholly attributed to the instrument and also wholly to the principal agent (IIIa, 237).

Later on, he attempts to solve the issue by accepting two kinds of causes:

> God, Who is the governor of the cosmos, intends some of His effects to be established by way of necessity, and others contingently. On this basis, He adapts different causes to them; for one group of effects there are necessary causes, but for another contingent causes. So, it falls under the order of divine providence not only that this effect is to be, but also that this effect is to be contingently, while another is to be necessarily. Because of this, some of the things that are subject to providence are necessary, whereas others are contingent and not at all necessary (IIIb, 56).

Aquinas attempts to talk himself out of the problem with his distinction between deterministic ("necessary") causes and indeterministic ("contingent") causes (for more on this, see Gevaert, 1965). Apart from remarking that it may be an all too easy circumvention of the issue, several questions present themselves here. For instance, whether causes as such, according to Aquinas, are not of a necessary character. So then, what are non-necessary causes? Furthermore, it is hard to comprehend how these two kinds of causes – which contradict each other – can both be upheld.

To Aquinas, the issue regarding the providence of God, related to the human being, as already stated, in general terms, presents itself in diverse forms. I want to mention only a few to point out how several unnecessary problems arise in his thinking due to his philosophical point of departure, which cannot be derived from the Scriptures. Due to his synthesis philosophy, Aquinas did not hold to a sound biblical idea of God nor a sound view of human beings. He could not possibly have a correct view of the relationship between God and human beings either. It is illustrated now with how he viewed the relation between God's providence and human (1.) freedom, (2.) prayer, (3.) evil, (4.) predestination, election and reprobation.

6. *Divine Providence and Human Freedom*
We will be dealing here with (1.) freedom of will, (2.) the freedom of choice, (3.) contingency and (4.) divine sovereignty (cf. also Vorster, 1965)

6.1 Freedom of Will

Aquinas borrowed his view of freedom from Aristotle: "that is free which is for its own sake according to the Philosopher in the beginning of the *Metaphysics*" (I, 271). This freedom is closely linked with the will so that Aquinas mostly speaks about freedom of will:

> Furthermore, 'that is free which is for its own sake,' and thus the free has the nature of that which is through itself. Now, first and primarily, will has liberty in acting, for according as someone acts voluntarily he is said to perform any given act freely (I, 241, 242).

As one who believes the Scriptures, it is noteworthy that Aquinas does not query the Aristotelian idea that freedom would mean existing *for one's own sake* – a completely unbiblical idea.

6.2 Freedom as The Freedom of Choice

The freedom of the will consists in his freedom of choice. To Aquinas, freedom is the freedom of choice. In other words, freedom is choosing from different options: "Free choice is said in relation to the things that one wills, not of necessity, but of his own accord. Thus, there is in us free choice in relation to our willing to run or to walk" (I, 270).

I would question Aquinas' view that freedom is the same as freedom of choice – at least when it comes to human religious freedom. Of course, I can choose whether I want to walk or run. But profound, religious freedom does not consist in my choice for or against God but is the very consequence of my desiring nothing but to obey His commandments.

According to Aquinas, only human beings possess the freedom of choice: "But on this account is man said to have free choice as opposed to the other animals because he is inclined to willing by judgement of the reason, and not by the impulse of nature as are the brutes" (I, 270). In this statement, what emerges once more is, amongst other things, the intellectualism of Aquinas under the influence of Aristotle: the intellect or human reason not only demands a freedom of choice but even guarantees that what is chosen will be good or right.

Sometimes Aquinas quotes Aristotle's definition of freedom in a slightly different way. Instead of "that is free which is for its own *sake*" it is quoted (from the same place in the *Metaphysics*) as: "the free is that which is its own *cause*" (II, 144).

Does Aquinas contradict himself here, or do I misunderstand him? For on the preceding pages, he taught that God as the primary cause governs everything. Now a human being is his own cause. Does not this sound rather like unbiblical human autonomy?

6.3 Freedom of Will and Contingency

Aquinas' "solution" is to connect the will with the doctrine of causality. Since the will is a *contingent* cause (cf. 5.2 above), freedom of will is possible for a human being:

> Now, the fact that the will is a contingent cause arises from its perfection, for it does not have power limited to one outcome but rather has the ability to produce this effect or that; for which reason it is contingent in regard to either one or the other. Therefore, it is more pertinent to divine providence to preserve liberty of will than contingency in natural causes (IIIa, 244, 245).

Several authors have written books before and after Aquinas (cf., e.g. Vorster, 1965) on freedom of choice, conducting lively debates on the nature of the will. One gets the impression that Aquinas wavered between determinism on the one hand and indeterminism on the other. His contemporaries had already accused him of a deterministic idea of God. Gevaert, for instance, (1965: 48, 49) writes the following on Aquinas' view of freedom:

> Freedom means the absence of determinism, not being determined, no fixed finality that was determined in advance by nature and is already written in her dynamic development. Positively seen, freedom means: self-determination regarding a particular good. A human being himself is the cause of his determination. Thomas often expresses this with a maxim from Aristotle: *liberum est quod sui causa est*. [Translated from the Dutch.]

6.4 Comments

On the one hand, Aquinas' deterministically coloured idea of God is unbiblical. On the other hand, his viewpoint, namely "the free man is he who acts for his own sake" (IIIb, 115), which he inherited from Aristotle, is far removed from what the Scriptures teach on human freedom. It could imply arbitrariness and lawlessness. According to the Scriptures, one should not act for his interest but in a way that honours God, in subordination to God's law. Then only will one be truly free.

Nor does freedom mean, according to the Scriptures, that one is not subject to "necessary causes" but to "contingent causes." Freedom has nothing to do with Aristotle's doctrine of causality. It means (on the negative side) to be released from sin and (on the positive side) again to be able to obey the law of God. The latter is only possible by the deliverance worked by Christ and under the guidance of the Holy Spirit. God's law indicates the direction of a human being's answer to his deliverance and new responsibility. Being free from sin to obey the law of God applies to both the central law of love and the different modal laws.

However, by "freedom to obey," I do not mean the same as the traditional "freedom *in bondage.*" For then, the age-old problem of determinism or indeterminism has not been overcome yet. Freedom would then be seen (deterministically) as bondage to the law. However, freedom does not consist of mere *bondage* to the law but *obedience* to the law.

Of course, God's law never becomes invalid. However, it can be obeyed or disobeyed. And obedience is only possible when a human being has been delivered from sin.

Therefore, freedom is not the ability to choose *either*, as Aquinas claims; this does not mean there is no such thing as the ability to choose. However, I would prefer to regard a human being's ability to choose as limited in choosing between walking and running. In man's (religious) relationship with God, one cannot consider freedom of choice. God firstly chooses a human being. It is not the human being that chooses God. All human beings can do, is to *respond*, either positively or negatively.

6.5 Human Freedom and Divine Sovereignty

It stands to reason that Aquinas could not combine his teaching on human freedom (which was coloured by the influence of Aristotle) with the sovereignty of the true God. In particular, he wrestles with the question of whether the providence of God excludes the human beings' freedom (of will) in a deterministic manner: "it would evidently be against the character of providence for all things to happen out of necessity. Therefore, divine providence does not impose necessity on things by entirely excluding contingency from things" (IIIa, 244).

Here again, we encounter Aquinas' earlier problematic distinction between the "necessary" (on God's side) and the "contingent" (on the side of human beings).

Because Aquinas did not acknowledge the radical distinction between God and human beings, and therefore cannot distinguish between a choice that is possible for human beings regarding created things but impossible regarding God, he has problems with the grace of God. Due to his synthesis philosophy, he is wavering all the time.

On the one hand, he teaches that a human being cannot attain his ultimate end without the help of God (cf. Ch. 147). His freedom of choice is not sufficient: "free choice is not sufficient without the external help of God" (IIIb, 253). Aquinas quoted several texts, which put all the emphasis on the work of God in the human being. For instance, he refers to John 6:44 and John 15:4 (cf. IIIb, 225), 2 Corinthians 5:14 (cf. IIIb, 226), Titus 3:5, Romans 9:16 and Lamentations 5:21 (cf. IIIb, 229).

For this reason, Aquinas also rejects the Pelagian view, which holds that a human being is redeemed purely from his own free will (cf. IIIb, 225). Aquinas opposes the Pelagians in several instances, particularly regarding their view of the will (cf., e.g. III, Ch. 14, 149, 155, 159 and 160).

On the other hand, Aquinas maintains that God does not force His grace on man – for a human being's freedom and ability of choice may not be destroyed: "God does not force us by His help to act rightly ... forced acts are not acts of virtues, since the main thing in virtue is choice " (IIIb,

227).

Despite his reprobation of the Pelagian point of view, Aquinas owes his great emphasis on man's freedom of will and ability to choose on that which is not distant from the Pelagians. Therefore, Reformed scholars often characterize Aquinas' viewpoint in the SCG as semi-Pelagian.

Aquinas was an *intellectualist* philosopher, while the thinking of Pelagians was *voluntarist*. According to Aquinas, the will acts based on the guidance from the intellect (following this viewpoint, one could say that wickedness stems from ignorance). This intellectualist tendency was also characteristic of the later Reformed Orthodoxy or Scholasticism, emphasizing the purity of doctrine in church and theology. The voluntarists (derived from Latin *voluntas* = will) held the exact opposite point of view, viz. that the will guides the intellect.

6.6 Comments

The hierarchical ontology of Aquinas prevents him from truly finding a solution to the issue under discussion. For according to him, God and the human being are parts of one being. And even if one considers God as much more significant than a human being – even ten thousand times greater – He (the transcendent One) remains a part of the same pyramid of being.

According to Aquinas' view, one can regard God and human beings either as rivals or as fellow workers – while neither of these viewpoints solves the problem. For instance, as rivals: God does everything, and therefore a human being can do nothing. Or the human being does everything, and, therefore, God can do nothing. Or, as fellow workers, God does the one half and the human being the other half. Likewise, the following effort to reach a balance does not hold good: God does everything, and the human being does everything, or God's work encompasses the work of human beings.

Aquinas' synthesis with the pagan ideas of Aristotle prevented him from reaching a Scriptural view of the relationship between God and man. The relationship between God and man is not that between a Primary and secondary cause. (God is not a cause – a cause is something of a cosmic nature.) The work of God and human beings cannot be compared. Provided one departs from the *radical* (instead of merely a *relative*) distinction between God and a human being, we as human beings still cannot fathom this problem. Still, at least we are prevented from searching for answers to false problems.

6.7 Determinism

Simultaneously we have to clear up a misunderstanding about Aquinas. Often it was claimed, from a Reformed angle, that Aquinas advocated the autonomy (being one's own law) or independence of the human being's natural abilities from God. But according to Aquinas, even before the fall, the human being could not by himself attain anything entirely without God who formed him, actualized him, and extended grace to him.

The most significant hazard in the work of Aquinas was not that he accepted a fully autonomous human being but rather that he leaned over to the other side too much. It seems as if God, by His eternal knowledge and the causal chain of being, controls the whole of creation to such an extent that no room is left for human responsibility despite what Aquinas says on free will.

Therefore, the protest of his contemporaries and later generations was not that Aquinas supposed man to be partly independent of God, but rather that he arrived at philosophical-theological determinism (cf. Venter, 1985: 100). For instance, the later Roman Catholic philosopher Suarez (1548-1617) rejects Aquinas' determinism and instead claims that God knows from eternity what the individual will choose and then by His grace intervenes to prevent human choices deviating from it.

How did Aquinas attempt to solve the second issue, namely that of divine providence and prayer?

7. Providence and Prayer

Some people assert that prayers avail nothing since God in His providence is immutable. Others claim that human prayers can change the providence of God. Of course, Aquinas could accept neither of these.

One has the same – futile – discrepancy between the omnipotence of God and the capability of human beings because they are placed on virtually the same level, and both are nomolised within a hierarchy of being.

7.1 Aquinas' Problem

In this light, Aquinas also read the Word of God. But the Scriptures can offer no final solution, for it is no use searching for solutions to false problems in the Holy Scriptures. Aquinas finds texts proclaiming both God's "changeability" (e.g. Is. 38:1-5 and Jer. 18:7-8 – cf. IIIb, 65) and his "unchangeability" (e.g. Num. 23:19, 1 Sam. 15:29 and Mal. 3:6 – cf. IIIb, 64). The error, however, lies in the fact that Aquinas reads these texts according to a philosophy that does not recognize the clear ontic distinction between God and man and their religious relationship.

7.2 Aquinas' Solution

Aquinas' solution in this case too, as we found – and rejected – before, is that the providence of God *already includes or encompasses* human prayers: "In this way, then, prayers are efficacious before God, yet they do not destroy the immutable order of divine providence, because this individual request that is granted to a certain petitioner falls under the order of divine providence" (IIIb, 62).

Later on, Aquinas distinguishes between a so-called universal and particular order in the providence of God intending to solve the problem. Prayers retain their power, not because they *change* the cosmic order but they are *part* of the cosmic order. Therefore, prayers keep their power; they cannot change the order of eternal control but rather they exist under such order. But nothing prevents some particular order, due to an inferior cause, from being changed through the efficacy of prayers. God transcends all causes (IIIb, 65) under His operation.

7.3 Comments

Aquinas' partial universalism is intimated here. But once again, the question confronts one: Is this distinction (between universal-individual) not too simple an evasion? The critical issue, namely the relationship between the two (the universal individual), remains unsolved.

The solution supplied by Aquinas, that the providence of God encompasses a human being's responsibility and his prayers – schematically represented by a circle with a point in the middle, is still supported by many Reformed people. It is, however, unacceptable. It finally amounts to a human being simply praying what God wants him to pray.

Interestingly, Aquinas is not at peace with texts speaking of God's changeability, repentance, wrath, etcetera. He stated that these should be understood metaphorically or figuratively (cf. IIIb, 66). Behind this lies again Aristotle's deterministic idea of God, namely God as the immutable (cf. Den Ottolander, 1965).

However, the wrath of God on sin and human repentance (when people are converted) may not be understood figuratively as understood biblically. It should be taken literally – otherwise, "our only comfort in life and death" becomes invalid. The next problem Aquinas struggled with was providence and evil.

8. Providence and Evil

According to his Aristotelian doctrine of causality, if Aquinas could say "God alone directly works on the choice made by man" (IIIb, 42), or "... man does choose in all cases the object in accord with God's operation within his will" (IIIb, 44), does it not imply that human choice and decisions are in any case not free or are determined by God? And that God, therefore, is also the Author of evil?

We will deal with the following four facets of Aquinas'- view of evil: (1.) It is something coincidental. (2.) A lack of the good. (3.) Negatively linked with the good. (4.) Both God and human beings are responsible for it.

8.1 Evil is Something Accidental

In Book II, the problem of evil confronted Aquinas (*malum*) (cf. Ch. 41). He says that God, as the ultimate good, can only be the cause of the good. Only in His *effects* can there originate accidental evil: "the first principle of all things is the one first good, in whose effects evil results accidentally" (II, 123).

Note how Aquinas once again takes refuge in the contingent or coincidental to end up in determinism (the questions I previously raised in this respect, therefore, still stand). Aquinas explained difficult texts like Isaiah 45:7 and Amos 3:6 as follows:

> Now, God is said to make or create evils, so far as He creates things which in themselves are good, yet are injurious to others; the wolf, though in its own kind a good of nature, is nevertheless evil to the sheep; so, too, is fire in relation to water, being dissolutive of the latter. He is said to create evils when He uses created things, which in themselves are good, to punish us for our evil doings (II, 123).

However, Aquinas could not stick to such a viewpoint. After standing by his idea that everything acts with a view to the good as their end, in Book III, in connection with his teaching on providence, the question nevertheless arises: but what about evil? His answer once more is that evil is not the *intention* of the one who acts – it is *accidental* (cf. III, Ch. 4):

> So, if this object is not good but bad, this will be apart from his intention. Therefore, an intelligent agent does not produce an evil result, unless it be apart from his intention. Since to tend to the good is common to the intelligent agent and to the agent that acts by natural instinct, evil does not result from the intention of any agent, except apart from the intention (IIIa, 42, 43).

Note how the intellectualism of Aquinas transpires again in this quotation. An intelligent being automatically pursues the good.

8.2 Evil is a Lack of the Good

Therefore, to Aquinas, evil is nothing more than an accidental shortcoming or defect. He further distinguishes between evil in a qualified sense. If, for instance, one has some or other defect, like not having two hands, and evil, in an unqualified sense, when there is a defect in the action itself (cf. IIIa, 44), the following is his concise summary definition of evil: "... evil is simply a privation of something which a subject is entitled by its origin to possess and which it ought to have, as we have said. Such is the meaning of the word "evil among all men" (IIIa, 48). Or still more concise: "Evil is the privation of good" (IIIa, 52).

But then the good must be the cause of the evil (cf. Ch. 10) – although Aquinas immediately sets a limit: "it is clear, both in the natural order and in the moral order, that evil is caused by good accidentally" (IIIa, 61). Clearly, Aquinas must have had in mind a relative (cosmic) good here; otherwise, God Himself (the Absolute Good) in the end again becomes the Cause of the evil.

8.3 Evil is Connected to the Good in a Negative Way

The following (third) step in Aquinas' argument is that evil is dependent on the good in a negative way – the good becomes the basis for the evil (cf. Ch. 11). The Bible does teach that evil (as the negative or opposite) can only sponge on the good, but this is not what Aquinas has in mind. He argues as follows: When evil is destroyed, the possibility for good to exist also comes to an end: "there must always continue to be a subject for evil, if evil is to endure" (IIIa, 63).

8.4 Comments

However, this view of evil differs entirely from that which the Word of God teaches. Within the confines of this chapter, it cannot be spelled out— compare, for instance, the reflections in (Berkouwer, 1958 and 1960). Berkouwer makes a few remarks, which boil down to the conclusion that the teaching of Aquinas has to be rejected. (1.) Evil is not something *accidental*. It was the result of a *deliberate* choice by Adam and Eve. (2.) Neither is it a (coincidental) *shortcoming*, but *rebellion* against God and

His law. (3.) Nor is it *essential for the good* but the opposite thereof. (4.) It has nothing to do with *causes and effects* but indicates the wrong *religious direction in* the life of a human being.

Evil arises, according to the Word of God, when a human being as subject to the law disobeys the law of God. At creation, everything was good, but as a consequence of the sin of human beings (disobedience to the law of God), evil entered creation. Christ redeems us so that we can once more do good, that is, obey the law of God. Evil, therefore, is not something applicable to God or His law, but only to human beings and the rest of creation, which has to suffer due to man's disobedience.

Since good and evil are bound up with the *religious direction* of one's life, it also permeates everything – including one's own heart – and cannot be localized in certain areas. Evil, therefore, is not merely a shortcoming or lack of good but something much more severe. Evil became possible because of sin (a wrong *direction*). Consequently, all kinds of *structural* shortcomings exist in the creature, illness and death being two examples.

The good is the radically *opposite* direction of evil. One evil in *itself* produces another. Behind it all lies the evil power of Satan. In his attempt to prevent God from being implicated as the cause of evil in the final instance, Aquinas even claims the opposite: good would not have existed if there was no evil. The good becomes dependent on evil. It seems that to Aquinas, there is a kind of dialectic relationship of dependence between good and evil.

That Aquinas at least wants to think in a consistently logical manner transpires from the next step.

8.5 The Cause of Evil Lies with Both the Secondary and the Primary Cause (God)

First, Aquinas again emphasizes that evil (as a defect) lies with the secondary causes: "so, it is possible in the case of things made and governed by God, for some defect and evil to be found, because of a defect of the secondary agents, even though there be no defect in God Himself" (IIIa, 238).

However, suppose he intends to think consistently. In that case, evil cannot be ascribed solely to secondary causes: "it is evident that bad actions, according as they are defective, are not from God but from defective proximate causes; but, in so far as they possess something of action and entity, they must be from God" (IIIa, 241).

Attempting to justify God as the cause of evil, Aquinas again says that many good things in creation would not have been there if there were no evil (For more arguments by Aquinas, cf. Venter, 1985: 96-97 and 1988: 172-173).

For instance, there would have been no patience in good people unless there was evil in the bad; there would have been no room for justice unless there was injustice; one would not have valued one's health unless one knew illness (cf. IIIa, 239, 240). His conclusion is: "Therefore, it is not the function of divine providence totally to exclude evils from things" (IIIa, 240). As "proof," he cites two texts: Isaiah 45:7: "I form the light and create darkness, I bring prosperity and create disaster; I, the LORD, do all these things" and Amos 3:6: "When disaster comes to a city, has not the LORD caused it?"

Later on, towards the end of Book III, Aquinas once more touches on the issue of evil (cf. Ch. 162). He quotes more texts which give the impression that God is the cause of sin (amongst others Exodus 10:1, Isaiah 63:17 and Romans 1:28). However, it seems as if Aquinas here draws back from the consequences of his deterministic viewpoint, for he says about these texts: "All these texts are to be understood in this way: God does not grant to some people his help in avoiding sin, while to others he does grant it" (IIIb, 266).

Aquinas attempts to argue simultaneously that evil does not come from God but that God's providence does not exclude evil altogether. God does not exclude it because evil is necessary for a variety of reasons. However, it does not originate from God but the creatures themselves.

Venter (1988: 174) rightly asks: "If evil is a necessary element of the creational order which was planned by God, made by Him and is ruled by Him, is not God then nevertheless the cause of the evil?"

8.6 Comments

Like Aristotle, Aquinas mistakenly calls God a cause and, thereby, reduces Him to something created. This whole issue flows on whether God is also is the cause, origin, or author of sin.

Therefore, Aquinas' problem here originates from his wrong idea of God. *On the one hand*, as a Christian, he wanted to acknowledge the God of the Scriptures. *On the other hand*, his attempt was thwarted and obscured by a pagan, Aristotelian idea of God. However, these two ideas are in direct conflict with each other. Despite his attempts to reconcile them, he does not succeed in doing so. Synthesis philosophy is always a *cul de sac*.

So how should we understand texts like Isaiah 45:7 and Amos 3:6? Currently, several biblical scholars accept that these words denote God's *judgement and punishment* and not that He *brings about sin*. The question about the *origin* of sin will, however, remain inexplicable. Even with the aid of Aristotle's doctrine of causality, Aquinas could not fathom it.

We have now reached the very last and probably most difficult of all the problems.

9. Predestination, Election and Reprobation

It is noteworthy that Aquinas only comes to God's election and reprobation in the last chapter (163) of Book III of the SCG, which deals with God's providence. Moreover, he deals with it very concisely – in only two pages (for more detail on this comparison, see the works by Friethoff, 1925 and Polman, 1936). But what he says in these two pages would have a decisive influence on Catholic and Protestant – even Reformed scholars – in the ages to follow. Therefore, in predestination and reprobation, the relationship between God and man reaches a climax. It concerns man's eternal weal and woe.

9.1 Predestination as An Eternal, Divine Decree

Aquinas had already pointed out that some people reach their ultimate aim due to God's gracious work, while others, who do not receive divine help, miss their ultimate aim. He then resumes:

> And since all things done by God are foreseen and ordered from eternity by His wisdom ... the aforementioned differentiation of men must be ordered by God from eternity, so that they are directed to their ultimate end... On the other hand, those whom He has decided from eternity not to give His grace, He is said to have reprobated or to have hated (IIIb, 267).

In the case of the elected, Aquinas quotes the well-known Ephesians 1: 4-5, and in the case of the rejected, he refers to Malachi 1: 2-3. Predestination, election and reprobation, therefore, to him, form part of God's providence.

9.2 *Further Explanation*

To this, Aquinas adds the following: (1.) the will and providence of God is the first but also the last cause of election and reprobation – one cannot look for more profound reasons "behind" this Cause. (2.) The Cause for election does not lie in human merit but solely in the grace of God. (3.) Probably for fear of divine determinism and human passivity, he reiterates: "it is possible to show that predestination and election impose no necessity by the same reasoning whereby we showed above (Chapter 72) that providence does not take away contingency from things" (IIIb, 267).

9.3 *Comments*

Once more, in the philosophy of Aquinas, one runs up against the dialectics between necessity and contingence or coincidence. This tension is not only between God and man but penetrates even Aquinas' idea of God. *On the one hand*, He determines everything from eternity and on *the other hand*, He still allows for coincidence. Are the two sides logically reconcilable? Is coincidence a biblical idea?

It should be noted in particular that Aquinas (in IIIb, 267 above) no less than three times reiterates that God determined election and reprobation *from eternity;* this is the main idea. However, the possible contingency or coincidence was necessary to prevent God from being regarded as the origin of evil.

Thus it would seem as if Aquinas' contemporaries were correct when they concluded that Aquinas' philosophy, despite all the intricate arguments to the opposite, could not conceal his deterministic idea of God.

9.4 The Historical Line Continued

Unfortunately, this deterministic trend carried forward into the Reformational tradition as well. We again encounter the doctrine of causality in Calvin (cf. his *Institutes*, Book 3, Chapter 14, par. 17 and 21). Aquinas' Scholasticism is even more pronounced in the work of his successor in Genèva, Beza. He accepted the Aristotelian ontology, doctrine of causality and logic as a "gift" from God and applied it to his doctrine of predestination as an eternal decree from a God who determines everything. This train of thought runs right through the whole of Reformed Orthodoxy (1550-1700), is present at the Synod of Dordt (1618-1619) and lives to this day with some Reformed people (cf. Chapter 1). Of course, there also were internal differences, for instance, between the superalapsarians and the infralapsarians.

The former group taught that God had already decided *before* the fall of man those He would elect and whom He would reject. The latter viewpoint could only mitigate such extreme determinism, teaching that God took his decision only *after* the fall. However, both groups uphold Aquinas' view of an eternal, unchangeable divine decision or decree to a greater or lesser extent.

Due to the idea that theology could study God (and His thoughts), which is nothing but speculation, God's providence and predestination became an *intellectual issue* instead of a *comfort accepted in profound faith*. This confusion between childlike faith and rational theology and the resulting overrating of theology above faith caused immense misery right through church history since Aquinas' day.

10. Conclusion
Finally, I draw the following conclusions from the investigation of this chapter.

10.1 The Hazard of Synthesis Philosophy
Firstly, synthesis philosophy decisively influences theological reflection; this was the outcome of this investigation.

10.2 The Hazard of Determinism
Secondly, despite many differences, one outstanding feature of this type of philosophy (and theology) repeatedly emerged in its deterministic character. Both God (by His own law) and human beings (by the divine law in them) are predestined, even regarding their own salvation. God, therefore, is immovable, immutable and in the (predestined) human being. Things like a sense of guilt and responsibility, which are realities, are inexplicable.

10.3 The Law-Idea as The Root Cause – Some Historical Glimpses
Thirdly, it became clear that "behind" this determinism lurks a particular idea of law. Both the "law" (*nomos*) and the "idea" are essential here.

Plato already viewed the ideas as a separate world of its own, serving as examples for humans in the visible world. The Neo-Platonism of Augustine shifted these ideas as blueprints for creation to God's intellect. Furthermore, Aquinas taught that God created these archetypes into creaturely things and rules and controls them accordingly.

As a result, the long history of the idea as a kind of guideline was not yet complete. During the period of rationalism (approximately 1600-1900), the idea still lived that (rational) ideas could govern the world; a new world could, thus, be created. However, a significant difference occurred with the Church Fathers and Medieval scholars of the preceding Christian synthesis philosophy. To the rationalists, the rational ideas no longer lie in God but the reason of human beings. It is no longer God's reason under discussion, but human reason is viewed as god. Unlike in Medieval (and afterwards in scholastic) thinking, when the ideas ruled because they were

God's ideas, reason had now become a god because its ideas ruled. However, the irrationalist schools of the modern world (e.g. "Lebensphilosophie," pragmatism and existentialism) gradually ousted reason. But these irrational schools did not entirely discard reason as it remained a practical necessity – ideas remain important. Current postmodernism continues this tendency.

10.4 A Felicitous Reversal

The *fourth* and last outcome of this chapter is the following discovery. Due to several factors, which include more accurate exegesis of the biblical message, since about the middle of the previous century, a reaction started against the determinism of Aquinas and his followers.

Since an erroneous view of divine sovereignty and human responsibility had such unpleasant consequences, especially in theology and the church, I will confine myself to this discipline and Reformed theology alone. Limited space only permits me to put the reader on the tracks of some sources (cf. also Van der Walt, 2011a, 2011b, 2011c, 2012a and 2012b.).

In Berkhouwer's well-known series *Dogmatische Studien* (Dogmatic studies), *De verkiezing Gods* appeared (*The election of God* in 1955). He raises serious questions about a deterministic doctrine of predestination. Holwerda (1958) later offered a new explanation of the expression "before the creation of the world" (in Ephesians 1:4), which questions an eternal, unchangeable divine decree. Spykman (1981) made a significant contribution to a new view of election and reprobation. Sinnema (1985), with his doctoral thesis and many other articles on Reformed scholastic thinking, made even more valuable contributions. Velema (1992) offers surprising new insights. Opposing the age-old idea that God was immovable and unchangeable (cf. Den Ottolander, 1965), Van Eck (1997) wrote a perceptive book *En toch beweegt Hij* (And yet He does move). Peels (2000) too criticized different traditional ideas of God in the light of the Scriptures. With this bit of good news, we can conclude this chapter.

10.5 Looking Ahead

In the next chapter, to conclude this series on Aquinas, we will be going full circle. For the last time, we will return to the subjects of the first chapter (synthesis philosophy and Scholasticism) because it could have created misunderstandings, needing to be answered in greater detail to some readers.

CHAPTER 6
CHRISTIANISING HELLENISM IMPLIES THE HELLENISATION OF THE CHRISTIAN FAITH

ONE MAY APPROACH THE encounter between Christian belief and Greek-Hellenist culture in two different ways: either from the perspectives of Christianization of Hellenism or the Hellenization of Christianity. This chapter deals with the second perspective, which is considered a result of the first.

Since the publication of his famous and massive (three-volume) Lehrbuch der Dogmengeschichte in 1886 and other works of Adolf von Harnack (1851-1930), the issue of the Hellenization of Christianity continues to be debated. According to Von Harnack, the accommodation between Christian faith and Greek-Hellenist philosophy during early Christian Patristic and Medieval thinking has to be evaluated negatively – it resulted in the intellectualization of original Christian beliefs into fixed theological dogmas.

It seems as if the founding fathers of Reformational philosophy, D.H.Th. Vollenhoven (1892-1978) and H. Dooyeweerd (1894-1977) more or less agreed with the viewpoint of Von Harnack. They merely employed a different term, "synthesis," to indicate the contamination resulting from an uncritical acceptance of Greek philosophy to explain Christian faith. However, a younger generation of Reformational scholars (e.g. Klapwijk and Helleman) questioned the fairness of characterizing other Christian thinkers as synthetic thinkers. They maintain that Christian theologians and philosophers of every age are children of their own times. Therefore, it is impossible to escape from their cultural-philosophical context. In contemporary Christian theological publications, something similar is taking place. What Von Harnack called "Hellinisation" and Vollenhoven indicated as "synthesis-thinking" is, to my mind, not taken seriously enough. (Van Asselt is taken as an example of a wider group of theologians.) According to its proponents, Reformed Orthodoxy (±1550-1700) only used Aristotelian-Thomist terminology and methods without any influence on the contents of its theology. Thus, one should not reject it as a synthesis but instead contribute towards its revival to indicate a new direction in contemporary Christianity.

At the end of five chapters on the philosophy of Thomas Aquinas (1224/5-1274) in his *Summa Contra Gentiles*, one could, therefore, pose the question, whether justice has been done to this Doctor Angelicus, characterizing his thinking (cf. the first chapter) as "synthetic." To provide an answer, in this contribution, I retrace his steps by offering a more detailed exposition and evaluation of synthetic and scholastic thinking. In conclusion, I again turn to Aquinas' fascination with Aristotle's philosophy despite the difficult opposition of some of his contemporaries.

1. Introduction: Motivation and Lay-out

IN THIS INTRODUCTION, (1.) we offer motivation as to why this chapter returns to the subject already briefly discussed in the first chapter and (2.) its outline is given.

1.1 Motivation

From two different perspectives, one can approach the meeting of Christian faith and Greek Hellenist culture (from approximately 50 AD). The first is from the Christianization of Hellenism and the second is the opposite, namely the Hellenization of Christianity. In this chapter, we are primarily concerned with the latter process – a consequence of the first. In Chapter one, this process was called "synthesis philosophy." It is necessary to return to it in detail. The following background sketch will explain why it is important.

1.1.1 Von Harnack on Hellenization
Ever since the publication of his famous and massive (three-volume) *Lehrbuch der Dogmengeschichte* (1886) and also the other works by the German scholar, Adolf von Harnack (1851-1930), the issue of the Hellenization of the Christian faith (cf. in particular Von Harnack, Part I:496-796 of the 1964-edition) has been an important point of debate. According to Von Harnack, the accommodation of Greek Hellenist thinking in the work of the early Christian Church Fathers and Medieval scholars led to the Christian faith being Hellenized or brought under Greek influence; that is, it was intellectualized to fixed theological dogmas. He, therefore, regarded Hellenization as a negative development for Christianity (for more on his view, cf. Helleman, 1994: 429 et seq.).

1.1.2 Vollenhoven and Dooyeweerd on Synthesis
These two fathers of a Reformational philosophy both have a critical attitude towards Christian synthesis philosophy. For Dooyeweerd, one can, for instance, refer to his publications of 1939 and 1949.

From the beginning, Vollenhoven was even more strongly opposed to synthesis philosophy (cf., e.g. Vollenhoven, 2005a: 405-406). He characterizes early Christian, Patristic and Medieval thinking (a sizable period from approximately 50-1550 AD) as synthesis philosophy and accordingly distinguishes between a period of *pre*-synthesis thinking (among the Greeks and Romans) and a period *after* the domination of Christian synthesis in Western history of philosophy (cf. Vollenhoven, 2005b: 29). Since this chapter will be discussing Vollenhoven's viewpoint in more detail below, we confine ourselves for the time being by stating that he did think anti-*synthetically* but not antithetically. We only add here that the anti-synthesis philosophy of Dooyeweerd and Vollenhoven also found followers worldwide. As far as South Africa is concerned, one can refer to E.A. Venter (s.a.) and Taljaard (1982).

1.1.3 Klapwijk's View of Synthesis Philosophy
Among the later followers of the founders of Reformational philosophy, Klapwijk, in particular (e.g. 1991, 1995), thought differently. His train of thought is briefly summarized, followed by a commentary.

Klapwijk's Point of View
Philosophy, according to Klapwijk, is the voice of a culture, articulating what lives within a culture. Christian thinkers also think within a specific cultural context from which they can never fully detach themselves, nor should they try to do it, since communication with non-Christian thinkers and concepts is essential (*religious* antithesis, according to Klapwijk, does not lead *eo ipso* to *philosophical* antithesis).

He, therefore, cannot identify himself with what he calls the anti-thetic viewpoint of Vollenhoven and Dooyeweerd. While Vollenhoven claims that true synthesis between the Christian faith on the one hand and contemporary philosophy, on the other hand, is not only *impermissible* but even *impossible*, Klapwijk asks: Then how can Vollenhoven resist something which is supposed to be essentially impossible? (Klapwijk, 1995: 178).

So how does Klapwijk himself see the relationship between Christian and non-Christian philosophy? According to Klapwijk, it is a fact (cf. Klapwijk, 1995: 182) that all Christian philosophers think both *antithetically* (in so far as they consider themselves alien towards worldly wisdom and want to be led by the revelation of God) and *synthetically* (in so far as they remain involved in the issues of their times). In this respect, Klapwijk refers to two sides of the well-known verse 2 Corinthians 10:5: *Antithetically:* "we demolish arguments and every pretension that sets itself up against the knowledge of God" and *synthetically:* "we take captive every thought to make it obedient to Christ."

In light of this, Klapwijk (instead of either accommodation or antithesis) proposes a transformational model. He admits that its application is not a simple matter. However, Klapwijk does not mean *external accommodation* to a non-Christian way of thinking, but the *critical processing* within a Christian worldview (cf. Klapwijk, 1995: 184, 185). Critical processing to him means melting down and purifying non-Christian ways of thinking so that they can be integrated within a Christian ontology in the service of God: this is what *normative* transformation means to Klapwijk.

However, he admits the possibility of *antinormative* or *inverted* transformation, which does not lead to the Christianization of non-Christian thinking, but, contrary to dechristianization or secularization of the Christian faith and philosophy. What renders it even more complex is that correct and inverted transformation often go hand in hand in the work of the same scholar because being open *to* the world is simultaneously being open *for* worldly ways of thinking (cf. Klapwijk, 1995: 187, 188).

Finally, Klapwijk thinks (cf. p. 189, 190) that his transformational philosophy will be more dynamic and contextual than his predecessors, Vollenhoven, Dooyeweerd and others.

Comment on Klapwijk's View

Klapwijk's (new) viewpoint on an antithetical attitude has already been scrutinized by several of his kindred spirits. Bos (1987: 135), for instance, maintains that Klapwijk's transformational philosophy entails only cosmetic changes. The contrast between antithesis and synthesis has only been substituted by two new concepts: normative anti-normative transformation.

Furthermore, Bos (1987: 137-138; 1996: 56-76) criticizes the *spolatio*-motive in Klapwijk's work, supporting his idea that, like the Israelites who later took gold from the Egyptians to melt it down and build a tabernacle for the Lord, Christians can take over non-Christian ways of thinking. According to Bos, this is a typical example of allegorical exegesis of the

Bible, which amounted to nothing less than a Hellenization of Christianity (cf. Choi, 2000: 136-144 for a detailed exposition of Klapwijk's viewpoint as well as criticism levelled at it). I confine myself to the following *four remarks*.

In the *first instance*, one must admit that some of Vollenhoven's predecessors, like Kuyper, were inclined to think anti*thetically:* Christian and non-Christian thinking are radically opposed. However, Vollenhoven thinks anti-*synthetically*.

In the second instance, Klapwijk also warns against anti-normative (inverted) transformation. Does this not on closer analysis mean the same that Vollenhoven meant with synthesis philosophy?

In the third instance, Vollenhoven (cf. 2.4 below) distinguishes between *spontaneous* (almost unconscious) synthesis philosophy and a *deliberate* synthesis between Christian faith and secular wisdom. Should not Klapwijk have taken this into account as well?

In the *fourth instance*, it is not true that Vollenhoven did not want to learn anything from non-Christian or synthetic philosophers. His thetic-critical method (cf. 2.11 below) contradicts such a suggestion as does his lifelong struggle with the history of the whole of Western philosophy.

Therefore, in my opinion, Klapwijk did lay significant new emphases. Still, his critique of Vollenhoven's synthesis view does not convince me We will go into Vollenhoven's viewpoint in more detail below.

1.1.4 Helleman's Sympathy with Synthesis Philosophy
Helleman (1990 & 1994a), just like Klapwijk, is critical of Vollenhoven's use of the term "synthesis." She also claims (cf. Helleman: 1994b: 462, 463) that the concept of "synthesis" in the Reformational philosophy of Vollenhoven and Dooyeweerd has more or less the same meaning as the "Hellenisation" of Von Harnack. About synthesis, she writes the following:

> It expresses a process which is in principle illegitimate, perhaps even impermissible or impossible for true faith ... In a synthesis the two component elements are essentially alien to one another. When combined the mix is unfortunate and detrimental (Helle-

man, 1994b: 463).

From the following quotation, however, both her rejection of the idea of synthesis as well as her own view becomes clear:

> If we are to regard interaction of Christianity and the Classics as synthesis, we will need to discern carefully the specific religious or cultural aspects which are juxtaposed, accommodated, and even compromised. To the extent that we recognized the primary religious character of Christianity and the nature of the classics to be primarily cultural, we may need to modify our use of the term 'synthesis' since the relative integrity of the two poles in the relationship is inevitably lost or threatened in a synthesis (Helleman, 1990: 19).

Here Helleman makes a clear distinction between culture (which includes philosophy) and religion. She maintains that it is wrong to effect a synthesis between pagan and Christian *religions*. Still, it is not to be regarded as synthesis when Christian scholars take over (cultural) *thinking* from pagan thinkers (cf., in particular, Helleman, 1990: 28, 29). Formulated differently: one should not compare Christian faith with heathen culture, only with heathen belief.

Although her viewpoint is not very clear (cf. Bos, 1996: 158, 179), it would furthermore seem as if classic culture and philosophy should be appreciated positively by Christians because, according to her, there is no specific Christian culture. Therefore, from her argument, it seems as if culture and philosophical thinking are supposed to be religiously neutral – a viewpoint that would be unacceptable to Vollenhoven and myself.

Another reason Helleman is less opposed to synthesis philosophy maybe because her research is mainly limited to early synthesis in the work of Patristic writers. As Vollenhoven has indicated, the synthesis philosophy of this period happened spontaneously and not deliberately, as happened, for instance, during the Middle Ages and in the work of Aquinas.

1.1.5 *The Debate By About The Nineties*

By about the nineties of the previous century, two important volumes were published. One of them deals with the classical heritage, while the other opens up the debate much wider.

Classical Philosophy
In a volume edited by Helleman (1990), indications are given on where the whole debate stands on how a Christian philosopher should position himself/herself towards the classical Graeco-Roman heritage. In the last chapter by Wolters (1990), for instance, in the line of what Bavinck wrote earlier, Niebuhr's well-known *Christ and culture* (1951) is used as a model to indicate the various possible attitudes taken by Christians. Wolters (1990: 194-195) summarizes the various attitudes as follows: (1.) grace *opposed to* nature, (2.) grace *perfecting* nature, (3.) grace *alongside* nature, (4.) grace *equals* nature, and (5.) grace *restoring* nature.

Wolters chooses the latter option because "it fully affirms the validity and legitimacy, in its own terms, of classical culture, and at the same time gives a religious critique of its perversion" (Wolters, 1990: 201). However, the categorization of Christian worldviews done by Bavinck, Niebuhr and their followers is currently no longer accepted without critique. It would most probably also have been unacceptable to Vollenhoven (cf. Van der Walt, 2012).

The More Broadly Based Debate
In the volume edited by Klapwijk, Griffioen & Groenewoud (1991), the whole scope of the debate is widened from the Christian's attitude towards ancient Graeco-Roman philosophy to the whole of Western philosophy. It is shown, for instance, how different philosophers (like Hegel, Tillich, Pannenberg and Gutierrez) tried to link Christianity with contemporary philosophy. With the closing essay by Klapwijk (1991), it is suggested that Klapwijk's own transformational model already mentioned in 1.1.3 (above) would be the (most) acceptable one.

1.1.6 The Struggle of Sweetman and Others
Finally, the fact that Reformational philosophers are currently still struggling with evaluating ancient Greek Hellenist philosophy becomes evident

from the volume edited by Sweetman (2007). Besides discussing again different historical characters (like Philo), the volume also contains Tol's (p. 127-160) essay on how Vollenhoven as a Christian philosopher saw classical antiquity. It is also important to study Sweetman's own introduction (p. 1-12) and epilogue (p. 267-289) carefully.

1.1.7 The Viewpoint of Some Contemporary Theologians
An outline has been given of the variety of views of (mostly Reformational) philosophers only. But in conclusion, something should be said on theological viewpoints about the Hellenization of Christianity (Von Harnack) or synthesis philosophy (Vollenhoven).

In general, theologians, even Reformed theologians, through the ages were not very conscious of the hazards attached to synthesis philosophy. Currently, it is no different as it becomes clear from the uncritical way Vos (1985 and 1990) condones the deliberate synthesis philosophy of Aquinas.

I will take only the essay by Van Asselt (1996) here as a representative example. His point of reference is taken as the sixteenth century Reformation on the one hand and Medieval theology on the other. The model of interpretation advocated by Van Asselt and many others is that of continuity. According to them, there is not much difference between the Middle Ages (± 500-1500), the Reformation (1500-1550 AD) and Reformed Orthodoxy (± 1550-1700) following the Reformation. Further, the detrimental role played in the Christian tradition by (e.g. Greek) philosophy is rejected as something merely *formal* (concerning the method of theologizing). The intention was not to have theological *contents* affected. Such a viewpoint, of course, does not at all tally with reality. Methods are not neutral (cf. Venter, 1981: 501 et seq.)

Due to this model of continuity and their naïve disregard for fundamental philosophical influences on theology, Van Asselt (*cum suis*) can also follow the reverse way into history and look for a new direction for the 21st century among philosophers like Aquinas, Duns Scotus and others who lived centuries ago.

Van Asselt *cum suis* can also follow the reverse way into history, looking for a new direction for the 21st century among philosophers like Aquinas, Duns Scotus, and others who lived centuries ago.

1.1.8 A Preliminary View

Earlier, I have already formulated my preliminary viewpoint in this respect (cf. Van der Walt, 2001a: 34) as follows. *First*, the Scriptures themselves bear clear witness that God's revelation does not completely ignore the culture in which it takes form but links up with it to some extent. Therefore, one could (possibly) deduct that God does not expect one to serve Him *outside* but *in* one's cultural clothes. I called this the principle of *relative continuity* (please note: *relative*). To this, I added the following:

> Apart from this *relative continuity* between Gospel and culture we do, however, also see a *radical discontinuity*. Without a degree of continuity the Gospel could never be relevant. Without discontinuity, it would not be able to challenge and change the culture in which it was embodied. It would become syncretized. The Biblical message is clear: The Gospel associated itself with different cultures – not to be domesticated, to become the captive of these cultures, but to liberate and transform them (Van der Walt, 2001a: 34).

So, in my opinion, the red warning lights begin flashing at the point where *relative* continuity is no longer relative so that the *radical* discontinuity no longer prevails. But if it is believed that the Christian faith and a specific culture mutually exclude each other in an antithetical way, then the Christian faith would hang in the air.

In my view, which shows correspondence with the Reformational approach in general as set out above, both uncritical continuity (synthesis or accommodation) between culture and the Christian faith and the opposite idea that the two could exist in total isolation from each other are rejected.

I admit that such a theory offers (like Klapwijk's transformational model) no simple solutions when one is confronted by concrete issues. In addition, it is merely a preliminary view, for the critical question can, of course, be posed whether such a view is not simply a modification of the method of paradox. For how can continuity and discontinuity go together? Perhaps this was why Aquinas, early in life, accepted the much easier solution of a nature-grace synthesis.

1.2 Lay-out

From the initial long motivation, it will be apparent that (as I did in Chapter one already) characterizing Aquinas (with Vollenhoven) as a synthesis philosopher would not be approved today but would be regarded as too harsh and judgmental. Hence, in this concluding chapter on Aquinas, I return to this issue in much greater detail.

The *following points* will be dealt with in succession: (1.)What exactly synthesis involves. (2.) What its basis is. (3.) How it differs from syncretism. (4.) Two kinds of synthesis philosophy. (5.)The various motives behind synthesis philosophy. (6.)That it is not merely a matter of terminology, method or form. (7.) The different methods according to which one can think synthetically. (8.) The hazards attached to these. (9.) That Vollenhoven's anti-synthetic philosophy implies a completely different view of the Western history of philosophy. (10.) What his thetic-critical method involves.

Since synthesis and Scholasticism are often not distinguished from each other, the following (second) central theme deals with what is understood by "scholasticism."

Finally (a third main section), we return to the fascination that Aquinas had with Aristotle's philosophy in particular. Questions, like the following, are answered: (1.) Why was the philosophy of the man from Stageira so popular in Aquinas' time? (2.) Was it not very difficult to attempt reconciling a pagan philosopher's ideas with the Scriptures? (3.) Did no one in the time of Aquinas object against his synthesis?

2. Synthesis Philosophy

When religions and cultures come into contact with one another, hybridization (acculturation) can occur, which also happened during the history of Christianity; the gradual Christianization of the West resulted in the Westernization of Christianity – first Hellenization, then Germanization

(Van der Walt, 2001a: 35). Several studies have been conducted on these processes, for instance, studies like that done by Fox (1986) and Wilken (1984) on the meeting of (pagan) Roman and Christian philosophy. Brown (1995) looks at the process from the perspective of Christianization, and Wilken (1984) looks the other way round at Christianity from the standpoint of Roman culture. Much has already been written on the later Christianization of German culture and the reverse process of Germanizing Christianity (cf., e.g. Fletcher, 1997 and Russell, 1994).

Similar processes are still taking place today. On our continent (especially since the beginning of the twentieth century), the Christianization of Africa, but simultaneously the Africanization of Christianity, has been in full swing (cf., e.g. Van der Walt, 2006). When do such processes (like Africanization) go too far and degenerate into synthesis or syncretism?

This chapter will be confined to the synthesis of Christian philosophy with non-biblical philosophical thinking from the Graeco-Roman world. Yet, it also contains pointers for today.

In the first instance, it is essential to get clarity on *the meaning of synthesis*.

2.1 What Synthesis Means

Synthesis originates when one combines biblical ideas with ideas from a non-Christian philosophy (Spier, 1959: 10) or stated the other way round (which amounts to the same) when one attempts to reconcile a pagan concept with themes from the revelation in Scripture (Vollenhoven, 2005a: 405). Although this synthesis philosophy reached a peak during Medieval philosophy, it is not confined to this period. It already occurred in the work of the Church Fathers, and continues until the present in the work of Christian thinkers.

For the sake of clarity, we have to say beforehand that calling someone's philosophy "synthesis" does not imply a judgment of his/her faith. Like Aquinas, one can be a devoted believer and still think synthetically.

2.2 Based on The Idea of Neutral Scholarship

Most of the time, philosophers who synthesize do not realize that being occupied with philosophy/theology is not a religiously neutral matter. There are fundamental religious differences between religious convictions (e.g. between pagan Greeks and Christians) that also determine a human being's scientific activity.

Vollenhoven, therefore, warns: "All human activity is controlled by religion, and so being occupied with philosophy is never neutral in the religious sense. Therefore, each philosophy should be conscious of its religious and thus non-scientific point of departure" (2005a: 406).

2.3 It Differs From Syncretism

Vollenhoven (2005a: 446) makes a clear distinction between synthesis and syncretism. As an explanatory example (cf. Venter, 1988: 82), we can use the early Christian and Medieval philosophers on the one hand and Manicheism and Gnosticism on the other hand. The latter blended, contorted and limited the role of Christ as the Redeemer with pagan ideas of other "redeemers" alongside Him (more on Gnosticism can be found in Bos, 1994: 1-23). During the time of the Church Fathers and the Middle Ages, philosophers, despite everything they added from Graeco-Roman philosophies, are still recognizable as Christian philosophers because they also accepted the biblical revelation on Christ.

Gort, Vroom, Fernhout and Wessels (1989) proved that the whole issue of syncretism is now a topical problem again. Van der Walt (2001b: 35) further shows that Western philosophers point out syncretistic trends in which traditional African religion and culture are blended with biblical ideas. However, often they (the Westerners) are not conscious of their syncretism between the Bible and Western culture.

2.4 Two Kinds of Synthesis

As mentioned above, Vollenhoven (2005a: 406) draws attention to the fact that one should distinguish between *unintentional* and *deliberate* synthesis philosophy. The former was mostly the case among the

Church Fathers, while thinkers during the Middle Ages followed the second course. It is the *deliberate* synthesis in particular which a Christian scholar should oppose. Because Christians, too, are children of their times, synthetic features will always occur to some extent. But if someone is *consciously resisting* while attempting to equip others to be more defendable against it, such a person should not be judged as a synthesis scholar. However, Aquinas was a deliberate synthesis thinker.

2.5 Different Motives

Vollenhoven (2011: 198) mentions different possible motives behind synthesis philosophy, including contemporary ones. (1.) Some Christian philosophers, as we have said, are not even conscious that they are thinking synthetically. (2.) Others think this way consciously because they want to be popular in the time in which they live. (3.) Still, others do not do it to be in vogue, but because it is too difficult and tiring to resist the spirit of one's own times. In the case of (2.) and (3.), egotistic motives can therefore come into play.

2.6 Synthesis is not merely a Matter of Terminology, and Methods are Not Neutral

Many theologians are of the opinion that they do not think in a synthetical manner because they are merely taking over some non-biblical *terms* from contemporary secular philosophy. Concepts or words are not empty receptacles that can be filled with any contents. Words carry meaning, have content. Spier rightly says:

> Synthesis philosophy begins where Christian scholars together with the terms, also take over the non-Christian content of the terms from renegade or pagan thought and believe that it can be united with Christian thought to form a whole. In this way, Thomistic philosophy in Roman Catholic circles has combined the ideas of Aristotle with Christian themes (1959: 10-11).

Methods are not neutral either as they are determined by one's worldview and philosophical points of departure, one's view of God, creation, human beings, particular epistemology, and so forth. As tangible evidence of this, I strongly recommend the excellent article by Hartvelt (1962) to the reader. He is one of the few Reformed theologians who realized what a decisive role originally philosophical methods have played in Reformational theology since the beginning of the Reformation. He also shows that these methods cannot be "justified" on biblical grounds but have been derived from the logic and philosophy of Aristotle.

According to Hartvelt, the first method is concerned with more than just listing information from the Scriptures. One's view of the relationship between God and human beings also comes into play. *In* the choice of method, one can cause dogma to *say* something – or to *withhold* it. Method means precision, planning, strategy, but also: pursuing a goal, letting the information say something, separately, according to its locus, but also in its totality.

2.7 Different Methods of Synthesis

Grabmann (reprinted 1956) is still a valuable source on methods used during the Middle Ages. Vollenhoven, too (2011: 202-206) did us an eminently valuable service by showing *how* Christian thinkers in the past and present reached their (unconscious as well as deliberate) synthesis through mainly three different methods (already mentioned briefly in Chapter 1, section 4.3).

2.7.1 Method of exegesis and eisegesis
The method of eisegesis and exegesis is the oldest. Early Christians, philosophically schooled in ancient philosophy, could first read unbiblical ideas into the Scriptures. And afterwards, with apparent approval from God's Word, read them out of the Scriptures again. This kind of synthesis philosophy was not original, for Jewish philosophers like Philo had already effected a synthesis with their Hellenist philosophical environment (cf. Runia, 1983, Doran, 1995 and Borgan, 1996).

Four Kinds of Hermeneutics

During the Middle Ages, a four-fold meaning of the Scriptures was usually still accepted (cf. De Lubac, 1959-1964): (1.) the literal meaning said what happened or what the *factual* position was, (2.) the allegorical meaning what one had to *believe*, (3.) the moral meaning indicated what one had to *do*, and (4.) the anagogical showed where one had to *go* or for what one had to *hope*. (In Latin: *Litera gesta docet, quid credas allegoria, moralis quid agas, quo tendas anagogia.*)

Nicolas van Lyra (obiit 1349 AD) articulated it in the following well-known poem:

> The letter shows us what God and our fathers did;
> The allegory shows us where our faith is hid;
> The moral meaning gives us rules of daily life;
> The anagoge shows us where we end our strife.

Allegorical exegesis
Jewish and Christian traditions employed allegorical hermeneutics (cf. Van der Walt, 1973: 196-200) to make it possible to carry out one's predisposing philosophical ideas into the Bible and guaranteeing the truth in a Biblicist manner. Individuals like the Jewish philosopher Philo from Alexandria (cf. Runia, 1983, 2007 and Helleman, 1994a: 107 et seq., 125 et seq., 159 et seq., 189 et seq. and 323 et seq.) and Christian thinkers like Origen (cf. Goud, 1991), Clemens (cf. Bos, 1991a and Helleman, 1994a: 323 et seq.) and Augustine (cf. Bos, 1991b) are important in this respect (Cf. also Smit, 1998: 275 et seq. for a good survey of the hermeneutics of early Christianity).

Biblicism
Vollenhoven also calls the method of eisegesis and exegesis the Biblicist method. As with all good things, the Bible has the potential to be misused. *How* one uses it depends on *what* the Bible is to you. To believers, it should not be just a source besides other sources of knowledge. It is God's authoritative *light* for the human being's direction in a life of faith. However, one does not look directly *into* the light on your desk or the

headlights of one's car. *By* the light of the Bible, one works to determine his/her direction.

Threefold Revelation
One can expect *too little* from the Bible. But one also misuses God's Word when one expects *too much* from it by expecting information and answers to every possible issue. Then one lapse into Biblicism – one reads one's own predisposed viewpoints into it and again – now with biblical sanction – from it.

The principle of "only Scripture" (*sola Scriptura*) can thus also be misunderstood and misused. It is important to remember that God's revelation is not confined to the Bible. He reveals Himself first in creation, then in His revelation in the Scriptures and finally in Christ. God presents human beings with one revelation but a three-fold one, distinguished but not separated. If one of these (e.g. the Bible) is overemphasized, we depreciate the other two. When one of these is underemphasized or depreciated (e.g. the creational revelation or the revelation incarnate in Christ), it easily leads to everything being expected from the Scriptures only – instead of looking at reality *in the light of* the Bible (the real meaning of *Sola Scriptura*)

Which philosophical ideas have been read into the Scriptures in this way? From the Church Fathers until the tenth or eleventh century, Plato was the hero in Christian synthesis philosophy – Aristotle became known only later. How was this possible, for in Plato, one is confronted by one of the most radical and consistent forms of heathen Greek philosophy? (Cf. Bos, 1996).

A second method to arrive at synthesis was as follows.

2.7.2 The Paradoxical Method
However, some assumed a paradoxical method as thinking Christians realized the danger of eisegesis and exegesis. They did observe the deep religious antithesis between pagan philosophy and biblical faith but still wanted to maintain both in the form of so-called double truth. Despite

this, their theologies/philosophies were contaminated.

For instance, Venter (1988: 82, 83) says of Tertullian (a representative of the method of paradox) the following. He may have had an antithetical attitude, but he did absorb non-Christian ideas in his philosophy in practice. It seems that the antithetical attitude could never succeed because we can never exceed our times' language and thought structures. The hybridization of Christian and non-Christian ideas is not something that can be avoided by drawing a line between groups (e.g. "believers" opposed to "philosophers") because this hybridization takes place in the thoughts of an individual – often without his willingness to do so. The third *method* was the following.

2.7.3 The Method of Nature and Grace
The last method, which had already originated in the sixth century but only flourished properly during Medieval philosophy, was nature and supra-nature or grace. According to this method, non-biblical philosophies were regarded as an "entrance hall" (*praeambula*) which the biblical message does not *reject*. These non-biblical philosophies perfect the biblical message.

Implications
Therefore, the nature-grace theme also implies that a Christian may practice science (except for the supernatural theology) independently from God's revelation in the Scriptures. In the profane (natural) sphere, pagan theories were introduced into Christianity and adapted where direct conflict occurred. But in this way, the impact of a Christian view on science, education, politics, labour, commerce, etcetera was obscured and ignored. Venter's comment on this is: "The greatest error of Medieval philosophy [including Thomas – BJvdW] was the division of the world into a sacred and a profane sphere – by doing this, they caused Christianity to adapt to the secular world" (Venter, 1985: 123).

Furthermore, one should consider the secularization of philosophy and philosophical or natural theology. Vollenhoven (2005a: 205) points out that even Aquinas' supernatural theology (*sacra doctrina*) was not biblically sound, free from the influence of pagan philosophical elements. Eisegesis-exegesis, used in conjunction with the nature-grace method (unbiblical philosophical ideas), were also subtly carried over into so-called holy theology. However, there are more hazards attached to this synthesis philosophy.

2.8 Hazards of Synthesis Philosophy

Vollenhoven (2005a: 406) maintains that any form of synthesis, no matter which method used to effect the synthesis, in the end, brings its revenge; it causes tension and damage. If one goes about synthesizing deliberately, too much that is authentic to the Christian faith is lost in the process of accommodation.

An Example
One could take Aquinas' synthesis between the biblical revelation about God and Aristotle's idea of god (cf. previous chapter). How is it possible to reconcile the heathen idea of an immovable god, who only thinks about himself all the time, who is absolute (therefore in no relationship) and who moreover predetermines everything, with the Bible – which teaches precisely the opposite?

Venter (1985: 38) therefore describes Aristotle's idea of the Godhead as "bloodless marble". Vollenhoven (2011: 204) calls it "something grisly." Spier (1959: 11) is, therefore, rightly of the opinion that synthetic philosophy obscures the truth of God's Word, undermines the power of the Christian faith, and in the field of science, delays the progress of God's kingdom.

No Slave of Aristotle's and yet...
It is true that Aquinas attempted to fit Aristotle into the tradition of the church and theology and did not want the opposite. He was, therefore, no slavish follower of Aristotle (he did not think like Aristotle but in an Aristotelising way), for it would undoubtedly have brought him into conflict with his faith and the tradition and authorities of the church (compare

Chapter one). But despite his good and honest intention, his interpreted Aristotelian philosophy did not keep on playing the part of merely a servant; it became a Trojan horse.

Unresolvable Tension

The significant problem with a synthesis theology or philosophy is that it can never be free from unresolvable, inherent tension. For iron and clay can never be truly united.

This tension can, for instance, be seen in the work of Evans (1980). The *artes liberales* was seen as a foundation for theological training. Still, because these sciences were based on ancient Greek philosophy, they stood in a relation of tension to theology as science which had to be based on the Scriptures.

Anachronistic Thinking

According to Vollenhoven (2011: 208), one grievously errs, as if in the synthesis philosophy of Aquinas, he/she attempts to turn Plato or Aristotle into that which is semi-Christian; in the first instance, it is historically incorrect. The pre-synthetic philosophers did not know the Gospel at all; they were utterly pagan. This does not mean that one should exalt oneself above them instead of having compassion for them. But having compassion does not mean declaring one ascribing to pagan philosophy as partly Christian. Therefore, one looks in vain for Christian themes in the work of Greek and Roman philosophers – it is a fool's errand.

Taken over by Aristotle

In the *second instance*, synthetical thinking is also hazardous to a Christian. Making Plato/Aristotle partly a Christian means adding something to the sphere of grace to get a complete Christian. Furthermore, you think you are taking over Plato/Aristotle for yourself and Christianity, but in the meantime, Platonism/Aristotelianism is taking possession of you and your Christian way of thinking. The *accommodation*, required by synthesis philosophy, quickly leads to the *capitulation* of the Christian faith, not only applied to the accommodation of Plato's and Aristotle's philosophies but also in the case of current efforts of reconciliation between the Christian faith and secular philosophy.

2.9 A Different View of the History of Western Thought

Instead of the continuity model of Van Asselt (1996) and others (cf. 1.1.7 above), Vollenhoven has an entirely different view of history. Taking Christian synthesis philosophy as his point of departure, he divides the history of Western philosophy into three significant periods (cf. Vollenhoven, 2005b: 29): (1.) the pre-synthesis thinking of the Greeks and Romans (from approximately six centuries BC to about 50 AD); (2.) the synthesis philosophy of the Church Fathers and the Middle Ages (from approximately 50 to about 1500 AD); (3.) the post-synthesis thinking (from approximately 1500 up to today). The latter period has a distinct anti-synthetic character and can be distinguished in two different schools. One starts with the Reformation, which wanted to break away from the synthesis between heathen philosophy and the Bible in order once more to do full justice to the Scriptures. The other school started with the Renaissance with the opposite motivation: it broke away from synthesis because it disliked the biblical element, wanting to revive ancient pagan culture and philosophies. These two tendencies of which the latter became the dominant one run right through to the present day.

2.10 A Permanent Temptation

Although it is no longer the dominating spirit, synthesis philosophy has never really disappeared among Christians – it remains a permanent temptation.

An example of this is the inception of Reformed Orthodoxy as early as the second generation of Reformational philosophers like Beza (Calvin's successor in Geneva). Because the insights acquired by the sixteenth-century Reformation had to be consolidated, extensive theological treatises originated, intended to defend, explain and systematize the new dogmas.

However, since no Christian philosophy was available, Aristotle was called in to help – just as earlier in the work of Aquinas and the Roman Catholic Contra-reformational movement after him. Musaeus, who wrote in the 17th century, is quite happy to see himself as a scholastic philosopher in a tradition going back to Aquinas. Protestant Orthodoxy became Protestant (also Reformed) Scholasticism (cf. Evans, McGrath & Galloway, 1986: 151 et seq.).

If one rejects synthesis philosophy, what, then, is the right way of thinking? Is it possible, since every philosopher is a child of his/her own era? What does it mean to reject synthesis (the way the 16th-century Reformers intended to do) because the secular element in it was unacceptable?

2.11 Thetic-Critical Philosophy

According to Vollenhoven (2005c: 6-8), a Christian should not think antithetically but thetic-critically. One cannot (thetically) philosophize without one's own preliminary viewpoint. But simultaneously, one can also (critically) learn from others. "Critical" includes both a positive and a negative side. The negative means, amongst other things, to think anti*synthetically*, that is, to reject synthesis philosophy as a Christian. Venter rightly says:

> A Christian philosopher does good when trying to learn from others. But merely polishing others' ideas to adapt them to one's faith in the end means that one's faith is combined with an idea structure which is foreign to it. The correct way is that we should take care that our Christian faith gives structure to our ideas, and that which we take over from others we should dismantle and restructure according to the structures of our faith (Venter, 1985: 11).

Apart from Vollenhoven's argument that synthesis philosophy reached its peak in the work of Aquinas, the latter is also called "the father of scholastic thinking." What are the differences and the relationships between the two? We will now address a second important subject.

3. Scholastic Philosophy

One would correctly regard Scholasticism as a type of synthesis philosophy. This tendency toward synthesis philosophy is also possible in evolutionism and existentialism.

McGrath (1988: 50) writes that "Scholasticism is probably one of the most despised intellectual movements in human history." Therefore, specific sources on Reformational philosophy ignore Scholasticism without even explaining what it entails, not realizing its significance for understanding the Reformational tradition.

Even if the concept "Scholasticism" is of ill repute today, it still is essential, if possible, to get greater clarity on it – also for this final chapter on the philosophy of Aquinas.

3.1 Stemming from Two Needs

McGrath (1988: 51) explains the inception of Medieval Scholasticism by referring to two needs that originated at the time. (1.) The need for *systematizing Christian theology* and developing it; (2.) The need to show that *theology* (and with it the Christian faith) *is a rational, scientific matter*. To meet these two needs, however, philosophy was necessary, being regarded as something rational: "This then is the essence of scholasticism: the demonstration of the inherent rationality of Christian theology by an appeal to philosophy" (McGrath, 1988: 51). It led to scholastic theologies, according to him, becoming "cathedrals of the intellect," encompassing the whole of reality. We already found this distinctly in the intellectualism of Aquinas.

Gaybba (1998: 29) concurs with this and shows how a mere two generations after the apostolic era, the use of philosophy made its appearance in theological thinking. And, since there was no truly Christian philosophy, especially Plato (in a Neo-Platonic version) became the philosophical pundit for Christian theologians until far into the Middle Ages before Aristotelian philosophy replaced Platonism.

3.2 Bound by Traditional Source

According to Vollenhoven (2005a: 371), the concept "Scholasticism" denotes the philosophical method of scholars with whom studying the heritage of their predecessors plays a more important part than their independent investigation. Scholasticism, for this reason, exhibits a substantial traditionalist character (cf. also Gaybba, 1998: 35, 36). The writings of the early Christian scholars were initially during the Middle Ages only collected (in *compilations*), later on, harmonized with one another (in *concordantiones*), which finally served as a base for their own opinions (in *sententiae*) and were used as teaching aids.

Hart briefly describes the situation during those days after the fall of the Roman Empire, the inundation of Europe by the German "barbarians," and the decline of the ancient culture and Christianity as follows:

> The preservation of culture and education came to rest in the hands of the clergy, mainly in the monasteries. Their primary interest was the passing on of the tradition of the Christian faith via the authority of the Church Fathers. This made for a traditionalistic, schoolishly-slavish clinging to traditional authority. And since this preservation consisted mainly of the propagation of remaining documents (by copying, making compilations, collections, concordances, etc.) and some hesitant interpretation, studies in grammar dominated the scene (1974: 102).

According to this description, Scholasticism does not necessarily imply the nature-grace theme or Aristotelising philosophy (1974: 102).

3.3 The Role of Logic

Venter (1985: 3, 4) rejects the concept that "Scholasticism" is supposedly the same as "unreformed" (Roman Catholic) thought (cf. the flourishing of scholastic thinking later on among Reformed Orthodoxy from approximately 1550-1700). According to Venter, the nature-grace theme only really became more prevalent during the thirteenth century. A "Scholasticism," as Venter explains, means (1.) incorporating a mostly ecclesiastical tradition of learning with the aid of strictly logical means within the context of philosophical schools, and (2.) adding in the same way new information to the systems. Logic did indeed take an essential role in scholastic thinking (cf. the impressive two volumes by De Rijk, 1962 & 1967).

3.4 Specific Methods

Grabmann (1956) and De Rijk (1977: 25) also discuss this facet of Scholasticism. They write that it denotes a theological and philosophical activity according to a specific method that (in both study and teaching) is characterized by a system of concepts, distinctions, the analysis of propositions, and particular ways of arguing in which the dialectic method is the dominant one (from p. 107 to 137, De Rijk discusses this dialectic method in detail).

3.5 A Wider Definition

All these definitions of what "Scholasticism" means point to different facets of this type of thinking: (1.) it originates from a specific need, (2.) it is markedly bound by tradition – even today, (3.) a certain type of logic takes an important role in it as well as (4.) a specific methodological approach. However, what is conspicuous in three of these definitions of Scholasticism is that they more or less concentrate on the *formal* aspect. Perhaps the contents are avoided because scholastic thinking can include diverse philosophical and theological directions and concepts.

McGrath (1988: 51), however, does not avoid the contents of Scholasticism and rightly so, in my opinion. He demonstrates how the Neo-Platonic, Augustinian philosophy (as the basis for a rational theology) by about 1270, despite vehement opposition from the conservative side, ousted Aristotle (called *"the philosopher"*). From then on, Aristotle's philosophy was employed to meet the two needs of Christian theology mentioned above (cf. 3.1). Polman (1961: 88-89) describes "Scholasticism" in which most of the previously mentioned elements are included. This term is derived from the Latin *scholasticus* and refers to teachers and students at cathedrals, convent schools, and universities.

Their philosophical-theological science practised was called "Scholasticism." Important traits were the following: (1.) A firm traditionalist approach since it only reproduced and systematized the heritage of the Church Fathers and the Greeks. (2.) A certain relationship developed between philosophy and theology in which philosophy was supposed to act as "handmaiden." (3.) Aristotle's influence grew steadily. (4.) A definite method was developed for reading, exegesis, commenting, speculating, debating and arguing – as emerges distinctly from the two *Summae* by Thomas Aquinas.

3.6 Conclusion

My personal opinion is, therefore, that one can hardly speak about Scholasticism during the heyday of the Middle Ages (from about 1250) without mentioning its Aristotelising character. The same applies to Lutheran and Reformed Scholasticism from approximately 1550 and contemporary theologians and philosophers who attempt to revive this kind of orthodoxy today.

I want to add as a second feature the dualism of nature-grace (supra nature). In the case of Aquinas, his Aristotelisation of Christianity was achieved employing his method of nature-supernature. I will first remark briefly about Aquinas' nature-grace dualism and then elaborate on the Aristotelian influence in his thinking.

3.6.1 Nature and Grace

The challenge which confronted the West at the time was not merely of a theological or philosophical kind but to effect unity between the Roman, German and Christian worldviews and cultures.

The underlying motive of unification which managed to mould these diverse elements into one 'community' we call the motive of 'Nature and Grace.' Simply stated, this motive understood the cosmos to consist of Nature, or man's external way of living from day to day (in sin), and Grace, the added dimension of 'new' life promised by Christianity. Whatever ideals would emerge from this synthesis of life-styles would at heart reflect this deeper duality of Nature and Grace.

In order to survive the fall of the Roman Empire, the Church and State somehow had to reach an alliance. Indeed, we can most fully express this reality in terms of the synthesis ideal of a *Christian Commonwealth (Corpus Christianum)*. Here Grace and Nature were to co-exist. The pope and the head of the state were 'equals.' The Roman Empire (now German) and the body of Christ were to be one.

It may be said of this ideal that it characteristically divided both man and cosmos into a duality consisting of a spiritual sphere and a natural one, maintaining that spirituality was attained through communion with God and naturally attained through rationality. The various expressions of this basic motive gave rise to both the plurality of Medieval cultural forms and the differences within scholastic thinking (Hart et al., 1974: 2, 3).

3.6.2 The Great Influence of Aristotle

The method of nature-grace enabled Aquinas (as has been abundantly proved by the previous chapters on his SCG) to attempt to reconcile Aristotle and the Scriptures. In these chapters, however, many questions were left unanswered, to which we now have to return. These are questions like the following: Why was Aristotle's philosophy in particular so popular at the time? Was it not very difficult, as well as irresponsible, to reconcile his ideas with the Word of God? Did nobody object against it?

Seeing that the reception and processing of philosophy according to the man from Stagira is an intricate tale, those interested are referred to the (unfortunately still unpublished but) excellent survey by Hart et al. (1974: 63-95). From this work, amongst other things, the following becomes clear: (1.) How at the universities of Paris and Oxford, the Neo-Platonic philosophy was gradually replaced by an Aristotelising one and what it contained. (2.) The fierce controversy that accompanied it, especially at the University of Paris – and also the role Aquinas played in it (cf. Hart et al., 1974: 84-86). (3.) Roman Catholic ecclesiastical authorities denounced the incorporation of Aristotelian philosophy in their theology. (4.) Later reactions (by eg Occam) to these ecclesiastical denunciations.

Here are a few flashes from the intricate and tense course of events.

4. Aquinas' Synthetic Accommodation of Aristotle's Philosophy

For the more significant part of the hey-days of the Middle Ages, Aristotle's philosophy played either a positive or a negative role.

4.1 A Broad Outline

I do not have the room to go into the philosophy of Aristotle himself here. I have to confine myself to start with the fact that this giant in the history of Western philosophy, not without reason, has always enjoyed attention within Reformational philosophy. Examples are Runner (1951), Vollenhoven (2011: 57-70, 118-126, 129-131) and various works by the Aristotle expert, Bos (e.g. 2003). I confine myself to an overview of Platonising and Aristotelising philosophy during the Middle Ages.

The history of *Medieval thinking* in main lines covered the following phases: (1.) an Augustinian-Boethian-Platonic; (2.) an Augustinian-Neo-Platonic-Aristotelian; (3.) a phase during which controversy began on the processing of Aristotle in Christianity and (4.) a phase of critique of Aristotle.

There was still minimal knowledge of Aristotle's logic during the first and partly the second phase of early Scholasticism. During the last, second, and especially during the third phase, the complete Aristotelian logic and his other works were discovered and translated into Latin, which was then utilized to introduce new information into the Christian tradition. However, during the final phase, the Aristotelian synthesis was queried.

4.2 The Reason for Aristotle's Popularity

According to Vos (1990: 70), the popularity of Aristotle's philosophy can be ascribed to the fact that philosophers of the thirteenth century provided a new scientific view of reality.

According to this view, the terrestrial world was no longer (the way it was in Augustinian Neo-Platonism) a mere "sign" of a higher world. Still, it was knowable as such by the natural intellect of human beings. Therefore, it was impossible to ignore Aristotle since it would mean stemming progress that would not last long. Such a strategy would be similar to us today attempting to avoid the scientific-technical problems of our times.

4.3 No Easy Task

One should, however, not assume that it was easy for Christian philosophers to accept Aristotle. The man from Stagira held, amongst others, the following views which were in direct conflict with the ecclesiastical and theological tradition of the time: (1.) he believed that the world had not been created but existed from all eternity; (2.) that the deity is an unchangeable, indifferent being who only thinks about himself and is the first cause and end of everything; (3.) that the soul of a human being is passive and has to be activated by a higher, supra-personal spiritual power; (4.) that human individual souls perish at the time of death since they are then once more taken up into the universal spirit; (5.) that knowledge can only be obtained via sensory experience. How, for instance, could the Aristotelian view of (3.), (4.) and (5.) be reconciled with the official teaching of the church?

4.4 Reactions to Aristotle's Philosophy

Aquinas had to reconcile Aristotle with the church and the doctrine of the church with Aristotle. I will once more explain the background briefly.

Aristotle was only discovered gradually in the Western world after many centuries (cf. Venter, 1988: 156). By the eleventh century, his logic was rediscovered. Via Arabic commentaries (who still read Aristotle from a Neo-Platonic perspective) during the late eleventh century, more of Aristotle's other works became known in the West. Only by the first half of the thirteenth century, the realization dawned that this was not the authentic Aristotle. Through translations from the original Greek into Latin, the real Aristotle first became known during the age in which Aquinas lived.

This history, especially the events at the University of Paris, is recounted in detail by Van Steenberghen (1955). He first describes how Aristotle gradually became known and was accepted and then the different reactions to him, namely an eclectic Aristotelianism, the more conservative Augustinian Aristotelianism (of amongst others Bonaventura) and the radical Aristotelianism (of, e.g. Siger of Brabant). As mentioned before, Hart et al. (1974: 63 et seq.) also present a short survey of this complex process, including the events at the University of Oxford.

Christian thinkers, therefore, reacted differently to this novelty. Some of them (e.g. Bonaventura) still shied away from Aristotle and preferred staying on the traditional Neoplatonic course (already paved by Augustine). Another group (e.g. the Averroists) leaned over to the other extreme by canonizing Aristotle (alongside the Scriptures), adhering to a double truth. A third, moderate group in the middle (e.g. Albertus Magnus and Aquinas) treated Aristotle with more caution and retained some Augustinian traditional elements. As shown in chapter one, even the moderation of Aquinas was, however, considered unorthodox by some of his contemporaries.

4.5 The Outcome of the Whole Course of Events

The reaction by the church initially was to ban the works of Aristotle without exception. Later on, it was realized that such an attempt was in vain; the condemnation was confined to his writings, considered to be a composition of "unorthodox" ideas (cf. Hart et al., 1974: 87). The condemnations were in particular levelled at the Averroist-Aristotelian line of Siger of Brabant, who attempted to reconcile Aristotle with the Scriptures through the method of paradox, the doctrine of double truth (cf. 2.7.2 above). Aquinas' method of nature-grace seemed to have been more acceptable, though not to everybody.

The condemnation (in 1277) by Bishop Tempier of Paris included no less than 219 errors, some of which were ideas of Aquinas. Eleven days after that, Robert Kilwardby, the Archbishop of Canterbury, applied this condemnation to the University of Oxford. His successor, John Peckham, repeated his predecessor's condemnation in 1284 and 1286 so that Thomist philosophy was forbidden at Oxford.

But the church could not stem the Aristotelian-Scholastic tide. In 1278, the Dominican Order declared the philosophy of Aquinas official doctrine of the order. And in 1323, Aquinas became the first person in history to be canonized by the Pope. Also, in 1325, the condemnation of particular views of Aquinas was retracted in the condemnation of 1277. Synthesis philosophy had triumphed!

4.6 Aristotle, Aristotelianism and Aristotle Interpretation

Finally, we have to point out that synthesis philosophy can have a very complex system as its outcome, so it is essential to use distinct terminology (cf. Vollenhoven, 2005a: 45). Aristotle himself underwent (according to Vollenhoven) a development through various phases. Trends linking up directly with some of his conceptions are designated "Aristotelianism." Other types of philosophy that are not directly connected with Aristotle's philosophy are called "Aristotle interpretations," such as Aquinas' subsistence theory. Aristotelianism and Aristotle's interpretations are therefore no longer the pure, original Aristotle. It has been combined, for instance, with Platonising elements (as in the SCG of Aquinas – cf. Vollenhoven, 2005a: 329).

5. Conclusion

In the earlier chapters, a mere philosophical dwarf dared to criticize a giant in the history of Western thought. My final conclusion is that, even though Aquinas wrote his *Summa Contra Gentiles* more than seven hundred years ago, one can still be challenged and enriched by his struggles as a Christian thinker. One can learn from his philosophy both in a negative and positive sense.

Negatively, one should be warned against any synthetic Christianity, aiming to compromise God's infallible revelation and contemporary, popular philosophy of whatever kind.

Positively, I want to refer to the balanced evaluation of two Reformational thinkers, viz. Spier and Hart.

Spier (1959: 93) justly writes that Aquinas "baptized" Aristotle to become a Christian but explains it as follows. He did not accept Aristotle's philosophy unquestioningly. On the one hand, he tried to cleanse generally accepted ideas presented as "Aristotelian" from their later interpretations. On the other hand, he let go of original Aristotelian ideas, which were irreconcilable with the Scriptures. He, therefore, was a foremost philosopher who embroidered his conception on an Aristotelian pattern.

One can also identify with Hart, who writes the following on Aquinas:

> Aquinas did not accept Aristotle wholesale; he only accepted that which he, too, considered to be true. He did not accept Aristotle, but the truth of Aristotle. Aquinas never quotes Aristotle with the implication that this statement is valid simply because Aristotle made it ... Out of his love for truth, Aquinas could not accept an equation between Aristotle with truth ... So Aquinas saw himself as a servant of truth (1974: 85).

CHAPTER 7
SEVEN CENTURIES OF NEO-THOMIST THINKING AFTER AQUINAS

IN THE PRECEDING CHAPTERS, the author investigated the philosophy of Thomas Aquinas (1224/1274), the doctor Angelicus of the Roman Catholic Church. In analyzing what happened to his heritage during the following seven centuries, this and the following chapter will conclude the book. As has been the case with many philosophical traditions, Aquinas was, since his death, interpreted by Neo-Thomist scholars in a great variety of ways.

The introduction provides some information about the interest of Reformational thinkers in Catholic Thomistic philosophy and vice versa. Then the question is asked how one should deal with an inherited tradition. Followed, thirdly, by a brief review of the revival of Thomist thinking, especially since the papal encyclical *Aeterni Patris* in the nineteenth century. The fourth section discusses the critical issue, viz., which Aquinas and whose Thomism? The next part investigates two methodologies of portraying the history of Neo-Thomism: according to different ontological types of conceptions in the interpretation of Aquinas, as well as a more chronological-historical method. Since the author regards neither of them as entirely satisfactory, the chapter is concluded with the prospect of an improved philosophical historiographical approach to describe and analyze Neo-Thomist thinking in philosophy and theology (see next chapter).

1. Introduction: How This Chapter Links up with Previous Chapters, The Motivation for It, Its Limitations and Lay-out

BY WAY OF INTRODUCTION, we indicate: (1.) How this chapter is related to the previous ones. (2.) The motivation for adding it. (3.) Its focus. (4.) The course the investigation will take.

1.1 Connection

In previous chapters, the author dealt with the philosophy of the important Medieval philosopher, Thomas Aquinas, in his *Summa Contra Gentiles*. This chapter and the one following it will conclude the book by asking what happened to his philosophical heritage during the more than seven centuries after his death up to today.

For the past seven hundred years, Thomistic followers have preserved his heritage by writing commentaries on his work and developing his ideas. In this way, a long tradition came into being comprised of a great variety of interpretations of the writings of the *doctor Angelicus*. The formation of such a (Neo)-Thomist school is not unusual. There are many examples in history of (re)interpretations of eminent philosophers, such as Neoplatonism, Neo-Kantianism, Neo-Calvinism (e.g. A. Kuyper) and many others. The first chapter already pointed out how various, even opposing, interpretations emerged at the International Thomas Conference (in Rome and Naples, 1974) commemorating the death of Aquinas seven centuries earlier.

These different readings of Aquinas were recently (Nov. 2012) once again emphasized in the lecture given by Walmsley (2012) during an International Conference in Johannesburg at the Catholic College of St. Augustine. The title of his lecture was already revealing: "Whose Thomism? Which Aquinas?"

1.2 Motivation

One could question whether this is not a case of occupying oneself with an archaeological-philosophical effort to revive old disputes. However, it was rightly said of Aquinas, even while he was still alive, that this "thick-headed bull" would keep on "bellowing" through the ages!

A second question is whether Reformational philosophers must take cognizance of Aquinas and Neo-Thomism. (During my years as a student, one of our professors warned us to beware of the "danger of Roman Catholicism"!) In answer, I, therefore, offer some motivation for this chapter.

1.2.1 Fellow-Christians

First, we should remember that Catholic philosophers are also Christians – our brothers and sisters in Christ. As will become evident, some of them advocated, apart from a Christian theology, also a Christian philosophy – as did Reformational philosophers. In addition, NeoThomism is one of the most prominent philosophical schools in the world (cf. Sahakian, 1969: 316) and produced some of the most influential theologians of the twentieth century. For instance, Van der Beek (2006) discusses the following Roman Catholic theologians: K. Raher, H. Urs von Balthasar, H. Kung, E. Schillebeekx and P. Schoonenberg.

1.2.2 Influence on Orthodox Reformed Theology

Secondly, it should be kept in mind (as already pointed out in previous chapters) that after the sixteenth-century Reformation from the middle of the seventeenth century and long afterwards, Thomist philosophy had a vast influence on Reformed Orthodox theology. Thomist philosophy emerged, for instance, in the *Synopsis Purioris Theologiae* (1625), written under the authority of the Synod of Dordt (cf. Van der Walt, 2011a and 2011b). That this scholastic attraction is lasting to this very day is confirmed by the fact that the first part of this work (containing three volumes, a total of 1500 pages) was once more (in Latin with an English translation) issued in 2013 by the well-known publisher Brill in Leiden.

1.2.3 Interrelations

In the third instance, in the teaching of Reformational philosophy at the Free University of Amsterdam, attention has always been given to Medieval philosophies (cf. Woldring, 2013). An excellent example of a thorough study of 933 pages is Zuidema (1936) on the philosophy of the late Medieval philosopher Willem van Ockham (1285-1349). Later examples are Smit (1950), who deals with new Roman Catholic views of history, and the publications by Aertsen (1982, 1983, 1984, 1990 and 1991), in which he focused on Aquinas.

Ever since the origin of Reformational philosophy in the thirties of the previous century, regular discussions have also occurred between Reformational philosophers (like Dooyeweerd) and Roman Catholic thinkers. (cf. e.g. Albers, 1955; Robbers, 1948: 124-126 and 1951: 119-120; Marlet, 1954; the contribution by Louet Feiser in Van Dijk & Stellingwerff, 1961: 18-35). During the International Conference at the 75th commemoration of the founding of the Society for Reformational Philosophy (Amsterdam, August 2011) once more papers were read by several Catholic-oriented speakers.

Within the circles of Reformed theology in the Netherlands, there has also been a lively interest in the past in developments within Roman Catholic theology (e.g. Berkouwer, 1948, 1964 and 1968; Meuleman, 1967; Wentsel, 1970 and Vandervelde, 1975).

1.2.4 Confronted by The Same Problems

In the fourth place, one should remember that the same problems often confront Christians of different convictions and denominations. One such issue is a Christian philosopher's attitude toward non-Christian secular philosophy and culture. Of course, this does not imply that the solutions to such burning questions would be similar for Roman Catholic and Reformational philosophers.

Both from the Roman Catholics and other churches' side, ecumenical debates have long since been taking place on possible ecclesiastical unity (possibly a climax will be reached in 2017, 500 years after Luther started ringing the Reformational bell). This kind of discussion was regularly encouraged by Pope Benedictus XVI (2005-2013), and from the side of the Evangelicals, it can be read in, for instance, Noll & Nystrom (2005).

1.2.5 Recent Attempts at a Synthesis
Finally, we point out that a movement that became known as Radical Orthodoxy attracts several followers in South Africa too. This group of philosophers like to hark back to Aquinas for inspiration – even though they admit that this is a "new" Aquinas, radically re-interpreted. Smith and others even attempt to combine this trend with specific insights of Reformational philosophy and, the other way round to "reform" Reformational philosophy in the light of Thomism (cf. Smith, 2004: 120 et seq., 155 et seq., 165 et seq. as well as Smith & Olthuis, 2006).

1.3 *Constraints*

It is impossible to do justice to such a long and complex tradition of more than seven centuries in a single chapter – it is merely possible to draw some main outlines.

Existing surveys of the history of Neo-Thomism are not very satisfactory since they usually merely mention the most important individuals chronologically (cf., e.g. Sassen & Delfgaauw, 1957; Hamman, 1960; Gilby, 1967). Or focus on different conceptual accents by different Neo-Thomist philosophers (cf., e.g. Ashley, 2006 and Haldane, 2005).

The mass of *theological* Thomist literature will only be touched on obliquely. This chapter is confined as far as possible to the Neo-Thomistic *philosophies* forming the foundation of the different theologies. The key issue (cf. the following chapter) is whether several basic, connected ideas could be regarded as typical of this philosophical tradition.

1.4 Lay-out

The following will be discussed: (1.) The way the followers of a certain tradition usually handle it. (2.) A short survey of the revival of Thomism, particularly since the end of the nineteenth and the beginning of the twentieth century. (3.) Two key issues: Which Aquinas? and Whose Thomism? will be discussed. (4.) Two methods by which Neo-Thomists recount the history of their tradition will be analyzed. One which mainly focuses on the types of conceptions, and a second, using a chronological-historical methodology. (5.) Because neither of these two methods seems to be fully satisfactory, the survey is concluded with the prospect of a final chapter in which the developments and shifts within Neo-Thomist philosophy (and by implication theology) are set out according to an improved method of philosophical historiography.

2. How a Tradition is Handled

Two vital introductory questions are: Exactly what does a tradition comprise? And: How is it usually handled? We here confine ourselves to philosophical traditions of a world-viewish nature.

2.1 What a Tradition Is

A tradition is the heritage left by predecessors to their successors. Our relationship with the past implies, according to Van der Hoeven, a responsibility towards those who left us a heritage (cf. Van der Hoeven, 1980: 21).

Such a view of tradition is related to one's view of history. Van der Hoeven formulates it as follows:

> History is that which concerns all of us, which takes us along in a forward movement. In it everything passes by, but in such a way that the passing by is still taken up in the forward movement. Therefore the past has never passed away, but is something all of us carry around with us. Even when we have taken leave of it, it keeps on speaking to us [Transl. from the Dutch.] (1974: 13).

He illustrates it as follows:

The relation of a human being with his parents can by way of analogy (nothing more) perhaps bring greater clarity. A human being only becomes really mature and independent, that is sees his own possibilities for the future more distinctly, when he learns to discover how much he has received from his parents, in particular regarding the points on which he differs most with them, their approach, habits, opinions, etc. [Transl. from the Dutch.]

Van der Hoeven, therefore, emphasizes the responsibility of those who receive a particular inherited tradition towards those who handed it down to them as an incomplete heritage. A tradition is consequently not something without obligations. But before saying something more in this regard, we first distinguish the various elements of a tradition.

2.2 *Elements of a Tradition*
Wolterstorff (1987) distinguishes the following four facets in any tradition.

A worldview tradition helps one understand everything in existence (the structural side) and how it *should be* (the normative element). In the case of philosophy, a (pre-scientific) worldview is developed into (scientific) reflection.

Secondly, such a philosophical tradition does not remain a mere theory but is expressed in practice in many ways.

Each tradition also has its own "story," usually penned down in important writings, through which it is handed down from one generation to the next. In the last instance, no tradition is infallible – it will always be an imperfect, human product. With this in mind, the next issue arises, namely, the handling of a tradition.

2.3 *How A Tradition Should be Handled*
The risk attached to any tradition is that it can become a stagnant, dead legacy from the past. Then tradition becomes the living faith of the deceased and traditionalism the dead faith of the living!

Because the Christian tradition from the past (among which the Thomist and Reformed) had a rather intellectualist approach, it is currently not very popular. The emphasis is more on practical experience (cf. Van der Stoep, Kuiper & Ramaker, 2007).

Vander Stelt (2005) shows how a classical view of being human runs right through the Christian tradition from as long ago as Plato and Aristotle. According to this anthropology, a human being (apart from his body) consists of three parts of the soul, namely reason (head), will (hand) and desire (heart). During the history of Christianity, emphasis was laid one-sidedly on one of these three.

Earlier in Reformed Orthodoxy (in Aquinas' intellectualism), great stress was put on rationality (the head). The right knowledge, teaching or doctrine (orthodoxy) was regarded as very important. Later on, the emphasis shifted to the will, the right conduct or deed (orthopraxy). As was the case in earlier periods, currently, the experience of the heart is given precedence. It is, therefore, a question of how intellectually coloured traditions can be transmitted within such a new spiritual climate.

Wolterstorff (1987: 11-12) recommends the following: (1.) *Being open* towards the tradition – even if one feels like changing or rejecting it. (2.) A *critical attitude,* asking questions like the following: Did the tradition have the correct view of reality and is it still pointing in a clear normative direction? Does it also find expression in concrete conduct? Is its story handed down to be relevant to our times and thus will be appealing to a new generation, inspire and motivate them? (3.) Its *creative development:* Any tradition demands correction, broadening and extending by its followers.

This shows similarity as to how the heritage of Aquinas was handled in the Neo-Thomist tradition, as will emerge from the next section.

3. A Brief Outline of the Neo-Thomist Tradition

"Neo-Thomism" has usually only been applied to the revival of this tradition since the end of the nineteenth century. In this outline, however, I use it for the complete history since Aquinas' death.

3.1 The Philosophy of Aquinas Canonized

Although in the previous chapter we did point out the initial opposition against the philosophy and theology of Aquinas, it did not last long. In 1318, the philosophy of *Doctor Communis* was declared official doctrine (*philosophia in ecclesia recepta*) of the Dominican Order (founded by Dominicus de Soto).

3.2 Influence on Other Orders

However, Aquinas' influence was not confined to this one order in the Roman Catholic Church. His influence soon spread to scholars of the Franciscan Order (founded in 1209) and the Order of the Jesuits (founded much later, in 1534).

These two orders, however, supported different kinds of anthropologies. Instead of the typical Thomist subsistence theory, it was either a *vinculum theory* or a semi-mystical view of being human. In opposition to the Thomist Dominicans' intellectualism, they also held voluntaristic views (more emphasis on the will than on the intellect).

Therefore, conflict could not be avoided, and the Franciscans and Jesuits are often designated as "unorthodox" Neo-Thomists. Examples of eminent earlier and later Thomist Jesuits are, for instance, Suarez (1548-1617), Rahner (1904-1984) and Marlet (1921-1997).

3.3 Decrees by Various Popes

Various papal decrees further contributed to preventing Aquinas' philosophy from petering out during history. The following significant events may be mentioned. In 1323, Pope John XXII declared Aquinas a saint. Aquinas' main theological work, the *Summa Theologiae*, later gained a place of honour alongside the Bible on the altar in the hall where the First Council of Trent met. Leo XII (1878-1903), in his encyclical *Aeterni Patris* of 1879, called Aquinas the *princeps* and *magister* who stands out far above the other scholastic intellectuals and pleaded for a revival of his philosophy. An encyclical is a circular letter from a pope himself to his bishops, priests, and the Roman Catholic Church (for a summary of this particular encyclical, cf. Meuleman, 1952 and Gilson, 1972: 37).

In *Pascendi Dominici Gregris* of 1907 against modernism, Pope Pius X (1903-1914) concurred with Pope Leo XII by prescribing scholastic philosophy (meaning mainly Aquinas) as foundational to the theological sciences. Benedictus XV (1914-1922) in 1917 regarded Aquinas' rational thinking as an example to lecturers and institutions. Pius XI (1922-1939), in his *Studiorum Ducem* of 1923, called Aquinas the common or universal teacher of the Roman Catholic Church, followed by the encyclical *Humani Generis* of Pius XII (1939-1958) in 1950. In this document, he did not oppose the Augustinian or Franciscan traditions in Neo-Thomism, but the *nouvelle theologie* (new theology) under the influence of existentialism in particular (cf. Meuleman, 1960). Once more, the philosophy of Aquinas was recommended since it would safeguard the foundations of the Christian faith.

In 1965 (directly after the Second Vatican Council of 1962-1965), Pope Paul VI, in a decree of 28 October, on the training of priests again emphasized the meaning of Aquinas' ideas for scientific development. Finally, in the encyclical *Fides et ratio* of Pope John Paul II (1978-2005), one once again finds (in the line of *Humani Generis*) accommodation of the Augustinian and Franciscan traditions. Augustinian and Franciscan traditions emphasize Thomism as the antipode for various irrationalist and relativist tendencies. Pope Benedictus XVI (2005-2013) followed the Augustinian tradition, and the latest pope, Francis, is of the Jesuit Order.

3.4 Nature and Grace

From these different ecclesiastical enunciations, it becomes evident that Catholic thinking from the higher, supernatural sphere of grace or faith (to which church and theology are regarded to belong) kept careful watch over the so-called lower, natural sphere of reason, science and philosophy. This kind of rational philosophy in which church leaders also had to be instructed was not to conflict with the Christian faith or undermine it but had to support it.

To Reformational philosophers, however, it remains a question whether Aquinas' synthesis with the pagan thinking of, for instance, Plato and Aristotle and the later syntheses of the Neo-Thomists with modern secular philosophies, did not constitute an obstacle, rather than offering support.

3.5 The Dutch-Belgian Contribution

Finally, we have to mention that, due to the dominating role currently played by English, the Dutch and Belgian contributions to the revival of Thomism have often been underrated by historiographers. This applies in particular to the Roman Catholic Universities of Nijmegen and Leuven to which Stryker Boudier (1985-1992) devotes his eight-volume work *Wijsgerig leven in Nederland, België en Luxemburg, 1880-1980*. Philosophical life in the Netherlands, Belgium and Luxemburg, 1880-1980 (Part 1 deals with the contributions by the Dominicans and Part 2 with that of the Jesuits).

He indicates how later Thomist philosophers, under the influence of newer philosophical trends and schools, deviated from Aquinas and other "fathers" (in Part 8 of 1992: 73 et seq., he also discusses what Roman Catholics imply by a Christian philosophy). As will become evident later (cf. the following chapter), the Netherlands and Belgium produced a substantial number of important Neo-Thomist philosophers.

4. Neo-Thomist Interpretations of Developments During Seven Centuries

Various Thomists themselves recount the history of Neo-Thomism. In addition to the sources later to be enumerated, we could mention Cessario (2003), Lonergan (2000) and Rowland (2012). Even writings dealing mainly with Aquinas often draw the lines further through history, (e.g. Nichols, 2002 and Elders, 2013). The well-known contemporary Roman Catholic philosopher MacIntyre (2009) also weaves the history of Thomism after Aquinas into his work. However, the intention of this chapter is not to set out a history of Neo-Thomism, but rather to draw attention to the problems concerning their different historiographies. We mention only a few examples.

4.1 Haldane

Haldane (2005: 1017) emphasizes the synthetic character of the Thomist tradition. Further, he distinguishes between the concept of "Thomism" in a narrower and a broader sense. To him, the narrower sense comprises the interpretations of and commentaries on Aquinas by sixteenth and seventeenth-century philosophers like Cajetanus (1469-1534) and others. He would probably also count De Vitoria (1468-1546) and possibly Zabarella (1532-1589) among these.

But already, in these early times, there were, according to Haldane, philosophers observing a connection between Aquinas' philosophy and that of, for instance, other Medieval philosophers. Suarez (1548-1617), for example, also used insights gained by Duns Scotus.

According to Haldane, even before, but especially after the Second Vatican Council (1962-1965), such a broader view gained popularity. Thomist philosophers began freely accommodating contemporary tendencies, for example, existentialism and phenomenology. However, this renders it more difficult to write a history of Neo-Thomism: "Not only have some self-proclaimed Thomists held positions with which Aquinas would probably have taken issue. Some have advanced claims that he would not have been able to understand" (Haldane, 2005: 1017).

Sassen & Delfgaauw (1957: 266) were confronted by the same issue already during the fifties of the previous century. Not only was it a fact that not all Thomists are Catholics, but the influence of various tendencies on Thomism often was so considerable "... that it is sometimes difficult to make out whether a certain philosopher should be regarded as a Thomist or not."

4.2 Delfgaauw

Delfgaauw (1952: 79 et seq.) attempts to distinguish between conservative, moderate and progressive Neo-Thomists and enumerates representatives of all three schools.

The conservatives thought that Aquinas' philosophy and theology merely needed to be explained anew for current times. The moderates did not want to change Aquinas' philosophy but were convinced that their own times presented numerous new issues which had not yet been topical in the time of the *Doctor Angelicus*. By far, most of the Neo-Thomists, however, belonged to the third group who believed that the philosophy of Aquinas could be followed in broad lines but could by no means be considered complete. Neo-Thomism could, according to them, only be a living philosophy if practised in perpetual contact with modern and contemporary philosophy.

Robbers (1951:82, 83) also follows this categorization into three types of Neo-Thomism and himself chooses the third (progressive) approach. Thus a great diversity of forms or shades of Neo-Thomism exists. As mentioned above, this was recently again accentuated by a lecture by Walmsley (2012) entitled "Whose Thomism? Which Aquinas?"

5. *Two Difficult Questions*
We begin with Walmsley's second question: Which Thomas? However, it cannot be isolated from his first question: Whose (Neo-)Thomism?

5.1 Which Aquinas?
To be a true *Thomist*, a philosopher has to consider Aquinas' thinking in some way or another. But to qualify as a true *Neo*-Thomist, one should also differ with it. Therefore, there should be both continuity and discontinuity. In the above-mentioned encyclical *Aeterni Patris* (of 04/08/1879), the issue, concisely put, is formulated as follows: *vetera novis augere et perficere* (the old should be enriched and perfected by the new).

To meet the two above-mentioned ecclesiastical directions first demands answering two vital questions. *First*, what were the essential traits of Aquinas' philosophy with which a Neo-Thomist should associate himself? *Secondly*, how much independence may a Neo-Thomist indulge in while remaining a Thomist? This, incidentally, applies to all three types of Neo-Thomism listed above because even the first two, distinguished by Delfgaauw, could not represent Aquinas neutrally and objectively.

5.2 Illustrating the Issue

Robbers (1951) is here used merely to illustrate how difficult it can be to answer the second question, which Aquinas?

Initially, he attempts to answer the question by trying to pin down which of the two had the more significant influence on Aquinas – Aristotelianism or (Neo-)Platonism. Following certain Aquinas interpretations, he chooses for the latter influence, which he discerns particularly in the central meaning of the doctrine of analogy in the work of Aquinas (p. 58).

Later on, however, he has to admit that distinct Aristotelian influence in the work of Aquinas cannot be denied either, and he writes: "Even if one could see the Platonism of Thomas as specified by Aristotelianism, likewise one can call his Aristotelianism specified by Platonism" (p. 69). Therefore, he finally prefers to identify an "Aristotelian Platonism" in the work of Aquinas (cf. p. 74).

However, it is not satisfactory to characterize the philosophy of Aquinas merely through reference to significant influences on his thinking, for Aquinas was an original thinker whose philosophy was not simply a combination of two other philosophers or schools of philosophy.

Robbers (1951: 80, 81) is, therefore, eventually compelled to enumerate some leading, characteristic features in the work of Aquinas. These are, according to him, Aquinas' teachings on the *analogia entis, materia et forma, actus et potentia* and *essentia et existentia*. He adds that this kind of philosophy was practised in a "Christian climate," in other words, it cannot be called Christian as such.

Is it not conspicuous that Robbers, in his description of the essential traits of Aquinas' thinking (and in his description of Neo-Thomism), makes no mention of the most important feature? Namely the distinction between a so-called natural and a supernatural sphere – with all the implications this has? Does he take this dualistic two realm doctrine so much for granted that it need not be mentioned? Or is it perhaps the deeply hidden driving force from which he as a Thomist departs?

5.3 Whose Thomism?

In the second instance, what does being a Neo-Thomist entail, according to Robbers (1951)? He admits (cf. p. 64) that this question is even more challenging to answer in clear terms. He merely states in general (p. 51) that Neo-Thomism should consist of two elements: One by which it is connected with Aquinas, and a second, whereby it can be considered a modern school of thought. Instead of distinct norms or guidelines for its modernity, Robbers falls back on what he previously described as characteristic of Aquinas.

Thus, he answers only one aspect, namely that of continuity and not the discontinuity with Aquinas, making modern Thomism a *new* kind of Thomism. Since Robbers advocates the third type of (progressive) Neo-Thomism, the answer probably is that. Just as Aquinas earlier attempted to combine Aristotelian and Platonic philosophies in synthesis with his Christian faith, Neo-Thomism may use the same synthesis method in the case of modern philosophical trends. Therefore, Robbers points out (p. 84 et seq.) that it would be following ecclesiastical enunciations, as, for instance, the *vetera novis augere* of *Aeterni Patris*.

It would seem (cf. Robbers, p. 52) as if he also departs from the (to my mind false) division between form and content. According to that, the "neutral" form and method of contemporary philosophies (accepted by the Neo-Thomists) would not influence the content of their Thomist (Christian) convictions. The same error is committed that Aquinas made seven centuries ago.

5.4 The Importance of a Development in the Philosophy of Aquinas

According to Vollenhoven (2000: 237-238), in understanding Aquinas, one must realize that significant shifts occurred due to development through several phases within his philosophy.

As was pointed out in Chapter one, Aquinas wrote his main philosophical work, the *Summa Contra Gentiles,* between 1258/9-1263/4, while he was still reading Aristotle through Platonising lenses. His theological *magnum opus*, the *Summa Theologiae,* however, originated during the following phase (1265-1274) when the influence of Aristotle on Aquinas' philosophy had increased, and it became clear that he was following a non-Platonising interpretation of Aristotle.

Therefore, Aquinas' followers will have to indicate with *which* concepts or writings of Aquinas they agree. Generally, such a distinction is not made by Neo-Thomists in Aquinas' own development. Thus some Neo-Thomists stressed the Platonic elements (e.g. the idea of participation), while others emphasized the Aristotelian features (e.g. the doctrine of causality, potency and act, matter and form). That brings us to the next point, namely that the history of Neo- Thomismis mainly mapped out according to two methods.

6. Two Historiographical Methods

The first method implies a more or less broad ontological-conceptual typology.

6.1 A Typological Classification

Ashley (2006: 44-45) uses this type of survey to attempt a systematic distinction between different kinds of Neo-Thomism. In his classification, one finds Platonising, Aristotelian, Augustinian, Existentialist, Phenomenological and Analytical Neo-Thomists. However, such a classification remains too vague, for what exactly is meant by "Platonising" etc.

(Neo-)Thomism? Would it not be possible to be more specific?

The same applies to Mitchell (2007: map no. 155, 156 and 172). His first map (no. 155) surveys medieval philosophy, subdivided into Islamic, Jewish and Christian philosophies. Among the latter, there is a distinction between Augustinians, Franciscans and Dominicans, and Aquinas as an important representative in the last-mentioned order.

The second map (no. 156) gives an outline of the 15th and 16th centuries, showing how Thomism had a significant influence on the Dominican Order (particularly at the University of Salamanca in Spain) and the Jesuits (particularly at the University of Coimbra in Portugal). In the first case, individuals like Cajetanus and De Vitoria were significant and in the latter, Suarez. According to this map, however, the Jesuits at the time were still thinking differently, especially in the line of Bonaventura. The third map (no. 172) gives a picture of 20th-century Neo-Thomism in the narrower meaning of the concept of the Thomist revival, which followed in response to *Aeterni Patris*.

Apart from being incomplete, the map is not very enlightening. For example, from Cardinal Désiré Mercier (1851-1926), who played an important role in the revival of Thomism, numerous lines on the map led to various philosophers, some of whom are merely mentioned among them early individuals (e.g. Etienne Gilson and other more recent philosophers like Alasdair MacIntyre). Other more recent philosophers are categorized according to concepts like "analytical," "metaphysical," and "transcendental."

6.2 A Chronological Account

Gilby (1967: 119-121) distinguishes between three meanings of the concept "Thomism" (in use since the fourteenth century) which correspond with three important periods in the history of this movement: (1.) Until the beginning of 1500, there was stiff competition between the various other Medieval schools and Thomism. (2.) From the 16th to the 18th century, Thomism enjoyed a golden age in Spain. (3.) From the second half of the nineteenth century (especially due to *Aeterni Patris*), a revival of Thomism began – regarded as the *philosophia perennis* of Roman Catholic thinking.

Since then, Thomists have been moving outwards in dialogue with numerous other philosophical traditions and disciplines and applied Thomist principles to contemporary social and political issues. Consequently, Gilby classifies the history chronologically into (1.) the thirteenth to the sixteenth centuries, (2.) the sixteenth to nineteenth and (3.) the nineteenth and twentieth centuries. In each period, he also mentions the most prominent philosophers and theologians.

7. Conclusion: The Necessity for a More Distinctly Philosophical Historiography

On the one hand, one has to admit that mapping the seven centuries-long Neo-Thomist traditions is not a simple matter. On the other hand, how it has been done up to now is confusing and therefore unsatisfactory. Consequently, a final chapter will investigate whether a more suitable method, which would offer both a better survey of and a deeper insight into Neo-Thomist philosophy, is available.

CHAPTER 8
A PROBLEM-HISTORICAL ANALYSIS OF NEO-THOMIST SCHOLARSHIP

The preceding chapter provided a broad overview of seven centuries of Neo-Thomist thinking in philosophy and theology and a discussion of the methodological attempts of various Neo-Thomists at describing this long history of the interpretations of Thomas Aquinas. As concluded in the previous chapter, a complex history, which was unable to provide an entirely satisfactory historiographical method, confronted these historiographers.

This chapter argues that a consistent problem-historical method may be more appropriate to do the job, providing both penetrating analysis and insight. The chapter develops as follows. The first part briefly describes the two main aspects of a philosophical conception, its ontological type and normative direction. The second part provides an analysis of "classic" Thomist ontology (purely cosmological thinking, an ontological hierarchy with a dualism, vertical partial universalism and a clear distinction between nature and supernature or grace) as well as its anthropology (a subsistence theory). From the third section onwards, *the focus is on the Thomist nature-grace distinction, describing the modern shifting perspectives on this central dogma, while the next section explains the underlying philosophical reasons for this remarkable departure from Aquinas' original viewpoint. Special attention is given to more recent irrationalist perspectives. The last (fifth) part is devoted to discussing a possible, more biblically oriented perspective on the ancient tension between the secular/profane and sacred/holy. In an increasingly secular world, Protestant Reformational thinkers are also challenged by the vital question of how one should view the relationship between nature and grace, culture and Christ, creation and redemption. If a Neo-Thomist view cannot help in this regard, in which direction should a Reformational philosophy be developed in the twenty-first century A.D.?*

1. Introduction

SOME PRELIMINARY REMARKS ARE required on how this chapter links up with the previous one and its layout.

1.1 Link

The previous seventh chapter concluded that Neo-Thomists could not offer a satisfactory philosophical account of the developments during the past seven centuries following their "father," Thomas Aquinas and that a better methodology should be found. Therefore, this chapter wants to investigate whether the consistent problem-historical method would be more appropriate for this purpose. Simultaneously, it also attempts to demonstrate that such a method can explain better than the standing theological studies of the remarkable shifts within Neo-Thomist thinking regarding a central dogma (the doctrine of nature-grace) in Roman Catholic philosophy (cf., e.g. Meuleman, 1951).

1.2 Lay-out

The argument is presented in the following phases. First, a brief definition is given of the two primary components of any philosophical and theological conception, its ontological type and normative direction. Subsequently (in the second part), analysis is offered of "classical" Thomist ontology, a purely cosmological philosophy. Our discussion will highlight an ontological hierarchy including a dualistic division, vertical partial universalism and a distinction between nature and grace (the supernatural), as well as typical Thomist anthropology (a subsistence theory).

From the third section onwards, the focus is on the two realm doctrine of nature-grace and the apparent shifts that have taken place during the past centuries concerning this central Roman Catholic dogma. A fourth section attempts to explain this remarkable departure from the original view of Aquinas from the perspective of certain underlying changes in philosophical views. Special attention is given to more recent irrationalist tendencies. The last (fifth) section is devoted to the possibility of a more biblically oriented view of the age-old (in my opinion fictitious) dualism between the profane/secular/worldly and the sacred/holy. Even to Protestant philosophers, this is an issue from which they have struggled to liberate themselves. How should they understand the relationship between nature and grace, culture and Christ, creation and redemption within the context of an increasingly secular 21st century?

2. Considering the Consistently Problem-Historical Method as a Possibility

The previous chapters have already mentioned (cf. also Vollenhoven, 2005; Runner, 1982 and Kok, 1998: 1-178) that a worldview and philosophy attempt to answer two fundamental questions. In the first instance, how existing reality *looks* according to one's view, and in the second instance, how it *should be*. The first is an *ontic* or *structural* question on what *exists* (reality), and the second is a *normative* or *directional question* on how one *should* think and act.

In his historiography of Western philosophy, Vollenhoven departs from the answers given to these two fundamental and historical questions scholars have posed. A response to the structural problem offers a specific philosophical ontology (or view of reality) and anthropology (or view of the human being). Answers to what should be normative for thinking and doing emerge in different philosophical *schools* or *currents* which point the direction for a specific time. Together, the type and current constitute the conception of a philosopher (For introductory, elementary explanations of Vollenhoven's method cf. Van der Walt, 2010a, 2013a, 2013b available in English in Van der Walt, 2014a: 47ff and 2014b:1-37).

2.1 The Character of Types

The interesting point is that the *types* of philosophies are not restricted to a certain age. After many of these originated as far back as ancient Greek philosophy, they emerged again in the works of various philosophers throughout history. An identical type of philosophy in the works of two different philosophers could therefore indicate the influence of one scholar (e.g. the master) on the other (e.g. the student or disciple) or of a philosophical school that could be in existence for a shorter or longer period. Accordingly, one would therefore expect more or less the same type of philosophy in the Neo-Thomist school. The standard type of philosophy would explain its consistent element (Vollenhoven, 2000: 184-259 mentions all the different philosophical types, of which Vollenhoven, 2005: 157-159 offers a brief survey).

2.2 The Nature of Schools or Trends

Unlike the type of philosophy that can live on for ages through generations and guarantee continuity in a tradition, a specific school, trend, or current lasts for only a limited time to be replaced afterward by a new normative direction. Therefore, schools are responsible for the variable or dynamic element in history (for an outline of the various schools in Western intellectual history, cf. Vollenhoven, 2005: 153-155).

Why do philosophical directions change all the time? According to Vollenhoven, this is the subjectivist idea of normativity, which already had its origin in Greek philosophy. What does he mean by subjectivism?

It implies that no clear distinction is made between law/norm and that (the subject) to which the law/norm applies. That which should be subject to norms/laws is wrongly elevated to become a norm itself. Formulated differently: what *is,* is also regarded as what *should be.*

Why do the various philosophical schools lead to constant change? Simply because there are so many things in creation that can be absolutized or elevated to normative status. In rationalist philosophy (± 1600-1900), the human mind was, for instance, absolutized as reason (*ratio*) as the essential standard for both theory and practice. Irrationalism, however, downgrades the reason without rejecting it entirely. In this mainstream (from approximately 1900) there are, however, internal differences. In vitalism, power or vitality is elevated to an absolute norm; in pragmatism, usefulness is viewed as the highest standard; in existentialism, human existential freedom has to point the direction (cf., e.g. Robbers, 1951).

2.3 The Influence of Schools on Types

As mentioned above, the combination of a certain type and specific normative current or school forms a specific philosopher's conception or system. But what is the relationship between the two main elements of a philosophical system? The dynamic element (normative school) can influence the type of philosophy. A particular kind of philosophy within rationalism is, for example, transformed when it also appears in subsequent irrationalist schools.

This chapter attempts to analyze Neo-Thomism according to this approach to the Western history of philosophy, both as far as its continuous ontological-anthropological features are concerned (the type of philosophy) and the different changing schools it passed throughout the past seven centuries.

3. The Type of Philosophy Fundamental to Thomism

First, attention will be given to several of Aquinas' disciples from the 16th and 17th centuries and subsequently from the 19th and 20th centuries to determine whether their type of philosophy remained the same.

3.1 Earlier Representatives

The founder of the Dominican Order, Dominicus de Soto (1491-1560), the classic commentator on Aquinas' *Summa Theologiae*, and T. De Vio Cajetanus (1469-1534), F. de Vitoria (1486-1546), attached to the famous university of Salamanca, Fr. de Suarez (1548-1617) and G. Zabarella (1532-1589), all still belong to the period or trend of the new age following the Middle Ages (cf. Vollenhoven, 2000: 257). Their philosophies also correspond to that of Aquinas during his second philosophical phase in which he wrote his two *Summae* (cf. Vollenhoven, 2000: 238).

3.2 More Recent Representatives

In the nineteenth and twentieth centuries, Aquinas' type of philosophy was more or less maintained. However, this takes place within new schools. Here are a few examples of how these philosophical currents changed. D. Mercier (1851-1926) was a neo-idealistic rationalist. However, the following philosophers did support some or other form of irrationalism: A.D. Sertillanges (1863-1948), H. Bergson (1860-1941) and M. Blondel (1861-1949) adhered to "Lebensphilosophie"; A. Gardeil (1859-1931) was a pragmatist and K. Rahner (1904-1984), J. Maritain (1882-1973) and M.F.J. Marlet (1921-1997) existentialists (cf. Vollenhoven, 2000).

Apart from these Roman Catholic philosophers, Vollenhoven (2000) also provides valuable information (according to type and current) on the following more recent individuals' philosophical conceptions: H. Urs von Balthazar (1905-1988), J. Danielou (1905-1974), L. La Velle (1883-1951), H. De Lubac (1896-1991), G. Marel (1889-1973), J. Maritain (1882-1973), P. Merlan (1897-1968), F. Sassen (1894-1971) and T. de Chardin (1881-1955). Vollenhoven (2000) was initially published already in 1962 by contemporary well-known Roman Catholic philosophers, like A. MacIntyre (1929-), C. Taylor (1931-) and others who were omitted (cf. Bartholomew & Goheen, 2013: 201 ff).

When a new school becomes a popular fashion, the older schools in philosophy are usually doubted. However, in a Christian academic milieu (mainly of a conservative nature), one often finds the opposite tendency: the perspective of a preceding, outdated philosophy criticizes contemporary philosophy.

For instance, Roman Catholic philosophers like Delfgaauw (1952: 110 et seq.) criticize the irrationalist schools, which depart from his rationalistic conviction. According to Delfgaauw, "Lebensphilosophie" causes a human being to be led by his instincts and not by his reason. The existentialists adhere to an idea of a blind, irrational choice for freedom. The pragmatists subordinate the human intellect and scholarship to useful conduct: science which is not of practical use is a luxury and is senseless. According to Delfgaauw, finally, pragmatism places the intellect in the service of the material prosperity of human beings.

Later on, we will show how this change in a normative direction led to the transformation of the typically Thomist doctrine of nature-grace.

3.3 A Brief Description of the Type of Philosophy of Neo-Thomism

The typification by Vollenhoven (2000: 238, 257) of the majority of these Thomist philosophers runs as follows: purely cosmological philosophy, dualism, vertical partial universalism and subsistence theory. What is implied by this Vollenhovian terminology? The first four concepts, in broad terms, describe the Thomist ontology or view of reality, and the last is its typical anthropology. The third chapter dealt with the ontology of Aquinas in his *Summa Contra Gentiles,* which is an extensive explanation of the above concepts (a brief refresher of the readers' memory).

3.3.1 Purely Cosmological Philosophy

Purely cosmological philosophy means that the origin of creation is not regarded as significant in this kind of thinking. Studying the existing *structural side* of cosmic things is the focus, while their *origin* and *development* are less important. Therefore, this type of philosophy implies a markedly static view in contrast to cosmogono-cosmological thinking, which, as the word denotes, does seek to pay attention to the genetic or dynamic. Older cosmological philosophers differ from other, later

Neo-Thomists (e.g. Blondel and Von Balthasar) with whom we will deal later.

3.3.2 Dualism

Dualism indicates that the existing reality consists of an original dichotomy, usually called the transcendent God and the non-transcendent universe. Within one hierarchy of being, a higher and a lower part is distinguished.

Such a view of reality, however, usually leads to all sorts of problems. For instance, what is the difference between God and creation and their relationship if they are merely higher and lower "parts" of the same hierarchy of being? This (false) issue leads to the "solution" that God is supposed to transcend and be immanent in creation. Then the next question arises: Exactly in what way is God present in creation? Or: How can He be in creation without creation becoming semi-divine (called pantheism) or God being cosmologized? Or the opposite: Does His transcendent being not imply that creation exists disconnected from God (called deism)? The only "solution" seems to be an always precarious balance between God's transcendence and His immanence.

Therefore, Neo-Thomism does not fully respect the *radical* distinction between God and His creation as found in the Bible. God and creation are not, biblically seen, in a *religious* relationship, but an *ontic* one of *analogy* (i.e. similarity in difference). In this way, creation participates in the divine. The highest quest of a human being becomes his supernatural deification.

3.3.3 Nature and Grace

Chapter one (subsections 4 and 5) has shown that the distinction between nature-grace is a *method* to effect a synthesis or compromise between biblical revelation and a prevalent extra-biblical philosophy. However, since a method is not something neutral or "formal," it has the result that reality itself is construed according to a double focused view: it consists of a natural, terrestrial and a supernatural, heavenly, divine sphere.

Since the transcendent is often associated with the supernatural, divine grace, and the non-transcendent with the natural cosmic things or spheres, all Thomist philosophers raise the question of what exactly the relationship and the difference between the two are supposed to be (chapter two discussed this issue in detail).

According to all Thomist philosophers, the *difference* between nature and grace is that the sphere of grace is something beyond reason, which one can only understand in faith. In contrast, nature is supposed to be accessible to human reason. Faith need not play any role in this domain.

The *relationship* between the two is that nature has an inherent quest (*desiderium naturale*) for the supernatural, which must be completed or perfected by divine grace.

Chapter two (subsection 6.1.3) stated that after Aquinas at an early stage, the Thomist philosophers already posed questions regarding this relationship (cf., e.g. O'Mahony, 1929). For instance: How can nature be a quest for the supernatural, since such a natural longing would no longer be purely natural? A natural consciousness of imperfection supposes at least something of a supernatural kind in nature.

The opposite question arises, seen from the side of grace. If nature is *perfected* by the supernatural (not *cancelled* – as Aquinas repeatedly emphasized), there would have to be something natural in the supernatural. This issue will be further investigated below (subsection 4).

3.3.4 Vertical Partial Universalism

Briefly put, partial universalism is an interim position between individualism and universalism. Individualism regards specific things as more important than the universal (this particular human being is more important than being human). Universalism teaches the exact opposite: being human is more important than this individual. However, both these viewpoints are erroneous since the universal and the individual are both *facets* of reality in their entirety. Vertical partial universalists see a higher-lower relationship between the universal and the individual. Classic Thomism regarded the form as the higher, universal and the matter as the lower, individual.

3.3.5 Subsistence theory

Chapter 4 already dealt with this kind of anthropology. In short, it boils down to the following: God creates every new human soul at some time or other (during conception or afterwards) into the human body, derived from the parents (a theory called creatianism). Since the soul comes from God as a separate substance (hence the name "subsistence theory" for this view of being human), it is supratemporal, supernatural and therefore, unlike the human body, immortal. After death, it also survives as a separate substance until the resurrection, reuniting with the resurrected body. (For a more biblically oriented view of a human being, cf. Van der Walt, 2010).

We have already mentioned above that a type of philosophy described does not stay consistent in succeeding normative currents. Subsequently, we will consider how the change to a new school also influenced Neo-Thomist philosophers' view of the central dogma of Thomism, viz., the relationship between nature and grace.

4. Shifts in Neo-Thomist Views of The Nature-Grace Theme

We will now demonstrate how a shift in view took place regarding the relationship between nature and grace, especially in more contemporary Thomist philosophy. Subsequently, we will point out the fundamental causes (sometimes due to a new school of thinking, but often at the same time also because of a new type of philosophy). Several studies have confirmed that Thomist philosophers, since 1920, advocated a different view from Aquinas on the relationship between nature and grace; from a Reformational angle, for instance, by Smit (1950), Meuleman (1960 and 1967) and later by Wentsel (1970). A comparison between the older views and the more recent ones reveals the difference.

According to Aquinas, nature has a passive potential for the supernatural. Grace realizes this potential and thereby fulfils the most profound possibilities and aspirations of nature. However, only by the intervention of God can the slumbering, unconscious quest of the natural human being be fully developed. Thus Aquinas accepted both a harmony and a strict distinction between the two spheres (cf. Polman, 1961: 367). The later twentieth-century Neo-Thomists would doubt this clear distinction made by Aquinas between nature and grace.

4.1 Earlier Views

Sixteenth-century debates already reveal problems with Aquinas. Cajetanus, who has already been mentioned (*obiit* 1534), attempted to solve the issue of the relationship between nature and grace by denying the (natural) longing or making it supernatural. On the other hand, Sylvester Ferrariensis (*obiit* 1528) queried the supernatural character of the object of the natural longing. Both philosophers, therefore, agree in so far as they reject a *positive directedness* of nature towards grace. Nature and grace exist *parallel alongside each other*. Nature is merely a *passive substratum* of the supernatural. Therefore, the Thomist concept *desiderium naturale* says nothing more than that nature *has an aptness* for taking up grace when God offers it (cf. Smit, 1950: 39).

4.2 Newer Tendencies

According to Smit (1950: 19), there were earlier signs (end of the 19th century) of objections against the two commentators as mentioned earlier on Aquinas' view, although the actual controversy about it only flared up after World War II. He describes the new opinions as follows. They all reject the idea that the natural sphere is an *altogether passive substratum* that can only be complemented by grace. According to them, there is a *positive relationship* between these two spheres. Formulated slightly differently (cf. Wentsel, 1970: 473), more recent Roman Catholic theology is grappling with the issue of whether the natural concept of a *desiderium* did not already imply grace. Therefore, the more recent Thomists are attempting, in different ways, to overcome the earlier substantial dualism in the two realm doctrine. Vandervelde (1975) shows that, due to this, a notable shift has also taken place in the work of Roman Catholic philosophers regarding the doctrine of original sin.

More recently, however, Zagzebski (1993: 3-4) wrote that a significant difference between Roman Catholic and Reformational philosophers is that the first continue to believe in an unaided human reason. While according to the latter group of Christian thinkers, the effects of the fall into sin on human reason were more radical.

4.3 Two Different Views

Smit (1950: 40 et seq.) also distinguishes two different directions among these 20th-century Neo-Thomists, a more static and dynamic direction.

The first (static) direction considers the natural desire to see God as an innate *ontic* urge of the human being to fulfill his being or existence. However, such a supernatural ultimate goal cannot, of course, be attained naturally. God is not compelled to answer to this longing either – that would jeopardize His divine freedom.

Smit has the following critique of this ontic (instead of religious) view of the relationship between God (supernature) and man (nature):

> It is once more evident here that the ontological and religious views of the basic relationship between God and human being mutually exclude each other. The first always entails a restriction on the second and the latter does not allow a restriction, precisely because of its integral character [Translated from the Dutch.] (1950: 42).

According to the biblical *religious* view, *all of* life is of a religious nature – there is no natural, religiously neutral territory.

The second, more recent view is the more dynamic, of which M. Blondel (1861-1949) was the primary representative. Seeing that he was an irrationalist, adherent of "Lebensphilosophie" or vitalism, he emphasized dynamic development and action instead of conceptual abstraction (typical of preceding rationalism). However, the theme of the natural human shortcoming, insufficiency (insatiable longing for supernatural grace), remains central in his philosophy.

4.4 Unsolved Issues

The key issue amongst Neo-Thomists is therefore not whether the distinction, nature grace, is biblically acceptable, but about where exactly the borderline between nature and grace should be drawn. Both the more structural and the dynamic views of Neo-Thomism are on thin ice in this reguard.

On the one hand, there is the risk that nature may from its *own power* reach its supernatural goal (cf. Smit, 1950: 41). Therefore, it is repeatedly emphasized that nature is *inefficax,* that is that reaching its supernatural end or *goal* goes entirely above the capacity of nature.

On the other hand, caution should be taken that the fact that God has created an innate longing for the supernatural in human beings does not result in an absolute *demand* by nature (human beings) reguarding divine grace (cf. Smit, 1950: 47). An affirmative answer to this would infringe on the undeservedness of grace and on God's right of decision. Some Thomist philosophers solve this problem by speaking not about an *absolute* but a *moral* demand from this side of nature.

It consequently becomes evident that the tension in the relationship between nature and grace is irresolveable (Smit 1950: 47), for instance, shows how the standpoint of H. de Lubac (1896-1991) finally reaches the point where nature is supernaturalized to such an extent and vanishes from the horizon and that the issue of the relationship between nature and grace is practically eliminated.

4.5 A Confimation

Wentsel (1970: 487-8) reaches the same conclusion. On the one hand, there is *continuity* in the Thomist tradtion, because nature and grace are still distinguished as two separate spheres. On the other hand, there is, however, also *discontinuity* or a clear shift, since nature and supernature are very closely connected. The distance between the Christian or the church and the world is almost obliterated: "After nature and grace were for a long time driven too far apart, a tendency can now be observed to identify the one with the other and allow them to merge (Wentsel, 1970:

488). [Translated from the Dutch.]

It is understandable that the Roman Catholic authorities in the papal encyclical *Humani Generis* (1950) spoke out agaisnt this new kind of Thomism and attempted to put in place various measures against it (cf. Meuleman, 1952).

An important question that has not been answeared, is what kind of philosophy is underlying these sometimes radically changed views of the age-old nature-grace theme – the next point of our invesigation.

5. The Philosophies "Behind" the Changed View of the relationship Between Nature and Grace

Since Smit (1950), Vandervelde (1975) and Wentsel (1970) do not offer a philosophical explination as to why the newer Thomists advocate a closer relationship between nature and supernature, we will now undertake to do this.

5.1 New Irrational Schools

The first reason is undoubtedly new philosophical trends, schools or normative views. It has been shown above with examples of some Neo-Thomist philosophers how their thinking reflects various rationalist and irrationalist currents. One example of the latter will here serve as an illustration.

5.2 K. Rahner as An Example of a New Philosophical Current

Rahner (1904-1984) teaches (cf. Wentsel, 1970: 167, 168 as well as Vandervelde, 1975: 109-126) that there is no contrast between nature and grace. Nature exisits on behalf of grace and grace purifies and fulfils nature – they are intrinsically involved. However, this happens in spite of the fact that Rahner's *type* of philosophy still corresponds with that of Aquinas (cf. 3 above and Vollenhoven 2000: 257).

Therefore, the chief reason for Rahner's new view on nature and grace is the new philosophical school he philosophized, namely existentialism, which emphasized human freedom and the dynamic-historic as opposed to the fixed and static nature of reality. In this respect, he concurs with, for instance, the view held by J. Maritain (1882-1973).

Despite this close involvement of the two spheres, Vandervelde (cf. one of the theses in his doctoral thesis) points out that the dualism and tension between a natural and a supernatural sphere constantly afflict Rahner's theology.

5.3 M. Blondel as An Example of Another Type of Philosophy

In some cases, however, it is not only new trends/schools/currents but, coupled with them, also new types of philosophies that cause a changed view of nature and grace. As an example, we mention M. Blondel (1861-1949). (H. Urs von Balthasar (1905-1988) holds a similar conception.) We will devote more time to this influential Roman Catholic philosopher of the previous century.

Blondel was not an existentialistic irrationalist but a vitalistic irrationalist philosopher. The distinctive trademark of his "Lebensphilosophie" is that the origin of the norms for human life lies in a vital life of power itself – a distinctly subjectivist idea of law that elevates things/matters to normative status.

Blondel's philosophical practice is unlike Aquinas' and Rahner's. Vollenhoven (2000: 245) characterizes it as follows: the cosmogono-cosmological, monistic, doctrine of priorities, and noetic. This philosophy's elements contribute to a closer, dynamic relationship instead of a separated, inflexible relationship between nature and grace.

As mentioned above, a cosmogonic philosophy, in contrast to the purely cosmological philosopher's structural thinking, emphasizes genetic thinking, which recognizes change in a dynamic creation. Monistic philosophers depart from an original unity (in contrast to the usual dualism of Thomism). Although plurality ensues from the unity, the unity always stays the final ideal – something that Blondel emphasizes in his teaching on nature-grace. Zuidema (1972) not only gives a good account of Blondel's ideas in this regard but also offers a discerning immanent critique. He concisely summarizes Blondel's whole philosophy in the following sentence: "Blondel takes his starting point in a supernatural idea of the natural to postulate employing this idea a natural doctrine of the supernatural" (Zuidema, 1972: 259).

5.4 An Apologetic Motive

Blondel's apologetic motive was communication with and persuasion of non-Christian philosophers by pretending that he was taking the same stand as these "non-believers" (cf. Meuleman, 1958). To effect this, Blondel departs from the supposition that the natural human being possesses a *manque*, a metaphysical disquiet, an ontological shortcoming or insatiable natural longing for supernatural grace.

Thus the basic pattern of Blondel's philosophy is (cf. Zuidema, 1972: 244): (1.) the human being is inadequate and imperfect because he is created; (2.) the human being as a creature senses in himself a need of fulfilment or redemption; (3.) God elevates the human being to the supernatural and thus obliterates the deficiency.

5.5 Inconsistency

Therefore, Blondel departs from a natural or immanent idea of the supernatural. Zuidema, however, poses the following critical question:

> Blondel will repeatedly point out that man's natural life is *se manque,* does not reach its goal and falls short of its destiny, if it does not culminate in a supranatural elevation and deification ... however, he has never seriously asked himself why natural-philosophical reason is an exception to this. What possible reason can there be that philosophy does not *se manque* when it does not culminate in a supranatural theology through a supranatural elevation? Along with scientific reason ... philosophy turns out to be the only thing in and on man which is to be an exception to the general rule of the insufficiency of the natural (1972: 232).

Zuidema's conclusion is: "Thus we encounter the extraordinary thesis in Blondel that philosophy is sufficient to demonstrate the insufficiency of everything natural with the exception of its own insufficiency on this point" (Zuidema, 1972: 232).

5.6 Failed Apologetics

The irrationalist Blondel, like Christian rationalist apologists through the ages, attempted to render the Christian faith acceptable to non-Christians by showing that such a faith is not irrational but rational precisely by admitting its own ontic shortcoming. However, Zuidema (1972: 252, 253) is not convinced that such an attempt can succeed. For modern human beings are convinced of their autonomy, they decide for themselves what is right – and will therefore not accept their natural deficiency. The secular philosopher prefers to live without God and will decline Blondel's supposed longing for a supernatural elevation.

Therefore, Zuidema's conclusion runs as follows: "Bondel's 'philosophical apologetics' is in my opinion doomed to failure. It harbours the seeds of its own self-destruction" (1972: 259).

Is it nevertheless permissible to call such apologetics a kind of Christian philosophy – as is often claimed nowadays?"

5.7 Champions of a Christian Philosophy?

Sassen & Delfgaauw (1957: 291-294) distinguish four different positions on the possibility of a Christian philosophy among Neo-Thomist philosophers. Some deny the possibility of a Christian philosophy in the natural sphere because of a clear separation of nature and grace. Only theology in the sphere of grace is considered to be Christian.

Others, for instance, like E. Gilson (1972), have a vague intermediate viewpoint. It seems that he is primarily concerned about the correct method *or* manner to be applied by Christian thinkers – as if a method were something neutral. For example, Gilson says about a Christian philosophy: "It is a *way* of philosophizing, namely the attitude of those who in their study of philosophy unites obedience to the Christian faith. This philosophical method, or attitude ... is *Christian philosophy* itself" (1972: 37) (A footnote shows that he is quoting from the *Aeterni Patris*.)

However, A mere Christian *attitude,* seen from a Reformational philosophical perspective, is not sufficient – the *result* or *content* of the philosophy should also be Christian. Formulated differently: A Christian's philosophy should specifically be Christian philosophy.

5.8 An Exceptional Viewpoint?

Since most Neo-Thomist philosophers agree that strictly and formally spoken philosophy can never earn the epithet "Christian," Blondel, however, is an exception. According to Blondel, the natural reason employing a purely philosophical direction reaches the admission of its insufficiency and the necessity of searching the Scriptures for answers to the problems it cannot solve by itself. If Thomist philosophy does not want to be Christian, it should, according to Blondel, be regarded as incomplete (cf. Sassen & Delfgaauw, 1957: 292 and Robbers 1948: 111). Accordingly, philosophy in a purely philosophical way reaches the admission of its insufficiency, and stands open to or longs for divine revelation.

5.9 Doomed to Failure

Robbers (1948: 111, cf. also 1949), a fellow Catholic, however, points out (our problem too) that this natural longing of philosophy for the supernatural revelation can in no way ensue from nature – it has to be something supernatural.

The Blondelian idea of a Christian philosophy, however, also differs from that of the Reformational tradition. Zuidema (1972: 231) points out that Blondel still maintains the idea of an autonomous, rational philosophy in the natural sphere and, thereby, rejects a truly integral Christian approach. Irrationalist Neo-Thomism has not yet been liberated from the belief in the autonomy of reason in the natural sphere. Their irrationalism seems to be confined to the domain of the supernatural.

In his earliest publications, today's well-known Catholic philosopher Alasdair MacIntyre still seemed to be open to an integral Christian philosophy when he wrote: "Religion as an activity divorced from other activities is without point. If religion is only a part of life, then religion has become optional. Only religion which is a way of living in every sphere either deserves to or can hope to survive" (MacIntyre, 1953: 9).

However, the age-old dualism between a so-called neutral natural sphere (the domain of reason and philosophy) and a Christian supernatural sphere (the domain of faith and theology) remains a stumbling block in the way of an integral Christian philosophy to every Catholic philosopher. They still cannot accept that one's Christian faith can and should also have a role to play in the inner reformation of scholarship (Cf. Noll & Turner, 2008). This concludes this investigation of Neo-Thomism. Finally, the question has to be raised on whether Reformational philosophy succeeded in replacing the nature-grace theme of Thomism and Neo-Thomism with a more biblically oriented view.

6. A Reformational Response

Reformational philosophers were convinced that the Neo–Thomist distinction between the spheres of nature and grace (or supernature) was, and still is, one of the most cardinal differences between Rome and the Reformation (cf. e.g. from a theological angle Berkouwer, 1948: 134 et seq.; Meuleman, 1967 and from a Christian philosophical perspective Vollenhoven, 1933; Dooyeweerd, 1959: 111 et seq.; Mekkes in various places in 1961 and 1965).

6.1 A False Problem

Although today Reformed philosophers advocate the two realm doctrine (cf., e.g. the discussion between Lief, 2012 and Van Drunen, 2012), to most Reformational philosophers the distinction between nature and grace implies a false problem which in the light of biblical revelation is unacceptable. It is based on the Christianization of an age-old pagan dualism between so-called profane and sacred spheres. Chapter one (subsection 4.4) already indicated that the nature-grace theme was an important method to effect a synthesis between extra-biblical and biblical ideas. Subsections 5.1 to 5.8 of the same chapter showed its detrimental implications for the entire Christian life and provided a biblical alternative.

6.2 The Correct Biblical Contrast

The Word of God does not know this distinction between natural and supernatural spheres. The biblical contrast is not that between nature and grace, but between sin and grace. Thus, wrote Bavinck (1894: 18) more than a hundred years ago, and other Reformational theologians and philosophers followed him (cf. e.g. Dooyeweerd, 1959; Olthuis, 1970; Spykman, 1992; Van der Walt, 2001 and Walsh & Middleton, 1984).

Vollenhoven (1933: 45), for instance, says that grace in the very first instance means divine favour extended to man. In the relationship of God with sinful people, it means His favour that has been forfeited. The opposite of grace is not nature or sin either, but the wrath of God.

Therefore, the Reformational tradition taught that the lives of human beings are religiously determined: the essence of a human being is to be in a covenant relationship with God, not just a so-called supernatural sphere of the life of the soul or spirit.

6.3 Modifications Offer No Solution

In the second instance, it is essential to point out that a mere reformulation or modification of the nature-grace dualism offers no solution. From the above account of the Neo-Thomist struggle with this central issue, it became distinctly evident that all of them attempted to retain it despite the tension it brought into their philosophy and numerous differences with Aquinas and fellow-Thomists faithful to this ancient doctrine.

According to a Reformational perspective, neither a diluted, rehashed, or reversed relation between the components of such a two realm doctrine can offer any solution. The only genuine solution from a biblical perspective is to take leave of the entire scheme of nature-grace as such.

However, it remains a question whether this happened within Reformational theology and philosophy.

6.4 Examples of Unfinished Reformation

As a test for answering this question, we mention only one example. One of the giants within Reformational tradition, Abraham Kuyper, is, for instance, receiving considerable attention, especially in the Anglo-Saxon world. For example, Kuipers (2011) published a comprehensive, annotated bibliography of Kuyper's writings.

Mouw (2012) published a volume in line with Kuyperian thinking in which he demonstrates what it means to think in a genuinely Reformational way. And also how, from such a perspective, one should react to the contemporary cultural environment – both individually and institutionally. Bishop & Kok (2013) have, besides a significant number of chapters on different aspects of Kuyper's philosophy, also a long list (on pp. 453-471) of chapters and books in English which were published from 1890 to 2012 on Kuyper's life, work and philosophy (cf. also Van der Walt, 2010b). A new Kuyper biography regarded as "definitive" has just seen the light from the hand of Bratt (2013).

Was this great thinker within the Reformational tradition able to evade the narcotic power of the nature-grace dualism fully? The discerning Reformational philosopher, Zuidema, does not think so. According to Zuidema (2013), Kuyper's teaching of general and special grace was merely a modification of the theme of nature-grace. Mekkes, in 1961 and 1965, also criticizes this doctrine in the works of both Kuyper and Bavinck. (cf. further Veenhof, 1994 and Heideman, 1959 for Bavinck's view.) Neither is Klapwijk (2013) without a critique of it.

There is good reason for the statement that Protestants and even Reformed theologians and church members in general, up to the present day, have not succeeded in cleansing themselves entirely from the blemish of some or other natural-supernatural dualism.

6.5 *The Alternative?*

However, the question is what a genuinely biblically-reformational view would entail, which could take the place of the Neo-Thomist idea of nature-grace. What should a Christian's relation be towards the increasingly secular thinking and culture in which he/she lives nowadays? What is the relationship between creation and salvation? It is clear that at the end of this investigation, there are still many unanswered questions that call for urgent further reflection.

Some examples from Protestant circles who are grappling with this issue are, for instance, Carter (2007), Carson (2008) and Klapwijk, Griffioen and Groenewoud (1991). It is also not only a Western problem. Christians in Africa are also struggling with it (e.g. Bediako, 1992 and Van der Walt, 2011). Nowadays, numerous worldviews, theologies, and philosophies alien to the Bible (e.g. individualism, consumerism, nationalism, relativism, scientific naturalism, and postmodern tribalism) confront Christians, compelling them to take a stand reguarding these issues (cf. Wilkens & Sanford, 2009).

This concluding chapter teaches at least one important lesson: the distinction in God's creation between a so-called natural and a so-called spiritual or religious sphere. We need to reject the tendency of Christians to divide between the sacred and the secular as against God's Word and will. Because life is religion, we must cherish *Coram Deo,* the reality that all of life is before the face of the Triune God.

The ideas of Thomas Aquinas (1225-1274), the most prominent Christian philosopher-theologian of the Middle Ages, were not confined to the so-called Dark Ages in Western history. In many different interpretations, the worldview of this intellectual giant reverberated during more than seven centuries up to today. Not only was he declared the *Doctor Angelicus* of the Roman Catholic Church, but his influence is also clearly discernible in Protestant church life, confessions and dogmatic works.

While this study consulted many works about Aquinas, it is based on a careful reading of the original Latin text of his *Summa Contra Gentiles,* his main philosophical work.

From an integral Christian philosophical historiography, this book analyzes both Aquinas' philosophy, the foundation of his theology, as well as many Neo-Thomist followers through the ages. It unveils the deepest religious, ontological, anthropological and epistemological presuppositions of their thinking.

The author furthermore indicates different stages in the development of Aquinas: from an initial Platonising orientation to a fully Aristotelising position.

Aquinas' synthesis between the revelation of God's Word and pagan Greek philosophy, already unacceptable by many of his contemporaries, proves to be untenable. The writer indicates how it resulted in many speculations, tensions and unsolvable problems in Aquinas. Thus he may serve as a warning today to Christian thinkers not to try to accommodate secular, biblically foreign ideas.

An additional feature of this work is that it openly acknowledges the lasting influence of Aquinas is also in the author's own Reformed theological-ecclesiastical tradition. This book is not only recommended for historians, philosophers and theologians, it will also benefit other thinking Christians to understand their roots and what it means to be a Christian today.

BIBLIOGRAPHY OF CHAPTERS 1 - 8

CHAPTER 1
Thomas Aquinas' philosophy in the "Summa Contra Gentiles"

1.1 *Original texts*
S.THOMAE AQUINATIS. 1935. *Summa Contra Gentiles seu De Veritate Catholicae Fidei*, (Reimpressio 21). Taurini (Italia): Marietti.

SANTO TOMAS DE AQUINO. 1967. *Summa Contra los Gentiles* (2 vol.). Latin-Spanish edition. (Eds. Carcedo, L.R. & Sierra, A.R.). Madrid: Biblioteca de Autores Christianos.

1.2 *Translations*
THOMAS AQUINAS. 1942-1960. *Summa Contra Gentiles; oder, Die Vertedingung der höchsten Wahrheiten. Aus dem lateinischen ins deutsche* übers. *und mit Ueberischten, Erläuterungen und Aristoteles-Texten versehen, von Helmut Fahsel.* Zürich: FraumünsterVerlag.
THOMAS AQUINAS. 1945. *Basic writings.* Part 1 & 2. (Ed. and annotated with an introd. by Anton C. Pegis.) New York: Random House.
THOMAS AQUINAS. 1950. *Of God and his creatures; an annotated transl. by Joseph Rickeby (with some abridgement) of the Summa Contra Gentiles.* Westminster: Caroll Press.

THOMAS AQUINAS. 1955. *On the truth of the Catholic faith (Summa Contra Gentiles)*. Book one: God. (Transl. with introd. and notes by A.C. Pegis.) New York: Doubleday.

THOMAS AQUINAS. 1956a. *On the truth of the Catholic Faith (Summa Contra Gentiles)*. Book two: Creation. (Transl. with an introd. and notes by J.F. Anderson.) New York: Doubleday.

THOMAS AQUINAS. 1956b. *On the truth of the Catholic Faith (Summa Contra Gentiles)*. Book three: Providence. (Part I. Transl. with an introd. and notes by V.J. Bourke.) New York: Doubleday.

THOMAS AQUINAS. 1956c. *On the truth of the Catholic Faith (Summa Contra Gentiles)*. Book three: Providence. (Part II. Transl. with an introd. and notes by C.J. O'Neil.) New York: Doubleday.

THOMAS AQUINAS. 1957. *On the truth of the Catholic Faith (Summa Contra Gentiles)*. Book four: Salvation. (Transl. with an introduction and notes by C.J. O'Neil.) New York: Doubleday.

2. Proceedings of the International Conference in Commemmoration of the Seventh Century of Aquinas' Death (17-24 April 1974 at Rome and Napels). Ed. by the seceretariat, A. Fernandez & A. Salizzoni.

1974. *Thommaso d'Aquino nel suo VII centenario Congresso Internazionale, Roma-Napoli, 17-24 aprile, 1974. Aquinas and the fundamental problems of our time*. (536 pp.)

1975. *Thomas d'Aquino nella storia del pensiero. Vol. I: Fonti del pensiero di S. Tommaso*. Napoli: Edizioni Domenicane Italiane. (470 pp.)

1976a. *Thommaso d'Aquino nella storia del pensiero. Vol. 2: Dal mediaevo ad oggi*. Napoli: Edizioni Domenicane Italiane. (645 pp.)

1976b. *Thommaso d'Aquino nel suo settimo centenario. Vol. 3: Dio e l'economia della salvezza*. Napoli: Edizioni Dome nicane Italiane. (488 pp.)

1976c. *Thommaso d'Aquino nel su settimo centenario.* Vol. 4: *Problemi di teologia.* Napoli: Edizioni Domenicane Italiane. (557 pp.)

3. Secondary Sources

AERTSEN, J.A. 1982. *"Natura et Creatura"; de denkweg van Thomas van Aquino.* 2 dele. Amsterdam: VU Boekhandel/Uitgeverij.

AERTSEN, J.A. 1991. Thomas Aquinas (1224/5-1274). In: Klapwijk, J., Griffioen, S. & Groenewoud, G. (Reds.), *Bringing into captivity every thought; capita selecta in the history of Christian evaluations of non-Christian philosophy.* Lanham: Univ. Press of America. pp. 95-122.

AETERNI PATRIS. 1948. Encycliek van Z.H. Pous Leo XIII van 4 Augustus 1879 over het herstel van de Christelijke Wijsbegeerte naar de geest van de H. Thomas van Aquino. (Vertaald door H. Boelaars.) Hilversum: Gooi & Sticht.

GAYBBA, B. 1998. Theology: the first 19 centuries. In: Maimela, S. & König, A. (Eds.), *Initiation into theology.* Pretoria: Van Schaik. pp. 27-48.

KOK, J.H. 1998. *Paterns of the Western mind; a Reformed Christian perspective.* Sioux Center, Iowa: Dordt College Press.

KRUGER, J.P. 2011. *Transcendence in immanence; a conversation with Jacques Derrida on space, time and meaning.* (D.Litt. & Phil. dissertation.) Pretoria: University of SA.

MARLET, M.Fr.J. 1954. *Grundlinien der kalvinistischen Philosophie der Gesetzesidee als christliche Transcendentalphilosophie.* München: Karl Zink.

MARLET, M.Fr.J. 1961. Wijsbegeerte der Wetsidee en Thomistisch denken. In: Van Dijk, W.J. & Stellingwerff, J. (Reds.), *Perspektief; feestbundel van de jongeren bij het vijf-en-twintig jarig bestaan van de Vereniging voor Calvinistische Wijsbegeerte.* Kampen: Kok. pp. 36-42.

MULLER, R.A. 2003. *Post-Reformation Dogmatics.* 4 Vols.

Grand Rapids, Michigan: Baker Academic.

ROBBERS, H. 1948. Het natuur-genade-schema als religieus grondmotief der scholastieke Wijsbegeerte. *Studia Catholica,* 23: 69-78.

ROBBERS, H. 1949. De Calvinistische Wijsbegeerte der Wet-sidee in gesprek met het Thomisme. *Studia Catholica,* 24: 161-171.

ROBBERS, H. 1961. *Neo-Thomisme en moderne wijsbegeerte.* Utrecht/ Brussel: Het Spectrum.

SMIT, J.H. 1965. *Rooms-Katolisisme en die wysbegeerte van die wetsidee, met besondere verwysing na die religieuse grondmotiewe.* (Unpublished M.A. dissertation.) Bloemfontein: UOVS.

SMIT, M.C. 1950. *De verhouding van Christendom en historie in de huidige Rooms Katolieke geschiedbeschouwing.* Kampen: Kok.

SMITH, K.A. 2004. *Introducing Radical Orthodoxy; mapping a post-secular theology.* Grand Rapids, Michigan: Baker Academic.

TALJAARD, J.A.L. 1976. *Polished lenses.* Potchefstroom: Pro Rege Pers.

TE VELDE, D. 2006. *Aquinas on God; "the divine science" in the "Summa Theologiae."* London: Ashgate.

TE VELDE, D. 2007. Metaphysics and the question of creation; Thomas Aquinas, Duns Scotus and us. In: Candler, P.M. & Cunningham, C. (Eds.), *Belief and metaphysics.* London: SCM Press.

TE VELDE, D. 2010a. *Paths beyond tracing; the connection of method and content in the doctrine of God, examined in Reformed Orthodoxy, Karl Barth and the Utrecht School.* Delft: Uburon.

TE VELDE, D. 2010b. Een positief beeld van Scholastiek. *Beweging,* 74(2): 34-37, Somer.

TOL, A. 2010. *Philosophy in the making; D.H.Th. Vollenhoven and the emergence of Reformed Philosophy.* Sioux Center, Iowa: Dordt College Press.

VAN ASSELT, W.J. & DEKKER, E. (Eds.) 2001. *Reformation and Scholasticism; an ecumenical enterprise.* Grand Rapids, Michigan: Baker Book House.

VAN ASSELT, W.J. 1996. De erfenis van de Gereformeerde

Scholastiek. *Kerk en Theologie*, 46: 126-136.

VAN DER WALT, B.J. 1968. *Die wysgerige konsepsie van Thomas van Aquino in sy "Summa Contra Gentiles" met spesiale verwysing na sy siening van teologie.* (Unpublished M.A. dissertation.) Potchefstroom: PU vir CHO.

VAN DER WALT, B.J. 1974a. *Die natuurlike teologie met be sondere aandag aan die visie daarop by Thomas van Aquino, Johannes Calvyn en die "Synopsis Purioris Theologiae" – 'n wysgerige ondersoek.* (Unpublished D.Phil. dissertation.) Potchefstroom. PU vir CHO.

VAN DER WALT, B.J. 1974b. Rooms-Katolieke bring hulde aan Thomas van Aquino. *Woord en Daad*, 15(143): 11-12, Augustus.

VAN DER WALT, B.J. 1974c. Thomas van Aquino en die fundamentele probleem van ons tyd. *Tydskrif vir Christelike Wetenskap*, 19: 10-20, September.

VAN DER WALT, B.J. 1975. Op die spore van Thomas van Aquino (1224-1274); „n biografiese skets. *Koers*, 40(1): 38-47.

VAN DER WALT, B.J. 1976. Thomas Aquinas' idea about wonders; a critical appraisal.

In: Thommaso d'Aquino nel su settimo centenario; atti del Congresso Internazionale, RomaNapoli, 17-24 aprile, 1974. Vol. 3: *Dio e léconomia della salvezza.* Napoli: Edizioni Domenicane Italiane. 470-480.

VAN DER WALT, B.J. 2011a. n' Klein wins maar n' groot verlies in die laat sestiende- en sewentiende-eeuse gereformeerde ortodoksie. n' Christelik-filosofiese benadering. *Tydskrif vir Christelike Wetenskap*, 47(1): 97-116.

VAN DER WALT, B.J. 2011b. Die "suiwer" Gereformeerde te ologie van 1625 sonder n "suiwer" filosofiese grondslag: Is dit moontlik? *Tydskrif vir Christelike Wetenskap*, 47(2): 1-34.

VAN DER WALT, B.J. 2011c. Die onsuiwer mensbeskouing, kenteorie en wetenskapsleer in die "Synopsis Purioris Theologiae" (1625). *Tydskrif vir Christelike Wetenskap*, 47(3): 49-86.

VAN DER WALT, B.J. 2011d. Goddelike soewereiniteit en menslike verantwoordelikheid volgens die sintesedenke van ongeveer die vyfde tot die sewentiende eeu; n' Christelikfilosofiese verkenning. *Tydskrif vir Christelike Wetenskap*, 47(4): 173-200.

VAN DER WALT, B.J. 2011e. Die Gereformeerd-Skolastieke visie op die verhouding tussen God en mens by F. Gomarus (1563-1641) en J. Arminius (1560-1609). *Tydskrif vir Geesteswetenskappe*, 51(3): 269-288.

VAN DER WALT, B.J. 2011f. Flagging philosophical minefields at the Synod of Dordt (1618-1619); Reformed Scholasticism reconsidered. *Koers*, 76(3): 505-538.

VAN DER WALT, B.J. 2012. Die religieuse rigting en die denke van Thomas van Aquino (1224/5-1274) en die implikasies daarvan vir vandag. *Tydskrif vir Christelike wetenskap*, 48(2): 223-249.

VAN DER WALT, B.J. 2012a. Die invloed van die Aristotelies-Skolastieke filosofie op die Dordtse Leerreëls (1619); 'n Christelik-filosofiese analise. *Tydskrif vir Christelike Wetenskap*, 48(1): 91-110.

VAN DER WALT, B.J. 2012b. Aristotelies-filosofiese invloede op die Sinode van Dordt (16181619) en die bevrydende perspektief van n' Reformatoriese filosofie op Goddelike soewereiniteit en menslike verantwoordelikheid. *Tydskrif vir Geesteswetenskappe*, 52(2): 147197.

VAN DER WALT, B.J. 2014a. *At the cradle of a Christian philosophy in Calvin, Vollenhoven, Stoker and Dooyeweerd.* Potchefstroom: The Institute for Contemporary Christianity in Africa.

VAN DER WALT, B.J. 2014b. *Constancy and change; historical types and trends in the passion of the Western mind.* Potchefstroom: The Institute for Contemporary Christianity in Africa.

VAN DER WALT, B.J. 2015. Die tragiese geestelike odussee van Lourens Ingelse; Anteunis Janse oor die spiritualiteit van die Nadere Reformasie. *Tydskrif vir Christelike Wetenskap*, 51(4): 43-67.

VAN DER WALT, B.J. 2016. Die godsdienstig-teologiese en filosofiese konteks van die negentiende eeuse Réveil in Nederland. *Tydskrif vir Christelike Wetenskap*, 52(2): 227-250.

VAN DER WALT, B.J. 2017a. Isaac da Costa se besware teen die gees van sy tyd. *Tydskrif vir Christelike Wetenskap*, 53(1).

VAN DER WALT, 2017b. Revolusie of reformasie? Die betekenis van G. Groen van Prinsterer (1801-1876) se besinning daaroor vir vandag. *Tydskrif vir Geesteswetenskappe*, 57 (3).

VAN STEENBERGHEN, F. 1955. *The philosophical movement in the thirteenth century*. Edinburgh: Nelson.

VENTER, E.A. s.j. *Die ontwikkeling van die Westerse denke*. Bloemfontein: SACUM.

VENTER, J.J. 1988. Pieke en lyne in die Westerse denkgeskiedenis. Deel 1: Antieke, Middeleeue, Renaissance. Potchefstroom: PU vir CHO (Dept. Sentrale Publikasies) Diktaat nr. 22 (88).

VOLLENHOVEN, D.H.Th. 2000. *Schematische Kaarten; filosofische concepties in probleemhistorisch verband*. (Eds. K.A. Bril & P.J. Boonstra.) Amstelveen: De Zaak Haes.

VOLLENHOVEN, D.H.Th. 2005a. *The problem-historical method and the history of philosophy*. (Ed. K.A. Bril.) Amstelveen: De Zaak Haes.

VOLLENHOVEN, D.H.Th. 2005b. *De probleem-historische methode en de geschiedenis van de wijsbegeerte*. (Ed. K.A. Bril.) Amstelveen: De Zaak Haes.

VOLLENHOVEN, D.H.Th. 2005c. *Wijsgerig Woordenboek*. (Red. K.A. Bril.) Amstelveen: De Zaak Haes.

VOLLENHOVEN, D.H.Th. 2005d. *Isagôgè Philosophiae – Introduction to Philosophy*. J.H. Kok & A. Tol. (Eds.) Sioux Center, Iowa: Dordt College Press.

VOLLENHOVEN, D.H.Th. 2011. *Gastcolleges Wijsbegeerte; erfenis voor het heden*. (Eds. K.A. Bril & R.A. Nijhoff.) Amsterdam: De Zaak Haes.

WHITE, J.R. 2006. *Pulpit crimes: the criminal mishandling of God's Word*. Birmingham, Alabama: Solid Ground Christian Books.

WUNDT, M. 1939. *Die deutsche Schulmetaphysik des 17. Jahrhunderts*. Tübingen: JCB Mohr (Paul Siebeck).

CHAPTER 2

AERTSEN, J.A. 1982. *"Natura et creatura"; de denkweg van Thomas van Aquino.* Amsterdam: VU Boekhandel/Uitgeverij.

AERTSEN, J.A. 1986. The circulation-motive and man in the thought of Thomas Aquinas. In: *Acts of the Sixth International Congress of Medieval Philosophy.* Louvain-la-Neuve. pp. 432-439.

AERTSEN, J.A. 1990. Aquinas and the classical heritage; a response. In: Wendy Helleman (Ed.) *Christianity and the classics; the acceptance of a heritage.* Lanham: University Press of America. pp. 83-90.

AERTSEN, J.A. 1991. Thomas Aquinas (1224/5-1274). In: Klapwijk, J., Griffioen, S. & Groenewoud, G. (Eds.), *Bringing into captivity every thought.* Lanham: Univ. Press of America. pp. 95-122.

BASTABLE, P.B. 1947. *Desire for God. Does man aspire naturally to the beautific vision? An analysis of this question and its history.* London/Dublin: Burns Oates & Washborne.

DEN OTTOLANDER, P. 1965. *"Deus immutabilis". Wijsgerige beschouwing over onveranderlijkheid en veranderlijkheid volgens de theologie van Sint Thomas en Karl Barth.*
Assen: Van Gorcum.

KUHLMANN, B.C. 1912. *Der Gesetzesbegriff beim Hl. Thomas von Aquin im Lichte des Rechtsstudiums seiner Zeit.* Bonn: Verlag von Peter Hanstein.

LOVEJOY, A.O. 1973. *The great chain of being; a history of an idea.* Cambridge, Massachusetts: Harvard Univ. Press.

MEIJER, B. 1944. *Het participatiebegrip in de thomistische circulatieleer. Verslag van de tiende algemene vergadering der Vereeniging voor Thomistische Wijsbegeerte.* (Bylage van *Studia Catholica*). Neijmegen: Dekker & Van de Vegt. pp. 55-71.

MEIJER, J.B.J. 1940. *Die eerste levensvraag in het intellectualisme van St. Thomas van Aquino en het integraal-realisme van Mau-*

rice Blondel. Roermond-Maaseik: J.J. Romen & Zonen.
PERSSON, E. 1957. *"Sacra doctrina"; reason and revelation in Aquinas.* (Transl. by R. Mackenzie.) Oxford: Basil Blackwell.
S.THOMAE AQUINATIS, 1935. *Summa Contra Gentiles seu de veritate Catholicae fidei.* Taurini: Marietti.
THOMAS AQUINAS. 1955-1957. *On the truth of the Catholic faith (Summa Contra Gentiles).* 5 Vols. New York: Doubleday (Image Books).
TOL, A. 2010. *Philosophy in the making; D.H. Th. Vollenhoven and the emergence of a reformed philosophy.* Sioux Center, Iowa: Dordt College Press.
VAN DEN BERG, I.J.M. 1958. *Inleiding tot het denken van Thomas van Aquino.* Assen/Amsterdam: Uitgeverij Born.
VAN DER WALT, B.J. 1968. *Die wysgerige konsepsie van Thomas in sy "Summa Contra Gentiles" met spesiale verwysing na sy siening van teologie.* Potchefstroom: PU vir CHO (M.A. dissertation).
VAN DER WALT, B.J. 1974. *Die natuurlike teologie met besondere aandag aan die visie daarop by Thomas van Aquino, Johannes Calvyn en die "Synopsis Purioris Theologiae" – 'n wysgerige ondersoek.* (D.Phil. dissertation). Potchefstroom: PU vir CHO.
VENTER, J.J. 1988. *Pieke en lyne in die Westerse denkgeskiedenis. Deel 1: Antieke, Middeleeue, Renaissance.* Potchefstroom: PU vir CHO (Dept. Sentrale Publikasies, Diktaat nr. 22(88)).
VOLLENHOVEN, D.H.Th. 2005a. *Wijsgerig Woordenboek.* K.A. Bril (Ed.). Amstelveen: De Zaak Haes.
VOLLENHOVEN, D.H.Th. 2005b. *Isagôgè Philosophiae – Introduction to Philosophy.* J.H. Kok & A. Tol. (Eds.) Sioux Center, Iowa: Dordt College Press.

CHAPTER 3
AERTSEN, J.A. 1991. Thomas Aquinas (1224/5 – 1274). In: Klapwijk, J., Griffioen, S. & Groenewald, G. (Eds.), *Bringing into captivity every thought.* Lanham: Univ. Press of America. pp. 95-122.

FABRO, C. 1961. *Participation et causalité selon St. Thomas d'Aquin.* Louvain/Paris: Vrin.

GEIGER, L.B. 1942. *La participation dans la Philosophie de S. Thomas d'Aquin.* Paris: J.Vrin.

HABBEL, J. 1928. *Die Analogie zwischen Gott und Welt nach Thomas von Aquin.* Regensburg.

HART, H., COOPER, J., DE KLERK, J., HULL, J. & VAN DER PLAATS, B. 1974. *Theorizing between Boethius and Occam; a preliminary survey.* Toronto: Institute for Christian Studies (Unpublished mimeograph).

HENLE, R.J. 1956. *Saint Thomas and Platonism.* The Hague: M. Nijhoff.

KLUBERTANZ, G.P. 1960. *St. Thomas Aquinas and analogy.* Chicago: Loyola Univ. Press.

KRÄMER, H.J. 1967. *De neo-platonische Seinsphilosophie und ihre Wirkung auf Thomas von Aquin.* Amsterdam: B.R. Gründer.

KRUGER, J.D. 2011. *Transcendence in immanence; a conversation with Jaques Derrida on space, time and meaning.* (D.Litt. & Phil. Dissertation.) Pretoria: Univ. of South Africa.

LYTTKENS, H. 1952. *The analogy between God and world; an investigation of its background and interpretation of its use by Thomas Aquinas.* Upsalla: Almqvist & Wiksells.

MCINERY, R.M. 1961. *The logic of analogy; an interpretation of St. Thomas Aquinas.* The Hague: M. Nijhoff.

MCINERY, R.M. 1968. *Studies in analogy.* The Hague: M. Nijhoff.

PHELAN, G.P. 1943. *St. Thomas and analogy.* Milwaukee: Marguette Univ.Press.

S. THOMAE AQUINATIS. 1935. *Summa Contra Gentiles seu De veritate Catholicaefidei.* Taurini: Marietti.

SCHÜTZ, L. 1895. *Thomas-Lexikon.* Paderborn: Ferdinand Schöningh.

SPIER, J.M. 1959. *Van Thales tot Sartre; wijsgeren uit oude en nieuwetijd*. Kampen: Kok.

THOMAS AQUINAS, 1955-1957. *On the truth of the Catholic faith* (Summa Contra Gentiles). 5 Vols. New York: Doubleday (Image Books).

VAN DER WALT, B.J. 1968. *Die wysgerige konsepsie van Thomas in sy "Summa Contra Gentiles" met spesiale verwysing na sy siening van teologie*. (M.A.dissertation.) Potchefstroom: PU vir CHO.

VAN DER WALT, B.J. 1974. *Die natuurlike teologie met besondere aandag aan die visie daarop by Thomas van Aquino, Johannes Calvyn en die "Synopsis Purioris Theologiae"* – 'n *wysgerige ondersoek*. (D.Phil. dissertation.) Potchefstroom: PU vir CHO.

VAN DER WALT, B.J. 1986. Die universalia-probleem gedurende die Middeleeue. In: Van der Walt, B.J., *Van Athene na Genève;* 'n *kort oorsig oor die geskiedenis van die Wysbegeerte vanaf die Grieke tot die Reformasie*. Potchefstroom: Pro Rege Pers, pp. 243-254.

VAN DER WALT, B.J. 2010. Imaging God in the contemporary world. In: Van der Walt, B.J., *At home in God's world*. Potchefstroom: Institute for Contemporary Christianity in Africa. pp 325-366.

VENTER, J.J. 1985. *Hoofprobleme van die Middeleeuse Wysbegeerte*. Potchefstroom: PU vir CHO (Dept. Sentrale Publikasies, Diktaat D65/79).

VENTER, J.J. 1988. *Pieke en lyne in die Westerse denkgeskiedenis. Band I: Antieke, Middeleeue, Renaissance*. Potchefstroom: PU vir CHO (Dept. Sentrale Publikasies, Diktaat 22/88).

VOLLENHOVEN, D.H.Th. 2000. *Schematische kaarten; filosofische concepties in probleemhistorisch verband*. K.A. Bril & P.J. Boonstra (Eds.) Amstelveen: De ZaakHaes.

VOLLENHOVEN, D.H.Th. 2005a. *Wijsgerig Woordenboek*. K.A. Bril (Ed.) Amstelveen: De ZaakHaes.

VOLLENHOVEN, D.H.Th. 2005b. *Isagôgè Philosophiae – Introduction to Philosophy*. J.H. Kok. & A. Tol. (Eds.) Sioux Center, Iowa: Dordt College Press.

VOLLENHOVEN, D.H.Th. 2011. *Gastcollegeswijsbegeerte;*

erfenis voor het heden. K.A. Bril & R.A. Nijhoff (Eds.) Amstelveen: De ZaakHaes.

CHAPTER 4

BERGER, H. 1968. *Op zoek naar identiteit; het Aristotelish substantiegrip en de mogelijkheid van een hedendaagse metafisika*. Nijmegen/Utrecht: Dekker & Van de Vegt.

DE GRIJS, F.J.A. 1967. *Goddelijk mensontwerp; een thematische studie over het beeld Gods in de mens volgens het Scriptura van Thomas van Aquino* (2 dele). Hilversum/Antwerpen: Paul Brand.

LAIS, H. 1951. *Die Gnadenlehre des hl. Thomas in der Summa Contra Gentiles und die Kommentar des Francis Sylvestris von Ferrara*. München: Kaiser Verlag.

NEUMANN, S. 1963. *Gegenstand und Methode der theoretische Wissenschaften nach Thomas von Aquin*. Münster (Westf.): Max Kramer.

NIEDE, E. 1928. *Glauben und Wissen nach Thomas van Aquin*. Freiburg im Breisgau: J.Waibel.

S.THOMAE AQUINATIS. 1935. *Summa Contra Gentilesseu De Veritate Catholicae Fidei*, (Reimpressio 21). Taurini (Italia): Marietti.

SCHEFFCZYK, L. (Ed.).1969. *Der Mensch als Bild Gottes*. Darmstadt: Wissenschaftliche Buchgesellschaft.

SIEWERTH, G. 1933. *Die Metaphysik der Erkenntnis nach Thomas von Aquin*. Teil 1: Die sinnliche Erkenntnis. München/Berlin: Kommissionsverlag von R. Oldenbourg.

SPIER, J.M. 1959. *Van Thales tot Sartre*. Kok: Kampen.

STINSON, C.H. 1966. *Reason and sin according to Aquinas and Calvin; the noetic effects of the fall of man*. Washington, D.C.: The Catholic University of America.

TER HORST, G. 2008. *De ontbinding van de substantie; een deconstructie van vorm en materie in de ontologie en kenleer van Thomas van Aquino*. Delft: Eburon.

THOMAS AQUINAS. 1955-1957. *On the truth of the Catholic Faith (Summa Contra Gentiles)*. 5 Volumes. New York: Doubleday.

TOL, A. 2010. *Philosophy in the making; D.H.Th. Vollenhoven and the emergence of Reformed Philosophy*. Sioux Center, Iowa: Dordt College Press.

VAN DER WALT, B.J. 1968. *Die wysgerige konsepsie van Thomas van Aquino in sy "Summa Contra Gentiles" met spesiale verwysing na sy siening van teologie*. (Unpublished M.A. dissertation.) Potchefstroom: PU vir CHO.

VAN DER WALT, B.J. 1974. *Die natuurlike teologie met besondere aandag aan die visie daarop by Thomas van Aquino, Johannes Calvyn en die "Synopsis Purioris Theologiae" – 'n wysgerige ondersoek*. (Unpublished D.Phil. dissertation.) Potchefstroom: PU vir CHO.

VAN DER WALT, B.J. 2010a. Imaging God in the contemporary world. In: Van der Walt, B.J., *At home in God's world*. Potchefstroom: Institute for Contemporary Christianity in Africa. pp. 325-366.

VAN DER WALT, B.J. 2010b. The biblical perspective on being human. In: Van der Walt, B.J., *At home in God's world*. Potchefstroom: The Institute for Contemporary Christianity in Africa. pp. 259-289.

VAN DER WALT, B.J. 2014. *At the cradle of a Christian philosophy: Calvin, Vollenhoven, Stoker and Dooyeweerd*. Potchefstroom: ICCA.

VENTER, J.J. 1985. *Hoofprobleme van die Middeleeuse Wysbegeerte*. Potchefstroom: PU vir CHO (Dept. Sentrale Publikasies, Diktaat D65/79).

VOLLENHOVEN, D.H.Th. 2000. *Schematische Kaarten; filosofische concepties in probleemhistorisch verband*. (K.A. Bril & P.J. Boonstra, Eds.). Amstelveen: De Zaak Haes.

VOLLENHOVEN, D.H.Th. 2011. *Gastcolleges Wijsbegeerte; erfenis voor het heden*. K.A. Bril & R.A. Nijhoff, Eds.). Amsterdam: De Zaak Haes.

CHAPTER 5

BERKOUWER, G.C. 1950. *De voorzienigheid Gods.* Kampen: Kok.

BERKOUWER, G.C. 1955. *De verkiezing Gods.* Kampen: Kok.

BERKOUWER, G.C. 1958. *De zonde. Deel 1: De oorsprong en kennis der zonde.* Kampen: Kok.

BERKOUWER, G.C. 1960. *De zonde. Deel 2: Wezen en verbreiding der zonde.* Kampen: Kok.

DE VOS, H. 1971. *De Bewijzen voor Gods bestaan; een systematisch-historische studie.* Groningen: Wolters-Noordhoff.

DEN OTTOLANDER, P. 1965. *"Deus immutabilis." Wijsgerige beschouwingen over onveranderlijkheid en veranderlikheid volgens de theologie van Sint Thomas en Karl Barth.* Assen: Van Gorcum.

FRIETHOFF, C. 1925. *De predestinatieleer van Thomas en Calvijn.* Zwolle: Waanders.

GEVAERT, J. 1965. *Contingent en noodzaakelijk bestaan volgens Thomas van Aquino.* Brussel: Palais der Academiën.

HICK, J., (Ed.). 1964. *The existence of God; readings.* London: Macmillan.

HOLWERDA, D. 1958. *De grondlegging der wêreld; zag Israel zijn uittocht als schepping?* Enschede: Boersma.

KLAPWIJK, J. 1994. Calvijn over de wijsbegeerte: oefening in ootmoedigheid. In: Zijlstra, A & Doornenbal, R.J.A. (Eds.), *Christelijke filosofie in beweging.* Amsterdam: Buijten & Schipperheijn. pp. 92-100.

KRÜGER, K. 1970. *Der Gottesbegriff der spekulativen Theologie.* Berlin: Walter de Gruyter & Co.

KRUGER, J.P. 2011 *Transcendence in immanence; a conversation with Jacques Derrida on space, time and meaning.* (D.Litt. et Phil. dissertation.) Pretoria: University of South Africa.

MIDDLETON, J.R. 2014. *A new heaven and a new earth; reclaiming Biblical eschatology.* Grand Rapids, Michigan: Baker Academic.

PEELS, H.G.L. 2000. *Heilig is Zijn Naam; onze Godsbeelden en de God van de Bijbel.* Bedum: Woord en Wêreld.

POLMAN, A.D.R. 1936. *De predestinasieleer bij Augustinus, Thomas van Aquino en Calvijn; een dogma-historische studie.* Franeker: Wever.

S.THOMAE AQUINATIS. 1935. *Summa Contra Gentiles seu De Veritate Catholicae Fidei,* (Reimpressio 21). Taurini (Italia): Marietti.

SINNEMA, D.W. 1985. *The issue of reprobation at the Synod of Dordt (1618-1619) in the light of the history of the doctrine.* (Ph.D. thesis.) Ann Arbor: University Microfilms International.

SPYKMAN, G.J. 1981. A new look at election and reprobation. In: Vander Goot, H. (Ed.), *Life is religion; essays dedicated to H.E. van Runner.* St. Catherines, Ontario: Paideia Press. pp. 171-191.

THOMAS AQUINAS. 1955-1957. *On the truth of the Catholic faith. Summa Contra Gentiles.* (5 Vols.) New York: Double Day (Image Books).

VAN DER WALT, B.J. 1968. *Die wysgerige konsepsie van Thomas van Aquino in sy "Summa Contra Gentiles" met spesiale verwysing na sy siening van teologie.* (Unpublished M.A. dissertation.) Potchefstroom: PU vir CHO.

VAN DER WALT, B.J. 1974. *Die natuurlike teologie met besondere aandag aan die visie daarop by Thomas van Aquino, Johannes Calvyn en die "Synopsis Purioris Theologia" – 'n wysgerige ondersoek.* (Unpublished D.Phil. dissertation.) Potchefstroom: PU vir CHO.

VAN DER WALT, B.J. 2011a. Goddelike soewereiniteit en menslike verantwoordelikheid volgens die sintesedenke van ongeveer die vyfde tot die sewentiende eeu. *Tydskrif vir Christelike Wetenskap,* 47(4): 173-200.

VAN DER WALT, B.J. 2011b. Die Gereformeerd-skolastieke

visie op die verhouding tussen God en mens by F. Gomarus (1563-1641) en J. Arminius (1560-1609). *Tydskrif vir Geesteswetenskappe,* 51(3): 269-288.

VAN DER WALT, B.J. 2011c. Flagging philosophical minefields at the Synod of Dordt 1618-1619); Reformed Scholasticism reconsidered. *Koers* 76(3): 505-538.

VAN DER WALT, B.J. 2012a. Die invloed van die Aristotelies-Skolastiese filosofie op die Dordtse Leerreëls (1619); 'n Christelik-filosofiese analise. *Tydskrif vir Christelike Wetenskap,* 48(1): 91-110.

VAN DER WALT, B.J. 2012b. Aristotelies-filosofiese invloede op die Sinode van Dordt (1618-1619) en die bevrydende perspektief van 'n Reformatoriese filosofie. *Tydskrif vir Geesteswetenskappe,* 52(2): 174-197.

VAN DER WALT, B.J. 2015a. Johan H. Bavinck in gesprek met Westerse en Oosterse mistiek: 'n boodskap vir vandag? *Tydskrif vir Christelike Wetenskap,* 51(2): 131-147.

VAN DER WALT, B.J. 20154b. Semi-mistieke spiritualiteit by J. Calvyn en A. Kuyper; die invloed daarvan tot op vandag. *Tydskrif vir Christelike Wetenskap,* 51(3): 99-124.

VAN DER WALT, B.J. 2015c. Die tragiese geestelike odussee van Lourens Ingelse; die spiritualiteit van die Nadere Reformasie. *Tydskrif vir Christelike Wetenskap,* 51(4): 43-67.

VAN DER WALT, B.J. 2015d. Mistiek: van verwarring na waarheid. *Koers,* 70(3).

VAN ECK, J. 1997. *En toch beweegt Hij; over de Godsleer in de Nederlandse belijdenisschriften.* Franeker: Uitgeverij Van Wijnen.

VELEMA, H. 1992. *Uitverkiezing? Jazeker! Maar hoe?* Kampen: Uitgeverij Van den Berg.

VENTER, J.J. 1985. *Hoofprobleme van die Middeleeuse Wysbegeerte.* Potchefstroom: PU vir CHO (Dept. Sentrale Publikasies, Diktaat 65/79).

VENTER, J.J. 1988. *Pieke en lyne in die Westerse denkgeskiede-*

nis. Band I: *Antieke, Middeleeue, Renaissance.* Potchefstroom: PU vir CHO (Dept. Sentrale Publikasies. Diktaat 22/88).

VORSTER, H. 1965. *Das Freiheitsverständnis bei Thomas von Aquin und Martin Luther.* Göttingen: Vandenhoeck & Ruprecht.

WEISCHEDEL, W. 1971 & 1972. *Der Gott der Philosophen; Gründlegung einer philosophische Theologie im Zeitalter des Nihilismus.* (Band 1 & 2). Darmstadt: Wissenschaftliche Buchgesellschaft.

CHAPTER 6

BORGAN, P. 1996. *Early Christianity and Hellenistic Judaism.* Edinburgh: Clark.

BOS, A.P. 1987. Transformation and deformation in Philosophy. *Philosophia Reformata,* 52: 120-140.

BOS, A.P. 1991a. Clement of Alexandria (150-215). In: Klapwijk, J., Griffioen, S. & Groenewoud, G. (Eds.), *Bringing into captivity every thought.* Lanham: Univ. Press of America. pp. 15-28.

BOS, A.P. 1991b. Augustine (354-430). In: Klapwijk, J., Griffioen, S. & Groenewoud, G. (Eds.), *Bringing into captivity every thought.* Lanham: Univ. Press of America. pp. 49-65.

BOS, A.P. 1994. Cosmic and meta-cosmic theology in Greek philosophy and Gnosticism. In: Helleman, W.E. (Ed.), *Hellenization revisited.* Lanham: Univ. Press of America. pp. 1-22.

BOS, A.P. 1996. *Geboeid door Plato.* Kampen: Kok.

BOS, A.P. 2003. *The soul and its instrumental body; a reinterpretation of Aristotle's philosophy of living nature.* Leiden: Brill.

BROWN, P. 1995. *Authority and the sacred; aspects of the Christianization of the Roman world.* Cambridge: Cambridge Univ. Press.

CHOI, Y.J. 2000. *Dialogue and antithesis; a philosophical study of the significance of Herman Dooyeweerd's transcendental critique.* (D.Phil. dissertation.) Potchefstroom: PU for CHE.

DE LUBAC, H. 1959-1964. *Exégèse medieval; les quatre sens de l'écriture.* 2 vols. Paris: Aubier.

DE RIJK, L.M. 1962 & 1967. *"Logica Modernorum"; a contribution to the history of early terminist logic.* 2 vols. Assen: Van Gorcum.

DE RIJK, L.M. 1977. *Middeleeuwse Wijsbegeerte; traditie en vernieuwing.* Assen: Van Gorcum.

DOOYEWEERD, H. 1939. Kuyper's wetenschapsleer. *Philosophia Reformata,* 4: 193-232.

DOOYEWEERD, H. 1949. *Reformatie en Scholastiek in de Wijsbegeerte.* Franeker: Wever.

DORAN, R. 1995. *Birth of a worldview; early Christianity in a Jewish and pagan context.* Boulder: Westview.

EVANS, G.R. 1980. *Old arts and new theology; the beginnings of theology as an academic discipline.* Oxford: Clarendon Press.

EVANS, G.R., MCGRATH, A.E. & GALLOWAY, A.D. 1986. *The history of Christian theology.* Vol 1: *The science of theology.* Grand Rapids, Michigan: Eerdmans.

FLETCHER, R. 1997. *The barbarian conversion; from paganism to Christianity.* New York: Henry Holt.

FOX, R.L. 1986. *Pagans and Christians in the Mediterranean world from the second century AD to the conversion of Constantine.* London: Penguin.

GAYBBA, B. 1998. Theology: the first 19 centuries. In: Maimela, S. & König, A. (Eds.), *Initiation into theology.* Pretoria: Van Schaik. pp. 27-48.

GORT, J.D., VROOM, H.M., FERNHOUT, R. & WESSELS, A. 1989. *Dialogue on syncretism; an interdisciplinary approach.* Grand Rapids, Michigan: Eerdmans.

GOUD, J.F. 1991. Origen (185-254). In: Klapwijk, J., Griffioen, S. & Groenewoud, G. (Eds.), *Bringing into captivity every thought.* Lanham: Univ. Press of America. pp. 29-48.

GRABMANN, M. 1956. *De Geschichte der scholastischen Methode.* 2 dele. Darmstadt: Wissenschaftliche Buchgesellschaft.

HART, H., COOPER, J., DE KERK, J., HULL, J. & VANDER PLAATS, B. 1974. *Theorizing between Boethius and Occam: a prelimi nary report.* Unpublished Mimeograph.Toronto: Institute for Christian Studies.

HARTVELT, G.P. 1962. Over de methode der dogmatiek in de eeuw der Reformatie. *Gereformeerd Theologisch Tijdschrift,* 62: 97-149.

HELLEMAN, W.E. 1990. Introduction. In: Helleman, W.E. (Ed.), *Christianity and the Classics; the acceptance of a heritage.* Lanham: Univ. Press of America. pp. 11-30.

HELLEMAN, W.E. (Ed.) 1994a. *Hellenization revisited.* Lanham: Univ. Press of America.

HELLEMAN, W.E. 1994b. Epilogue. In: Helleman, W.E. (Ed.), *Hellenization revisited; Shaping a Christian response within the Greco-Roman World.* Lanham: Univ. Press of America. pp. 429-511.

KLAPWIJK, J. 1991. The idea of transformational philosophy. In: Klapwijk, J., Griffioen, S. & Groenewoud, G. (Eds.), *Bringing into captivity every thought.* Lanham: Univ. Press of America. pp. 241-266.

KLAPWIJK, J. 1995. Antithese, synthese en de idee van transformationele filosofie. In: Klapwijk, J. *Transformationele filosofie.* (Eds. R. van Woudenberg & S. Griffioen.) Kampen: Kok Agora. pp. 175-193.

KLAPWIJK, J. GRIFFIOEN, S. & GROENEWOUD, G. (Eds.), 1991. *Bringing into captivity every thought; capita selecta, in the history of Christian evaluations of non-Christian philosophy.* Lanham: Univ. Press of America.

MCGRATH, A.E. 1988. *Reformational thought; an introduction.* Oxford: Basil Blackwell.

NIEBUHR, H.R. 1951. *Christ and culture.* New York: Harper & Row.

POLMAN, A.D.R. 1961. Scholastiek. In: Grosheide, F.W. & Van Itterzon, G.P. (Eds.), *Christelijke Encyclopedie.* Deel 6. Kampen: Kok. pp. 88-89.

RUNIA, D.T. 1983. *Philo of Alexandria and the "Timaeus" of Plato.* Amsterdam: VU Boekhandel.

RUNIA, D.T. 2007. Philo in the Reformational tradition. In: Sweetman, R. (Ed.), *In the Phrygian mode; neo-Calvinism, Antiquity and the lamentations of Reformational philosophy.* Toronto: ICS and Lanham: Univ. Press of America. pp. 195-212.

RUNNER, H.E. 1951. *The development of Aristotle illustrated from the earliest books of the Physics.* Kampen: Kok.

RUSSELL, J.C. 1994. *The Germanization of Early Medieval Christianity; a sociological approach to religious transformation.* New York: Oxford Univ. Press.

SMIT, D.J. 1998. Biblical hermeneutics: the first 19 centuries & Biblical hermeneutics: the 20th century. In: Maimela, S. & König, A. *Initiation into theology.* Pretoria: Van Schaik. pp. 275-296 & 297-318.

SPIER, J.M. 1959. *Van Thales tot Sartre.* Kampen: Kok.

SWEETMAN, R. 2007. (Ed.) *In the Phrygian mode; neo-Calvinism, Antiquity and the lamentations of Reformational philosophy.* Toronto: Institute for Christian Studies and Lanham: Univ. Press of America.

TALJAARD, J.A.L. 1982. *Kort oorsig van die geskiedenis van die Wysbegeerte deur D.H.Th. Vollenhoven (1956) – 'n verwerking in Afrikaans.* (Diktaat nr. 5/82.) Potchefstroom: PU vir CHO.

TOL, A. 2007. Vollenhoven on early Classical Antiquity. In: Sweetman, R. (Ed.), *In the Phrygian mode.* Toronto: ICS and Lanham: Univ. Press of America. pp. 127-160.

VAN ASSELT, W.J. 1996. De erfenis van de Gereformeerde Scholastiek. *Kerk en Theologie,* 46: 126-136.

VAN DER WALT, B.J. 1973. Eisegesis-exegesis, paradox and nature-grace; methods of synthesis in Medieval philosophy. *Philosophia Reformata,* 38: 191-211.

VAN DER WALT, B.J. 2001a. Culture, worldview and religion. *Philosophia Reformata,* 66: 23-38.

VAN DER WALT, B.J. 2001b. Why the salt has lost its quality; the influence of dualistic worldviews on Christianity. In: Van der Walt, B.J., *Transformed by the renewing of your mind*. Potchefstroom: Institute for Contemporary Christianity in Africa. pp. 1-42.

VAN DER WALT, B.J. 2006. *When African and Western cultures meet*. Potchefstroom: The Institute for Contemporary Christianity in Africa.

VAN DER WALT, B.J. 2012. Flying on the wings of Vollenhoven's radical Christian worldview; a reconsideration of the usual typology of Chris tian worldviews. *Koers*, 77 (1): 56-69.

VAN STEENBERGHEN, F. 1955. *The philosophical movement of the thirteenth century*. Edinburgh: Nelson.

VENTER, E.A. s.j. *Die ontwikkeling van die Westerse denke*. Bloemfontein: SACUM.

VENTER, J.J. 1981. *Geloofsgebonde denke by Anselmus; 'n studie van sy wysgerige metode*. (D.Phil. dissertation) Potchefstroom: PU vir CHO.

VENTER, J.J. 1985. *Hoofprobleme van die Middeleeuse Wysbegeerte*. (Diktaat 65/79.) Potchefstroom: PU vir CHO, Dept. Sentrale Publikasies.

VENTER, J.J. 1988. Pieke en lyne in die Westerse Wysbegeerte. (Diktaat nr. 22/88.) Potchefstroom: PU vir CHO. Dept. Sentrale Publikasies.

VOLLENHOVEN, D.H.Th. 2005a. *Wijsgerig Woordenboek*. Bril, K.A. (Ed.). Amstelveen: De Zaak Haes.

VOLLENHOVEN, D.H.Th. 2005b. *The problem-historical-method and the history of philosophy*. Bril, K.A. (Ed.). Amstelveen: De Zaak Haes.

VOLLENHOVEN, D.H.Th. 2005c. *Isagôgè Philosophiae; introduction to philosophy*. J. Kok & A. Tol (Eds.). Sioux Center, Iowa: Dordt College Press.

VOLLENHOVEN, D.H.Th. 2011. *Gastcolleges Wijsbegeerte; erfenis voor het heden*. Bril, K.A. & Nijhoff, R.A. (Eds.). Amstelveen:

De Zaak Haes.

VON HARNACK, A. 1964. *Lehrbuch der Dogmengeschichte* (3 dele). Darmstadt: Wissenschaftlich Buchgesellschaft.

VOS, A. 1985. *Aquinas, Calvin and contemporary Protestant thought; a critique of Protestant views on the thought of Thomas Aquinas.* Grand Rapids, Michigan: Eerdmans.

VOS, A. 1990. As the philosopher says; Thomas Aquinas and the classical heritage. In: Helleman, W.E. (Ed.), *Christianity and the classics; the acceptance of a heritage.* Lanham: Univ. Press of America. pp. 69-82.

WILKEN, R. 1984. *The Christians as the Romans saw them.* New Haven, Yale University.

WOLTERS, A.M. 1990. Christianity and the classics: a typology of attitudes. In: Helleman, W.E. (Ed.), *Christianity and the Classics: the acceptance of a heritage.* Lanham: Univ. Press of America. pp. 189-203.

CHAPTER 7

AERTSEN, J.A. 1982. *Natura et creatura: de denkweg van Thomas van Aquino.* (2 dele). Amsterdam: VU Boekhandel (Proefskrif).

AERTSEN, J.A. 1983. Het zijnde en de goede zijn omkeerbaar. In: Van Vollenhoven, Th. (Ed.) *Zin en zijn, metafysische beschouwingen over de goede.* Baarn: Ambo. pp. 32-45.

AERTSEN, J.A. 1984. *Middeleeuwse beschouwingen over waarheid: adaequatio rei et intellectus.* Amsterdam: Vrije Universiteit (Inougurele rede).

AERTSEN, J.A. 1990. Aquinas and the classical heritage. In: Helleman, W.E. (Ed). *Christianity and the Classics; the acceptance of a heritage.* Lanham: Univ. Press of America. pp. 83-90.

AERTSEN, J.A. 1991. Thomas Aquinas (1224/5-1274). In: Klapwijk, J., Grirffioen, S. & Groenewoud, G. (Eds.). *Bringing into captivity every thought; capita selecta in the history of Christian evaluations of non-Christian philosophy*. Lanham: Univ. Press of America. pp. 95-122.

ALBERS, O.J.L. 1955. *Het natuurrecht volgens de Wijsbegeerte der Wetsidee; een kritische beschouwing*. Nijmegen: Drukkerij Gebr. Janssen.

ASHLEY, B. 2006. *Way towards wisdom; an interdisciplinary and intercultural introduction to metaphysics*. Notre Dame, Indiana: Univ. of Notre Dame Press.

BERKOUWER, G.C. 1948. *Conflict met Rome*. Kampen: Kok.

BERKOUWER, G.C. 1964. *Vatikaans Concilie en Nieuwe Theologie*. Kampen, Kok.

BERKOUWER, G.C. 1968. *Nabetrachting op het Concilie*. Kampen: Kok.

CESSARIO, R. 2003. *A short history of Thomism*. New York: Catholic Univ. Press of America.

DELFGAAUW, B. 1952. *Beknopte geschiedenis der wijsbegeerte; deel 3: de hedendaagse wijsbegeerte*. Baarn: Het Wereldvenster.

ELDERS, L. 2013. *Thomas van Aquino; een inleiding tot zijn leven en denke*. Almere: Parthenon.

GILBY, T. 1967. Thomism. In: Edwards, P. (Ed.), *The Encyclopdia of Philosophy*. New York/London: Macmillan Pub. Co. pp. 119-121.

GILSON, E. 1972. What is Christian philosophy? In: Bronstein, D.J., Krikorian, Y.H.S. & Wiener, P.P. (Eds.), *Basic problems of philosophy*. Englewood Cliffs, New Jersey: PrenticeHall.

HALDANE, J. 2005. Thomism. In: Craig, E. (Ed.) *The shorter Routledge Encyclopedia of Philosophy*. London/New York: Routledge, pp. 1017-1018.

HAMMAN, A. 1960. Neuscholastik. In: Galling, K. (Red.) *Die Religion in Geschichte und Gegenwart*. (Deel 4).Tübingen: JCB Mohr (Paul Siebeck). pp. 1434-1437.

LONERGAN, B. 2000. *Grace and freedom; opperative grace in the thought of Thomas Aquinas*. (Volume 1 of Lonergan's Collected

Works. Ed. by F.E. Crowe & R.M. Doran.) Toronto: Univ. Press of Toronto.

LOUET FEISER, J.J. 1961. De bijdrage van de Wijsbegeerte der Wetsidee tot de vernieuwing van het philosophisch inzicht. In: W.K. van Dijk & J. Stellingwerff (Eds.) *Perspectief*. Kampen: Kok. pp. 18-35.

MACINTYRE, A. 2009. *God, philosophy and universities; a selective history of the Catholic philosophical tradition*. London: Continuum.

MARLET, M. 1954. *Gründlinien der kalvinistische Philosophie der Gesetzidee als christliche transcendental Philosophie*. München: Karl Zink.

MEULEMAN, G.E. 1952. *De Encyclick Humani Generis*. Kampen: Kok.

MEULEMAN, G.E. 1960. Nieuwe theologie. In: Grosheide, F.W. & Van Itterzon, G.A. (Eds.) *Christelijke Encyclopedie*, deel 5. Kampen: Kok. pp. 209-211.

MEULEMAN, G.E. 1967. Natuur en genade. In: Berkhof, H. *et al. Protestantse verkenningen na Vaticanum II*. 's-Gravenhage: Boekencentrum.

MITCHELL, C.V. 2007. *Charts of philosophy and philosophers*. Grand Rapids, Michigan: Zondervan.

NICHOLS, A. 2002. *Discovering Aquinas; an introduction to his life, work and influence*. Grand Rapids, Michigan: Eerdmans.

NOLL, M.A. & NYSTROM, C. 2005. *Is the Reformation over? An Evangelical assessment of contemporary Roman Catholicism*. Grand Rapids, Michigan: Baker Academic.

ROBBERS, H. 1948. *Wijsbegeerte en openbaring*. Brussel: Het Spectrum.

ROBBERS, H. 1951. *Neo-Thomisme en moderne wijsbegeerte*. Utrecht/Brussel: Het Spectrum.

ROWLAND, T. 2012. A Symphony of theological renewal. *The Tablet*, 16-17, November.

SAHAKIAN, W.S. 1969. *Outline-history of philosophy*. New

York: Barnes & Noble.
SASSEN, F. & DELFGAUW, B. 1957. *Wijsbegeerte van onze tijd.* Antwerpen/Amsterdam: Standaard-Boekhandel.
SMIT, M.C. 1950. *De verhouding van Christendom en historie in de huidige RoomsKatholieke geschiedbeschouwing.* Kampen: Kok.
SMITH, J.K.A. & OLTHUIS, J.H. (Eds.) 2006. *Radical Orthodoxy and the Reformed tradition.* Grand Rapids, MI: Baker Academic.
SMITH, J.K.A. 2004. *Radical Orthodoxy; mapping a post-secular theology.* Grand Rapids, Michigan: Baker Book House.
STRYKER BOUDIER, C.E.M. 1985-1992. *Wijsgerig leven in Nederland, België en Luxemburg 1880-1980.* (8 dele.) Nijmegen/Baarn: Ambo.
VAN DER BEEK, A. 2006. *Van Kant tot Kuitert; de belangrijkste theologen van de 19e en 20e eeuw.* Kampen: Kok.
VAN DER HOEVEN, J. 1974. Einde van eentijdperk? In: Van Riessen, H., Goudzwaard, B., Rookmaker, H.R. en Van der Hoeven, J., *Macht en onmacht van de twintigste eeuw.* Amsterdam: Buijten & Schipperheijn. pp. 112-142.
VAN DER HOEVEN, J. 1980. *Peilingen; korte exploraties in wijsgerig stroomgebied.* Amsterdam: Buijten & Schipperheijn.
VAN DER STOEP, J., KUIPER, R. & RAMAKER, T. (Eds.) 2007. *Alles wat je hart begeert; Christelijke oriëntatie in een op belevinggerichte cultuur.* Amsterdam: Buijten & Schipperheijn.
VAN DER WALT, B.J. 2011a. Die "suiwer" Gereformeerde teologie sonder 'n "suiwer" filosofiese grondslag: is dit moontlik? *Tydskrif vir Christelike Wetenskap,* 47(2): 1-33.
VAN DER WALT, B.J. 2011b. 'n Onsuiwer mensbeskouing, kenteorie en wetenskapsleer in die *Synopsis Purioris Theologiae (1625).Tydskrif vir Christelike Wetenskap,* 47(3): 49-86.
VANDER STELT, J.C. 2005. "Faculty psychology" and theology. In: Kok, J.H. (Ed.), *Ways of knowing in concert.* Sioux Center, Iowa: Dordt College Press. p. 45-60.
VANDERVELDE, G. 1975. *Original sin; two major trends in*

contemporary Roman Catholic reinterpretation. Amsterdam: Rodolphi.

VOLLENHOVEN, D.H.Th. 2000. *Schematische Kaarten; filosofische concepties in probleemhistorisch verband.* (Eds. K.A. Bril & P.J. Boonstra). Amstelveen: De ZaakHaes.

VOLLENHOVEN, D.H.Th. 2005. *The problem-historical method and the history of philosophy.* (Ed. K.A. Bril.) Amstelveen: De Zaak Haes.

WALMSLEY, G. 2012. Whose Thomism? Which Aquinas? Paper delivered at an international conference at St. Augustine's College, Johannesburg on 3 November 2012.

WENTSEL, B. 1970. *Natuur en genade; een introductie in en confrontatie met de jongste ontwikkelingen in de Rooms-Katolieke teologie inzake dit thema.* Kampen: J.H. Kok.

WOLDRING, H.E.S. 2013. *Een handvol filosofen; geschiedenis van de filosofiebeoefening aan de Vrije Universiteit in Amsterdam van 1880 tot 2012.* Hilversum: Verloren.

WOLTERSTORFF, N. 1987. *Keeping faith.* Grand Rapids, Michigan: Calvin College Press.

ZUIDEMA, S.U. 1936. *De philosophie van Occam in zijn Com mentaar op de Sententiën.* (2 dele). Hilversum: Schipper.

CHAPTER 8

BARTHOLOMEW, C.G. & GOHEEN, M.W. 2013. *Christian philosophy.* Grand Rapids, Michigan: Barker Academic.

BAVINCK, H. 1894. *De algemene genade.* Kampen: Kok.

BEDIAKO, K. 1992. *Theology and identity; Christian thought in the second century and in modern Africa.* Oxford: Regnum Books.

BERKOUWER, G.C. 1948. *Conflict met Rome.* Kampen: Kok.

BISHOP, J. & KOK, J.H. (Eds.) 2013. *On Kuyper; a collection of readings on the life, work and legacy of Abraham Kuyper.* Sioux Center, Iowa: Dordt College Press.

BRATT, J.D. 2013. *Abraham Kuyper; modern Calvinist, Chris-*

tian democrat. Grand Rapids, Michigan: Eerdmans.

CARSON, D.A. 2008. *Christ and culture revisited.* Grand Rapids, Michigan: Eerdmans.

CARTER, C.A. 2007. *Rethinking Christ and culture; a post-Christendom perspective.* Grand Rapids, Michigan: Brazos.

DELFGAAUW, B. 1952. *Beknopte geschiedenis der wijsbegeerte;* deel 3: de hedendaagse wijsbegeerte. Baarn: Het Wereldvenster.

DOOYEWEERD, H. 1959. *Vernieuwing en bezinning; rondom het reformatorish grondmotief.* Zutphen: J.B. van den Brink & Co.

GILSON, E. 1972. What is Christian philosophy? In: Bronstein, D.J., Krikorian, Y.H. & Wiener, P.P. (Eds.), *Basic problems of philosophy.* EnglewoodCliffs, New Yersey: Prentice-Hall. pp. 30-40.

HEIDEMAN, E.P. 1959. *The relation of revelation and reason in E. Brunner and H. Bavinck.* Assen: Van Gorcum.

KLAPWIJK, J. 2013. Antithesis and common grace. In: Bishop, J. & Kok, J.H. (Eds.), *On Kuyper; a collection of readings on the life, work and legacy of Abraham Kuyper.* Sioux Center, Iowa: Dordt College Press. pp. 287-302.

KLAPWIJK, J., GRIFFIOEN, S. & GROENEWOUD, G. (Eds.) 1991. *Bringing into captivity every thought; capita selecta in the history of Christian evaluations of non-Christian philosophy.* Lanham: Univ. Press of America.

KOK, J.H. 1998. *Patterns of the Western mind; a Reformed Christian perspective.* Sioux Center, Iowa: Dordt College Press.

KUIPERS, T. 2011. *Abraham Kuyper; an annotated bibliography, 1857-2012.* Leiden: Brill.

LIEF, J. 2012. The two kingdoms perspective and theological method: why I still disagree with David van Drunen. *Pro Rege,* 41(1):1-5, Sept.

MACINTYRE, A. 1953. *Marxism: an interpretation.* London: SCM Press.

MEKKES, J.P.A. 1961. *Scheppingsopenbaring en wijsbegeerte.*

Kampen: Kok. (Also available in an English translation of 2010: *Creation, revelation and philosophy*. Sioux Center, Iowa: Dordt College Press).

MEKKES, J.P.A. 1965. *Teken en motief der creatuur*. Amsterdam: Buijten & Schipperheijn.

MEULEMAN, G.E. 1951. *De ontwikkeling van het dogma in de Rooms Katolieke theologie*. Kampen: Kok.

MEULEMAN, G.E. 1952. *De encycliek "Humani generis"*. Kampen: Kok.

MEULEMAN, G.E. 1958. *Maurice Blondel en de apologetiek*. Kampen: Kok.

MEULEMAN, G.E. 1960. Nieuwe Theologie. In: Grosheide, F.W. & Van Itterzon, G.P. (Eds.) *Christelijke Encyclopedie,* deel 5. Kampen: Kok. pp. 209-211.

MEULEMAN, G.E. 1967. Natuur en genade. In: Berkhof, H. et al. *Protestantse verkenningen na Vaticanum II*. s'Gravenhave: Boekencentrum.

MOUW, R.J. 2012. *The challenges of cultural discipleship; essays in the line of Abraham Kuyper*. Grand Rapids, Michigan: Eerdmans.

NOLL, M.A. & TURNER, J. 2008. *The future of Christian learning; an Evangelical and Catholic dialogue*. Grand Rapids, Michigan: Brazos Press.

O'MAHONY, J.E. 1929. *The desire of God in the philosophy of St. Thomas Aquinas*. London: Longman Green.

OLTHUIS, J.H. 1970. Must the church become secular? In: Olthuis, J.A., Hart, H., Seerveld, G.C., Zylstra, B. & Olthuis, J.A. *Out of concern for the church*. Toronto: Wedge Pub. Foundation. pp.105-125.

POLMAN, A.D.R. 1961. Thomas van Aquino. In: Grosheide, F.W. & Van Itterzon, G.P. (Eds.) *Christelijke Encyclopedie,* deel 6. Kampen: Kok. pp. 366-368.

ROBBERS, H. 1948. *Wijsbegeerte en openbaring*. Brussel: Het

Spectrum.

ROBBERS, H. 1949. Het Calvinistische wijsbegeerte in gesprek met het Thomisme. *Studia Catholica*, 24: 161-171.

ROBBERS, H. 1951. *Neo-Thomisme en moderne wijsbegeerte*. Utrecht/Brussel: Het Spectrum.

RUNNER, H.E. 1982. *The relation of the Bible to learning*. Jordan Station, Ontario: Paideia Press.

SASSEN, F. & DELFGAAUW, B. 1957. *Wijsbegeerte van onze tijd*. Antwerpen/Amsterdam: Standaard-Boekhandel.

SMIT, M.C. 1950. *De verhouding van Christendom en historie in de huidige Rooms-Katolieke geschiedbeschouwing*. Kampen: J.H. Kok.

SPYKMAN, G.J. 1992. *Reformational theology; a new paradigm in doing dogmatics*. Grand Rapids, Michigan: Eerdmans.

VAN DER WALT, B.J. 2001. Why the lost has lost its quality; the influence of dualistic worldviews on Christianity. In: Van der Walt, B.J., *Transformed by the renewing of your mind*. Potchefstroom: The Institute for Contemporary Christianity in Africa. pp. 1-42.

VAN DER WALT, B.J. 2010. A biblical perspective on being human. In: Van der Walt, B.J., *At home in God's world*. Potchefstroom: The Institute for Contemporary Christianity in Africa. pp. 259-289.

VAN DER WALT, B.J. 2010a. A new paradigm for doing Christian philosophy: D.H.Th. Vollenhoven. In: Van der Walt, B.J., *At home in God's world*. Potchefstroom: The Institute for Contemporary Christianity in Africa. pp. 152-182.

VAN DER WALT, B.J. 2010b. Wêreldwye belangstelling in die Kuyperiaanse Reformatoriese lewensvisie. *Tydskrif vir Christelike Wetenskap*, 46(1): 43-60.

VAN DER WALT, B.J. 2011. An evangelical voice in Africa: the worldview background of the theology of Tokunboh Adeyemo (01/10/1944-17/03/2010). *In die Skriflig*, 45(4):919-956.

VAN DER WALT, B.J. 2013a. Hoe om die geskiedenis van die filosofie weer te gee: 'n Verkenning van wysgerige historiografiese probleme en metodes. *Tydskrif vir Geesteswetenskappe,* 53(1):1-15, Maart.

VAN DER WALT, B.J. 2013b. 'n Skrifmatige perspektief op die Westerse intellektuele denke: die ontstaan en kontoere van en vrae oor die konsekwent probleem-historiese metode. *Tydskrif vir Geesteswetenskappe,* 53 (1): 1-15) (3). September.

VAN DER WALT, B.J. 2014a. *At the cradle of a Christian philosophy: Calvin, Vollenhoven, Stoker and Dooyeweerd.* Potchefstroom: Institute for Contemporary Christianity in Africa.

VAN DER WALT, B.J. 2014b. *Constancy and change; historical types and trends in the passion of the Western mind.* Potchefstroom: Institute for Contemporary Christianity in Africa.

VAN DRUNEN, D. 2012. The two kingdoms and Reformed Christianity; why recovering an old paradigm is hisitorically sound, biblically grounded and practically useful. *Pro Rege,* 40(3): 31-18, March.

VANDERVELDE, G. 1975. *Original sin; two major trends in contemporary Roman Catholic reinterpretation.* Amsterdam: Rodolphi.

VEENHOF, J. 1994. *The relationship between nature and grace according to H. Bavinck.* Potchefstroom: Institute for Reformational Studies. (Study pamphlet, no. 322, October).

VOLLENHOVEN, D.H.Th. 1933. *Het Calvinisme en de reformatie van de wijsbegeerte.* Amsterdam: Paris.

VOLLENHOVEN, D.H.Th. 2000. *Schematische Kaarten; filosofische concepties in probleemhistorisch verband.* (K.A. Bril & P.J. Boonstra, Eds.) Amstelveen: De ZaakHaes.

VOLLENHOVEN, D.H.Th. 2005. *The problem-historical method and the history of philosophy.* (K.A. Bril, Ed.) Amstelveen: De Zaak Haes.

WALSH, B.J. & MIDDLETON, J.R. 1984. *The transforming vision.* Downers Grove, Illinois: InterVarsity Press.

WENTSEL, B. 1970. *Natuur en genade; een introductie in en confrontatie met de jongste ontwikkelingen in de Rooms-Katolieke te-*

ologie inzake dit thema. Kampen: J.H. Kok.

WILKENS, S. & SANFORD, M.L. 2009. *Hidden worldviews; eight cultural stories that shape our lives*. Downers Grove, Illinois: InterVarsity Press Academic.

ZAGZEBSKI, I. (Ed.) 1993. *Rational faith; Catholic responses to Reformed Eipistemology*. Notre Dame, Indiana: University of Notre Dame Press.

ZUIDEMA, S.U. 1972. Maurice Blondel and the method of immanence. In: Zuidema, S.U. *Communication and confrontation*. Assen/Kampen: Van Gorcum/Kok. pp. 227-262.

ZUIDEMA, S.U. 2013. Common grace and Christian action in Abraham Kuyper. In: Bishop, S. & Kok, J.H. (Eds.) *On Kuyper: a collection of readings on the life, work and legacy of Abraham Kuyper*. Sioux Center, Iowa: Dordt College Press. pp. 247-286.

Subject Index - Thomas Aquinas and the Neo-Thomist Tradition

A

abortion, 83
Africanization, 150
angels, 49, 50, 116
anthropology, 7, 9, 27,
    47, 57, 70, 76, 77, 78,
    79, 80, 85, 88, 103,
    178, 189, 191, 195,
    198
Aquinas' philosophy, 2,
    3, 7, 8, 16, 18, 24, 25, 35,
    36, 38, 39, 43, 50, 51, 54,
    56, 59, 65, 72, 74, 99, 109,
    134, 179, 182, 183, 186,
    210, 213
Aristotle's philosophy, 19,
    41, 103, 108, 140, 149,
    165, 166, 169, 170, 229
Aristotelian Philosophy, 20,
    158, 161, 165
Aristotelianising philosophy,
    19, 20
Aristotelianism, 18, 20, 23, 158,
    168, 169, 184
Augustinian philosophy, 163

B

Biblicism, 26, 154, 155

C

Catholic philosophy, 55, 190

Christian Aristotelianism, 20, 23
Christian philosophers, 15, 26, 58,
    142, 151, 152, 167, 204
Christian philosophy, 1, 5, 7, 15, 60,
    142, 150, 160, 161, 173, 181, 205, 206,
    207, 215, 231, 235, 239
Christian theology, 7, 22(add), 106,
    161, 163, 173, 230
Christian thinkers, 25, 140, 142,
    150, 153, 154, 168, 200, 205, 211
Christian worldviews, 146, 164
Christianity, 7, 21, 25, 31, 33,
    102, 139, 140, 141, 144, 145, 146,
    147, 149, 150, 154, 156, 158, 162,
    164, 166, 169, 178, 218, 220, 223,
    225, 229, 230, 231, 232, 233, 234,
    241, 242
contemporary philosophy, 142, 146,
    183, 195
cosmological philosophy, 57, 59, 191,
    195
cosmos, 8, 36, 38, 39, 40, 43, 50, 51,
    54, 56, 65, 66, 77, 78, 103, 106, 111,
    114, 117, 119, 164, 165
creatianism, 82, 83, 84, 198
creation, 17, 30, 35, 36, 39, 40, 43,
    45, 46, 52, 53, 54, 55, 56, 58, 59,
    60, 61, 62, 63, 64, 65, 68, 70, 74, 75,
    76, 77, 83, 104, 105, 106, 107, 111, 114,
    115, 117, 125, 130, 131, 135, 136, 152, 155,
    190, 191, 193, 195, 196, 203, 209, 210,
    216

D

death, 2, 5, 8, 16, 20, 86, 87,
    88, 127, 130, 167, 171, 172, 178,
    198
determinism, 45, 73, 74, 121,
    122, 125, 128, 133, 134, 135,
    136
divine law/*lex divina*, 49
divine sovereignty, 12, 74, 120,
    123, 136
doctrine of analogy, 67, 69, 70,
    184
doctrine of nature-grace, 27, 52,
    190, 191, 195
doctrine of participation, 52, 67,
    70, 71, 72, 76
dualism, 27, 30, 32, 39, 57, 63, 64,
    75, 85, 164, 189, 191, 195, 199, 203,
    207, 208, 209

E

earth, 73, 112, 113, 226
eisegesis, 26, 48, 110, 153, 154, 155
election, 45, 74, 102, 104, 119, 132,
    133, 134, 136, 227
empiricism, 90, 92
epistemology, 7, 9, 57, 76, 77, 78,
    80, 89, 90, 92, 95, 98, 99, 103, 153
eternity, 44, 45, 48, 60, 64, 65, 74,
    81, 88, 98, 117, 125, 133, 134, 167
evil, 9, 30, 61, 83, 102, 104, 107,
    119, 127-131, 134
exegesis, 26, 48, 51, 110, 111, 136,

143, 153, 154, 155, 157, 164, 232
exemplars, 44, 45, 52, 56, 58, 60,
   62, 64, 69, 70, 71, 72, 73, 75, 81,
   98, 109
existentialism, 16, 136, 161, 180, 182,
   193, 202

G

Germanization, 149, 232
Graeco-Roman philosophy, 146
Greek-Hellenist culture, 139
Greek philosophy, 12, 14, 25, 27,
   33, 37, 39, 55, 75, 86, 140, 155,
   158, 192, 211

H

Hellenism, 139, 141
Hellenization, 139, 141,
144, 147, 149, 229, 231
heretics, 22, 25
human freedom, 9, 102,
104, 122, 123, 202
hybridization, 149, 156

I

illumination, 95, 99
intellective soul, 78, 79,
   80, 81, 82, 84, 85, 86, 87, 88,
   89, 93, 94
intellectual creatures, 46, 110,
115, 116
intellectualism, 46, 80, 85, 92,
   115, 120, 128, 161, 178, 179

intellectus agens, 90, 94, 95, 96
intellectus possibilis, 90, 96
irrationalism, 193, 194, 204
Islamic faith, 23

L

law, 8, 11, 33, 35, 36, 38-53,
    54, 55, 56, 59, 60, 62, 63, 64,
    65, 66, 67, 68, 69, 70, 71, 73,
    74, 75, 77, 78, 79, 87, 90, 92,
    96, 98, 99, 103, 105, 109, 110,
    111, 112, 116, 117, 122, 125, 130,
    135, 192, 203

M

Medieval philosophy, 2, 150,
156, 232
Medieval theology, 147
monism, 63, 64

N

natural law/*lex naturalis*, 49
natural theology, 8, 39, 92, 99,
    106, 109, 110, 156
nature-grace theme, 28, 156, 162,
    163, 198, 205
neo-Calvinism, 172
neo-Kantianism, 172
neo-Platonism, 43, 72, 135, 166
neo-Platonic philosophy, 43, 165
neo-Thomism, 2, 7, 8, 9, 171, 173,
    175, 178, 180, 181, 182, 183, 184, 185,
    186, 187, 193, 195, 196, 201, 206, 207

neo-Thomist philosophers, 175, 181, 198, 202, 205, 206
nomology, 51, 56, 77, 79, 92, 103

P

pagan philosophy, 25, 26, 27, 31, 33, 155, 158
pantheism, 39, 63, 196
paradoxical method, 155
partial universalism, 56, 66, 75, 127, 189, 191, 195, 197
phantasma/phantasms, 90, 93, 94, 95, 96
phenomenology, 1, 182
Platonism, 43, 72, 135, 158, 161, 162, 166,184, 222
pragmatism, 136, 193, 195
prayer, 102, 104, 119, 125
Protestant Scholasticism, 14, 74
providence, 9, 17, 45, 47, 57, 101, 102, 104, 105, 106, 107, 109, 112-119, 1 21, 123, 125-127, 128, 131, 132, 133, 134

R

Radical Orthodoxy, 7, 15, 100, 175, 216, 237
rationalism, 85, 135, 193, 200
redemption, 17, 32, 39, 61, 85, 104, 105, 190, 191, 204
Reformational philosophers, 7, 58, 146, 159, 173, 174, 180, 200, 207
Reformational philosophy, 2, 5, 7,

11, 13, 15, 46, 77, 99, 139, 141, 142, 144, 161, 166, 174, 175, 190, 207, 232
Reformational thinkers, 169, 171, 190
Reformational tradition, 103, 134, 161, 206, 208, 209, 232
Reformed Scholasticism, 6, 46, 164, 190, 218, 228
Reformed Orthodox theology, 15, 99, 173
Reformed scholastic theology, 77
Reformed theology, 13, 14, 136, 174
reprobation, 102, 104, 119, 124, 132, 133, 134, 136, 227
Roman Catholic philosophers, 14, 194, 195, 200
Roman Catholic theology, 174, 199
Roman culture, 150

S

Scholasticism, 6, 11, 14, 15, 46, 53, 55, 74, 124, 134, 137, 149, 160, 161-164, 166, 216, 218, 228
scholastic philosophy, 12, 14, 16, 161, 180
scholastic theology, 11, 77
secular philosophy, 152, 159, 174
similitudo, 39, 43, 46, 47, 52, 68, 70, 79, 97
soul, 3, 78-89, 93, 94, 95, 97,

98, 167, 178, 198, 208, 229
syncretism, 149, 150, 151, 230
synthesis thinking, 12, 14, 18, 20, 21, 22, 24, 26, 33, 37, 113, 141, 159
synthetic philosophy, 5, 30, 149, 157
synthesis philosophy, 14, 33, 36, 43, 77, 99, 103, 108, 110, 119, 123, 132, 135, 137, 141, 142, 144, 145, 147, 149, 150, 151, 152, 153, 155, 157, 158, 159, 160, 161, 169

T

Thomism, 2, 7, 8, 9, 16, 99, 171, 173, 175, 176, 178, 180, 181, 182, 183, 184, 185, 186, 187, 193, 195, 196, 197, 198, 201, 202, 203, 206, 207, 235, 238
Thomist philosophers, 175, 181, 182, 195, 197, 198, 201, 202, 205, 206
Thomist philosophy, 1, 2, 3, 168, 173, 176, 188, 198, 206
traducianism, 84
traducianists, 82, 83
Trinity, 48

W

Western culture, 18, 151
Western philosophy, 1, 2, 24,
    144, 146, 159, 166, 191

Scripture Index - Thomas Aquinas and the Neo-Thomist Tradition

GENESIS

Genesis 1:26 – 46, 81, 112
Genesis 2:2 – 83
Genesis 2:7 – 82
Genesis 2:15 – 112
Genesis 3:5 – 111

EXODUS

Exodus 10:1 – 131
Exodus 18:21-22 – 115

NUMBERS

Numbers 23:19 – 126

I SAMUEL

1 Samuel 15:29 – 126

JOB

Job 11:7 – 48

PSALMS

Psalm 33:15 – 82
Psalm 139:8 – 113

PROVERBS

Proverbs 8:7 – 25
Proverbs 11:29 – 115
Proverbs 16:4 – 111
Proverbs 21:1 – 118

ISAIAH
Isaiah 26:12 – 118
Isaiah 38:1-5 – 126
Isaiah 45:7 – 128, 131, 132
Isaiah 63:17 – 131

JEREMIAH
Jeremiah 18:7-8 – 126
Jeremiah 23:24 – 113

LAMENTATIONS
Lamentations 5:21 – 123

AMOS
Amos 3:6 – 128, 131, 132

MALACHI
Malachi 1:2-3 – 133
Malachi 3:6 – 126

JOHN
John 1:5 – 62
John 6:44 – 123
John 15:4 – 123
John 15:5 – 118

ROMANS
Romans 1:28 – 131
Romans 9:16 – 123
Romans 11:36 – 51, 111

1 CORINTHIANS

1 Corinthians 3:9 – 114
1 Corinthians 15:53-54 – 89

2 CORINTHIANS

2 Corinthians 5:14 – 123
2 Corinthians 10:5 – 142

EPHESIANS

Ephesians 1:4 – 136
Ephesians 1:4-5 – 133

PHILIPPIANS

Philippians 2:13 – 118

COLOSSIANS

Colossians 1:15 – 49

1 TIMOTHY

1 Timothy 6:16 – 89

TITUS

Titus 3:5 – 123

REVELATION

Revelation 22:13 – 111

Name Index

A

A'Brakel 13
Adam 61, 111, 129
Aertsen, J.A. 17, 29, 51, 52, 72, 73, 174
Aeterni Patris 14, 171, 179, 183, 185, 187, 205
Albers, O.J.L. 174
Alexandria 154, 229, 232
Amsterdam 174, 215, 219, 220, 221, 222, 225, 226, 234, 237, 238, 241, 242
Aquinas, Thomas 1, 2, 3, 5, 7, 8, 9, 11, 12, 14, 15, 16, 17, 18, 19, 20, 21, 22, 23, 24, 25, 26, 27, 28, 29, 30, 31, 32, 33, 35, 36, 37, 38, 39, 40, 41, 42, 43, 44, 45, 46, 47, 48, 49, 50, 51, 52, 53, 54, 55, 56, 57, 58, 59, 60, 61, 62, 63, 64, 65, 66, 67, 68, 69, 70, 71, 72, 73, 74, 75, 76, 77, 78, 79, 80, 81, 82, 83, 84, 85, 86, 87, 88, 89, 90, 91, 92, 93, 94, 95, 96, 97, 98, 99, 100, 101, 102, 103, 104, 105, 106, 107, 108, 109, 110, 111, 112, 113, 114, 115, 116, 117, 118, 119, 120, 121, 122, 123, 124, 125, 126, 127, 128, 129, 130, 131, 132, 133, 134, 135, 136, 137, 140, 145, 147, 148, 149, 150, 152, 157, 158, 160, 161, 164, 165, 166, 167, 168, 169, 170, 171, 172, 173, 174, 175, 176, 178, 179, 180, 181, 182, 183, 184, 185, 186, 189, 190, 191, 193, 194, 195, 197, 198, 199, 202, 203, 208, 210, 211, 213, 214, 215, 216, 217, 220, 221, 222, 234, 235, 236, 238, 240, 244, 253
Archbishop of Canterbury 20, 168
Aristotle 12, 18, 19, 20, 21, 22, 23, 25, 31, 33, 36, 37, 39, 40, 41, 42, 49, 50, 55, 57, 62, 64, 72, 75, 86, 87, 88, 92, 94, 95, 103, 105, 106, 107, 108, 109, 110, 111, 112, 114, 115, 116, 117, 120, 121, 122, 123, 124, 127, 132, 140, 149, 152, 153, 155, 157, 158, 159, 160, 163, 164, 165, 166, 167, 168, 169, 170, 178, 181, 185, 186, 229, 232, 244
Arminius 6, 218, 228
Asalo of St.Victor 19
Ashley 175, 186
At the cradle of a Christian philosophy in Calvin, Vollenhoven, Stoker and Dooyeweerd 7
Augustine 12, 19, 20, 43, 60, 72, 135, 154, 168, 173, 229, 238
Augustinians 62, 186
Averroës 20, 37

Averroists 26, 168
Avicenna 18, 19, 22

B

Bartholomew, C.G. 194
Bastable, P.B. 53
Bavinck, Herman 7, 14, 74, 99, 146, 208, 209, 228, 239, 242
Bediako, K. 210
Belgium 181
Berger 86, 88
Bergson 194
Berkouwer 102, 129, 174, 207
Beza 11, 12, 14, 134, 159
Bible 14, 23, 25, 26, 27, 30, 31, 32, 33, 37, 48, 53, 70, 82, 87, 89, 103, 106, 110, 111, 129, 144, 151, 154, 155, 157, 159, 179, 196, 210, 241
Biblicists 27
Bilderdijk 13
Bishop J. 107
Bishop Tempier 168, 209, 239, 243
Blondel, M. 53, 194, 196, 200, 203, 204, 205, 206, 221, 240, 243
Boëthius the Dacian 20
Bonaventura 168, 187
Borgan 153
Bos, A.P. 143, 145, 151, 154, 155, 166
Boudier, Stryker 181
Bratt 209
Brill 174, 229, 239
Brown 150

C

Cajetanus 182, 187, 194, 199
Calvin 7, 12, 14, 15, 134, 159, 218, 224, 225, 234, 238, 242
Calvin College 15, 238
Canons of Dordt 6, 11
Carson, D.A. 210
Carter, C.A. 210
Catholic College of St. Augustine 173
Catholics 35, 175, 181, 182
Cessario, R. 181
Choi, Y.J. 144
Christ and culture 146, 231, 239

Christianity 7, 21, 25, 31, 33, 102, 139, 140, 141, 144, 145, 146, 147, 149, 150, 154, 156, 158, 162, 164, 166, 169, 178, 218, 220, 223, 225, 229, 230, 231, 232, 233, 234, 241, 242, 245
Christians 23, 24, 25, 32, 82, 103, 104, 113, 143, 145, 146, 151, 152, 153, 155, 159, 173, 174, 205, 210, 211, 230, 234
Church Fathers 24, 33, 135, 141, 150, 151, 152, 155, 159, 162, 164
Clemens 154
Coletto, Renato 3, 10
Commentary on the Gospel of John 62
Constancy and change: historical types and trends in the passion of the Western mind 8
Council of Lyon 20
Council of Trent 179

D

Da Costa, Isaac 13
Danielou 194
Danielou, J 194
de Chardin, T 194
De Grijs, F.J.A 79
Dekker 15, 220, 224
Delfgaauw, B. 175, 182, 183, 195, 205, 206
De Lubac, H. 154, 194
Den Ottolander, P. 40, 127, 136
De Rijk, L.M. 163
De verkiezing Gods Sappeared (The election of God in 1955) 136
De Vitoria, F. 182, 187
De Vos 106
Die wysgerige konsepsie van Thomas van Aquino in sy "Summa Contra Gentiles" 8
Dogmatische Studien (Dogmatic studies) 136
Dominican Order 19, 169, 186, 194
Dominicans 19, 179, 181, 186
Dominicus de Soto 179, 194
Dooyeweerd, Herman 2, 7, 11, 13, 15, 77, 88, 100, 139, 141, 142, 143, 144, 174, 207, 208, 218, 225, 229, 242
Doran, R. 153, 236
Doubleday 17, 38, 57, 79, 104, 105, 214, 221, 223, 225
Duns Scotus 7, 147, 148, 182, 216

E

Egyptians 143
Elders, L. 181
Encyclopedia of Holy Theology 7
En toch beweegt Hij (And yet He does move) 136
Europe 162
European Reveil 13
Evangelicals 175
Evans, G.R. 158, 160
Eve 111, 129

F

Fabro, C. 70, 72
Feiser, Louet 174
Fernhout, R 151
Ferrariensis, Sylvester 199
Fides et ratio 180
Fletcher, R. 150
Fosso Nova 20
Fox, R.L. 150
Franciscan Order 179
Franciscans 5, 19, 179, 186
Free University of Amsterdam 174
Friethoff, C. 132
Fr. Suarez 11, 12, 73, 74, 99, 125, 179, 182, 187, 194

G

Galloway, A.D. 160
Gardeil, A. 194
Gaybba, B. 21, 161, 162
Geiger, L.B. 70, 72
Genèva 14, 134
Germany 14
Gevaert, J. 119, 121
Gilby, T. 175, 187
Gilson, E. 180, 187, 205
Gnosticism 151, 229
God 6, 8, 9, 17, 23, 24, 25, 26, 27, 28, 29, 31, 33, 36, 37, 38, 39, 40, 41, 42, 43, 44, 45, 46, 47, 48, 49, 50, 51, 52, 53, 54, 55, 56, 57, 58, 59, 60, 62, 63, 64, 67, 68, 69, 70, 71, 72, 73, 74, 75, 76, 77, 78, 79, 81,

82, 83, 84, 86, 87, 88, 89, 90, 92, 95, 97, 98, 99, 101, 102, 103, 104, 105, 106, 107, 108, 109, 110, 111, 112, 113, 114, 115, 116, 117, 118, 119, 120, 121, 122, 123, 124, 125, 126, 127, 128, 129, 130, 131, 132, 133, 134, 135, 136, 142, 143, 148, 152, 153, 154, 155, 156, 157, 165, 169, 196, 198, 199, 200, 201, 204, 205, 208, 210, 211, 213, 214, 216, 218, 219, 220, 222, 223, 225, 226, 227, 228, 236, 240, 241
God's providence 17, 47, 57, 101, 102, 104, 105, 114, 117, 119, 131, 132, 133, 134
Goheen, M.W. 194
Gomarus, F. 6, 218
Gort, J.D. 151
Goud, J.F. 154
Grabmann, M. 153, 163
Grand Rapids 15, 216, 226, 230, 234, 236, 237, 238, 239, 240, 241
Greeks 58, 141, 151, 159, 164
Griffioen, S. 146, 210, 215, 220, 221, 229, 230, 231
Groenewoud, G. 146, 210, 215, 220, 229, 230, 231, 234
Gutierrez, G. 146

H

Habbel, J. 67
Haldane, J. 175, 182
Hamman, A. 175
Hart 62, 162, 165, 168, 169, 170, 240
Hartvelt 153
Hartvelt, G.P. 153
Hegel, G.W.F. 146
Heideman, E.P. 209
Helleman, W.E. 140, 141, 144, 145, 146, 154, 220, 229, 231, 234
Hibernus, Petrus 19
Hick, J. 106
Holwerda, D. 136
Holy Spirit 85, 111, 122
Humani Generis 180, 202, 236

I

In die Skriflig 13, 241
International Thomas Conference 16, 172
Introducing Radical Orthodoxy 7, 216
Israelites 143
Italy 19, 20, 37

J

Jesuit Order 180
Jesuits 5, 179, 181, 186, 187
Jews 22
Johannesburg 173, 238

K

Kilwardby, Robert 168
Klapwijk, J. 103, 140, 142, 143, 144, 146, 148, 209, 210, 221, 229, 230, 231
Klubertanz, G.P. 67
Koers 6, 217, 218, 228, 233
Kok, J.H. 28, 33, 191, 209, 215, 216, 219, 221, 223, 224, 226, 229, 231, 232, 233, 235, 236, 237, 238, 239, 240, 241, 243
Kruger, J.P. 16, 64, 114
Krüger, K. 106
Kuhlmann, B.C. 49
Kuiper, R. 178
Kuipers, T. 209
Kung, H. 173
Kuyper 7
Kuyper, Abraham 7, 99, 103, 144, 172, 208, 209, 228, 230, 238, 239, 240, 243

L

Lais, H. 90, 99
La Velle, L. 194
Lebensphilosophie 136, 194, 195, 200, 203
Lehrbuch der Dogmengeschichte 139, 141, 234
Leiden 13, 174, 229, 239
Lief, J. 207
Lonergan, B. 181, 235
Lovejoy, A.O. 49
Luther, Martin 21, 175, 229
Luxemburg 181, 237
Lyttkens, H. 67

M

MacIntyre, Alasdair 187, 194, 206, 207
Magnus, Albertus 19, 20, 22, 168

Manicheism 151
Marel, G. 194
Maritain, J 194, 203
Marlet, M.F.J. 15, 174, 179, 194
McGrath, A.E. 160, 161, 163
McInery, R.M. 67
Meijer, J.B.J. 52, 53
Mekkes, J.P.A. 207, 209
Mercier, Désiré 187, 194
Merlan, P. 194
Metaphysics 120, 121, 216
Meuleman, G.E. 174, 180, 190, 198, 202, 204, 207
Middle Ages 14, 24, 31, 33, 90, 145, 147, 151, 152, 153, 154, 159, 161, 162, 164, 166, 194, 210
Middleton, J.R. 112, 208
Milbank, John 7
Mitchell, C.V. 186
Moses 37
Mouw, R.J. 209
Müller, R.A. 15
Musaeus 160
Muslims 22, 23

N

Naples 8, 18, 19, 20, 172
Nelson, Marietjie 10, 219, 233
Neo-Thomists 5, 9, 53, 176, 179, 182, 183, 185, 186, 189, 190, 196, 199, 200
Netherlands 7, 13, 15, 174, 181
Neumann, S. 90
New Testament 22
Nichols, A. 181
Nicomachean Ethics 108
Niebuhr, H.R. 146
Niede, E. 90, 99
Noll, M.A. 175, 207
Northwest University 3, 10
Nystrom, C. 175

O

Old Testament 22

Olthuis, J.H. 7, 175, 208, 240
O'Mahony, J.E. 197
Order of the Jesuits 179
Origen 81, 154, 230
Oxford 165, 168, 221, 230, 231, 232, 238

P

Pannenberg, W. 146
Paris 19, 20, 23, 165, 167, 168, 222, 230, 242
Pascendi Dominici Gregris 180
Paul 37, 180, 219, 224, 235
Peckham, John 168
Peels, H.G.L 136
Pelagians 123, 124
Persson, E. 40
Phelan, G.P. 67
Philo 147, 153, 154, 232
Pisa 37
Plato 20, 21, 37, 43, 50, 55, 62, 72, 81, 86, 95, 135, 155, 158, 159, 161, 178, 229, 232
Plotinus 43
Polman, A.D.R 132, 163, 199
Pope Benedictus XV & XVI 175, 180
Pope Francis I 180, 224
Pope Gregory IX 19
Pope John Paul II 180
Pope John XXII 179
Pope Leo XII 180
Pope Leo XIII 14
Pope Paul VI 180
Pope Pius X 180
Pope Pius XI 180
Pope Pius XII 180
Pope Urbanus IV 19
Portugal 186
Potchefstroom 3, 10, 216, 217, 218, 219, 221, 223, 225, 227, 228, 229, 232, 233, 241, 242
Protestants 32, 35, 209

R

Radical Orthodoxy and the Reformed Tradition 7

Rahner, K. 179, 194, 202, 203
Ramaker, T. 178
Raymundus from Pennaforte 22
Reformation 5, 13, 24, 29, 147, 153, 159, 173, 207, 208, 215, 216, 236
Reformed Dogmatics 7
Reformed theologians 7, 26, 32, 45, 79, 82, 99, 100, 103, 114, 117, 147, 153, 209
Reformers 29, 160
Renaissance 24, 31, 159, 219, 221, 223, 229
Robbers, H. 15, 16, 174, 183, 184, 185, 193, 206
Roman Catholic Church 5, 31, 32, 103, 171, 179, 180, 210
Roman Empire 162, 165
Romans 51, 111, 123, 131, 141, 159, 234, 254
Rome 8, 19, 20, 29, 172, 207, 214, 235, 238
Runia, D.T. 153, 154
Runner, H.E. 166, 191, 227
Russell, J.C. 150

S

Sahakian, W.S. 173
Sanford, M.L. 210
Santo Thomas de Aquino 17
Sassen 175, 182, 194, 205, 206
SCG 17, 18, 19, 21, 22, 23, 25, 26, 27, 37, 38, 40, 43, 47, 51, 52, 54, 56, 57, 61, 65, 66, 74, 79, 84, 95, 99, 104, 105, 124, 132, 165, 169
Scheffczyk, L. 79
Schilder, K. 103
Schillebeekx, E. 173
Schoonenberg, P. 173
Schütz, L. 57
Scriptures 18, 20, 24, 25, 26, 29, 40, 43, 49, 53, 60, 61, 62, 64, 69, 79, 83, 87, 103, 108, 110, 111, 118, 119, 120, 122, 126, 132, 136, 148, 149, 153, 154, 155, 156, 158, 159, 165, 168, 170, 206
Second Vatican Council 180, 182
Sertillanges, A.D. 194
Siewerth, G. 90
Siger of Brabant 168
Sinnema, D.W. 136
Smit, D.J. 154
Smith, J.A.K 7, 15, 175
Smit, J.H. 15

Smit, M.C. 2, 16, 174, 198, 199, 200, 201, 202
Smytegeld 13
Society for Reformational Philosophy 174
Solomon 115, 116
South Africa 7, 13, 16, 33, 142, 175, 222, 226
Spain 22, 186, 187
Spier, J.M. 65, 89, 97, 150, 152, 157, 169
Spykman, G.J. 136, 208
Stageira 19, 25, 149
Stagira 165, 167
Stellingwerff, J. 174, 215, 236
S. Thomae Aquinatis 17, 38, 57, 104
Stinson, C.H. 99
Stoker, Hendrik, G. 7, 11, 13, 15, 77, 100, 218, 225, 242
Studiorum Ducem 180
Suarez, F. 11, 12, 73, 74, 99, 125, 179, 182, 187, 194
Summa Contra Gentiles 8, 11, 17, 35, 37, 38, 55, 56, 77, 79, 101, 102, 104, 140, 169, 172, 185, 195, 210, 213, 214, 217, 221, 222, 223, 225, 227
Summa Theologiae 17, 22, 37, 40, 52, 105, 179, 186, 194, 216
Sweetman, R. 146, 147, 232
Synod of Dordt 6, 12, 45, 74, 134, 173, 218, 228
Synod of Orange 27, 28
Synopsis Purioris Theologiae 6, 11, 13, 103, 173, 217, 221, 223, 225, 237

T

Taljaard, J.A.L. 15, 142
Taylor, C. 194
Ter Horst, G. 86
Terracina 20
Tertullian 26, 156
Te Velde, D. 15
Thomas Lexicon 57
Tillich, P. 146
Tol, A. 15, 54, 98, 99, 147, 219, 221, 223, 233
Traini, Francesco 37
Turner, J. 207
Tydskrif vir Christelike Wetenskap/Journal for Christian Scholarship 6, 7, 8, 217, 218, 219, 227, 228, 237, 241, 242
Tydskrif vir Geesteswetenskappe 6, 218, 219, 228, 242

U

University of Coimbra 186
University of Leiden 13
University of Leuven 181
University of Naples 18, 19
University of Nijmegen 181
University of Oxford 168
University of Paris 23, 165, 167
University of Salamanca 186
Ursinus, Z. 12
Urs von Balthasar 173, 203

V

Van Asselt, W.J. 15, 140, 147, 159
van Brabant, Singer 20
Van den Berg, I.J.M. 37, 228
Van der Beek, A. 173
Van der Hoeven, J. 176, 177, 237
Vander Stelt, J.C. 178, 181
Van der Stoep, J. 178
Vandervelde, G. 174, 199, 202, 203
Van der Walt, B.J. 2, 10, 12, 13, 16, 17, 18, 22, 38, 52, 57, 61, 65, 67, 70, 72, 79, 84, 87, 88, 99, 104, 106, 111, 136, 146, 148, 150, 151, 154, 173, 192, 198, 208, 209, 210, 223, 225, 233, 241
Van der Walt, Hannetjie 10
Van Dijk, W.K. 174, 215
Van Drunen, David 207
Van Eck, J. 136
van Lyra, Nicolas 154
van Moerbeke, William 19
van Ockham 174
Van Ockham, William 45, 46, 174
van Prinsterer, Groen 13, 103, 219
Van Steenberghen, F. 23, 167
Veenhof, J. 209
Velema, H. 136
Venter, E.A. 16, 23, 25, 30, 31, 142
Venter, J.J. 45, 58, 59, 65, 67, 70, 72, 90, 106, 125, 131, 142, 147, 151, 156, 157, 160, 162, 167
Vollenhoven, D.H. Th. 2, 7, 11, 13, 15, 20, 22, 24, 26, 27, 29, 33, 39, 53,

54, 57, 58, 59, 62, 63, 66, 74, 88, 99, 139, 140, 141, 142, 143, 144, 145, 146, 147, 149, 150, 151, 152, 153, 154, 156, 157, 158, 159, 160, 162, 166, 169, 185, 191, 192, 194, 195, 202, 203, 207, 208, 216, 218, 221, 225, 232, 233, 234, 241, 242
Von Harnack, Aldolf 139, 140, 141, 144, 147
Vorster, H. 119, 121
Vos, A. 106, 147, 166
Vroom, H.M. 151

W

Walmsley, G. 172, 183
Walsh, B.J. 208
Weischedel, W. 106
Wentsel, B. 174, 198, 199, 201, 202
Wessels, A. 151
Wijsgerig leven in Nederland, België en Luxemburg, 1880-1980. 181
Wilken, R. 150
Wilkens, S. 210
Woldring, H.E.S. 174
Wolters, A.M. 146, 226
Wolterstorff, N. 177, 178
Word of God 23, 24, 48, 75, 112, 113, 114, 126, 129, 130, 165, 208
World War II 199
Wundt, M. 14

Z

Zabarella, G. 11, 12, 182, 194
Zagzebski, I. 200
Zuidema, S.U. 2, 174, 203, 204, 205, 206, 209, 243

www.ingramcontent.com/pod-product-compliance
Lightning Source LLC
Chambersburg PA
CBHW071900290426
44110CB00013B/1221